Dictionary of Maya Hieroglyphs

Dictionary of Maya Hieroglyphs

JOHN MONTGOMERY

HIPPOCRENE BOOKS, INC.
New York

For information, address:
HIPPOCRENE BOOKS, INC.
171 Madison Avenue
New York, NY 10016

Library of Congress Cataloging-in-Publication Data

Montgomery, John, 1951–
    Dictionary of Maya hieroglyphs / John Montgomery.
        p.   cm.
    Includes indexes.
    ISBN 0-7818-0862-6
    1. Mayan languages—Writing—Dictionaries.   2. Inscriptions, Mayan—
Dictionaries.   I. Title.

F1435.3.W75 m66 2002   2002068597
497'.415—dc21   CIP

Book design and composition by Susan A. Ahlquist, East Hampton, NY.

Printed in the United States of America.

In memory of

Ben Leaf

ACKNOWLEDGMENTS

Many individuals contributed to this dictionary. I would like to thank Barbara MacLeod for her generous "on the ground" time spent discussing verb morphology and the problem of hard and soft j (j versus h). Similarly, Phil Wanyerka, Robert Wald, and Marc Zender took time to discuss a variety of dictionary entries, especially in regard to verbal inflection and orthography. Of exceptional note was the help provided by Donald Hales in identifying T-numbers and his generous loan of many of the photographs that I used to generate the illustrations for the dictionary entries. Others who contributed significantly include John Harris and Linda Quist, both of whom helped find hard-to-locate examples of spellings. No one assisted more vigorously than my editor at Hippocrene, Caroline Gates, whose suggestions and skills immeasurably improved the organization of the dictionary and the method of presentation. Of course my wife, son, and daughter deserve credit for their unfailing patience and support. Any and all errors, especially in the interpretation of the glyphs, remain the responsibility of the author.

CONTENTS

ACKNOWLEDGMENTS   vi

INTRODUCTION   1

THE LANGUAGE OF MAYA HIEROGLYPHIC WRITING   5

PRONUNCIATION GUIDE   7
    Glottal Stops   7
    Vowels   8
    Consonants   8
    Orthography   9

CONVENTIONS FOR TRANSCRIBING GLYPHS   11

GUIDE TO DICTIONARY ENTRIES   15

GUIDE TO ABBREVIATIONS AND TERMS   17

DICTIONARY OF MAYA HIEROGLYPHS   23
    a   25
    b'   39
    ch   47
    ch'   71
    e   87
    i   91
    j   105
    k   129
    k'   141
    l   157

m	165
n	177
o	189
p	199
s	211
t	221
tz	241
tz'	247
u	253
w	261
x	275
y	279
Emblem Glyphs	307
Lords of the Night	319

INDICES — 321

LANGUAGE INDICES — 323
Mayan — 323
English — 346
Spanish — 370

INDEX OF VISUAL ELEMENTS — 393

SUBJECT INDICES — 399
Numbers — 399
Days — 400
Months — 400
Long Count — 401
Phonetic Signs — 401
Verbs/Verbal Phrases — 403
Pronouns — 409
Adjectives — 409
T-Numbers — 411

INTRODUCTION

> [D]ecipherment has now proceeded to the point where it
> may possibly be doubted whether history as such was
> ever recorded on the monuments.
>
> —Sylvanus G. Morley,
> *Inscriptions at Copán*, 1920

Archaeologist, epigrapher, public speaker extraordinaire, Sylvanus "Vay" Morley proved remarkably wrong when he pronounced Maya inscriptions devoid of historical content. Indeed, decipherment has progressed to the point where, today, investigators can finally and definitively say that not only was Morley mistaken about content, he was wrong in pronouncing the script unreadable in the Mayan language.

Despite remarkable progress in deciphering the script in recent years, resources indispensable to learning Maya hieroglyphic inscriptions or gaining a more thorough knowledge of the script remain curiously nonexistent. Epigraphers—those who decipher ancient inscriptions—themselves lack formal material for study, despite decades of new discoveries. Resources that do exist are widely scattered in academic and private libraries, or are available only as obscure workshop notebooks or hard-to-reach private files.

This dictionary of Maya hieroglyphs attempts to fill this void by presenting a selection of more than 1,200 entries that include the most common glyphs and glyph compounds. Aimed at anyone interested in the subject, and in particular newcomers to decipherment and travelers to the Maya area, it presents a convenient inventory of basic glyphic signs, together with cross-references that identify specific categories of hieroglyphs and subject matter. Scholars will find the dictionary useful as an easily accessible reference to a broad range of hieroglyphs, including some of the more recent and cutting-edge decipherments.

While I have attempted a more or less complete inventory of signs with phonetic values, I have refrained from an exhaustive selection of complex glyph groups. Such a dictionary of every known reading would run to thousands of entries, even if confined to only those examples that are reasonably secure. A catalog of all the known individual names featured in Maya inscriptions alone would include hundreds of items, a possibility for a future publication but outside the scope of the present volume.

I have chosen primarily the most important and trustworthy decipherments, ones largely free of controversy and vital to understanding the Maya script. As a sampling of the full range of hieroglyphic material, entries represent major subjects, verbs, and other glyphic constructions, as well as elements of key importance to the script's literary structure. To maintain the dictionary's "general" focus I have selected illustrations mainly from Late Classic texts (c. A.D. 600–900)—the height of Maya civilization and the peak epoch of the script's uniformity. These restrictions notwithstanding, entries include glyphs that, although of some uncertainty, lie on the cutting edge of decipherment and were chosen to indicate the direction of current research. Selections of this type include glyphs recently identified as plural suffixes, first- and second-person pronouns, and other tentative grammatical features. In other words, I maintain significant conservatism throughout these pages while cautiously extending the range of entries into somewhat untested territory. Entries of the latter class represent a very small percentage of the overall total.

Because few Emblem Glyphs have accepted or completely intelligible readings, the dictionary presents this class of hieroglyphs as a separate section according to the name of the archaeological site to which the Emblem Glyph corresponds, rather than the Mayan name deciphered by epigraphers. When known, cross-references by Mayan name have been added. For example, the main sign of the Tikal Emblem can be found in the dictionary under **MUTUL**, its accepted phonetic reading. This allows for consistency of use, and for future, possibly more accurate decipherments. Similarly, an additional section lists the Lords of the Night, not all of whose components have been fully deciphered.

Personal names have not been included except when significantly related to other entries. Thus, "shield" is given as the primary definition of **PAKAL**, followed by a notation that **PAKAL** serves as the name of several Palenque kings. Also not included are the names of most locations, especially ones associated with local features related to individual sites.

So that users can quickly find any entry in a variety of useful ways, supplemental indices list glyphs by language—Mayan, English, and Spanish—

and by major subject categories. The latter include mathematical items, calendrical and grammatical elements, phonetic signs, and visual or *iconographic* features. A final index lists entries by T-number, the number assigned to each glyph in the "Thompson Catalog" or *Catalog of Maya Hieroglyphs* published in 1962 by the University of Oklahoma Press.

Breakthroughs in glyph decipherment over the last several decades have offered extraordinarily rich and exciting readings, and have revealed how the script closely reflects the Mayan language in a variety of ways. This dictionary tries to make decipherment of the script more accessible while providing a useful tool for future exploration of the glyphic texts. Hopefully the reader will find that these goals have been met.

THE LANGUAGE OF MAYA HIEROGLYPHIC WRITING

Distribution of Mayan languages in modern and ancient times suggests that the hieroglyphs record a dialect of the Ch'olan group, represented today by dialects of Ch'ol, Ch'ontal, and Ch'orti, and by extinct Ch'olti. Originally distributed across the base of the Yucatán Peninsula as far as western Honduras, ancient Ch'olan corresponded precisely with those areas where Classic Period hieroglyphic texts (*ca.* A.D. 300–900) were the most concentrated and in use for the longest period of time.

Historically, groups of speakers of Yucatec and its sub-dialects encroached or intruded upon this Ch'olan core, and scholars have argued that many areas of the ancient Maya territory included mixed or contiguous populations of Ch'olan and Yucatec speakers. Yet when we turn to spellings from Classic Period inscriptions, an ambiguous situation arises where inscriptions do not conform entirely to one language nor the other, and not all of the proposed verbal inflectional patterns of the script survive in modern or colonial languages. In some cases, expected Ch'olan spellings were proven erroneous when the same glyph was found to incorporate unequivocal Yucatec spellings. In one example, the name of the Palenque king formerly called Chan Bahlum, or Snake Jaguar, had to be revised when epigraphers realized that the presence of the phonetic complement **ka** clearly indicated Yucatec *kan* "snake," rather than Ch'olan *chan*.

Epigraphers David Stuart, Stephen Houston, and John Robertson have proposed that Maya hieroglyphs record a distinctive, specialized "scribal language," a version preserved only in ancient inscriptions. They refer to this language as Classical Mayan. Although their ideas remain untested and unproven, they have neatly explained one of the more vexing problems facing decipherment today. The situation in which a language in its written form represents a "high" or elite language is called *diglossia*, as in ancient Egypt for example, where the written language expressed peculiar traditions missing from the spoken language.

This idea of a scribal language helps to explain the script's remarkable uniformity. Although each city's inscriptions had their idiosyncrasies, the script preserved quite similar conventions from city to city throughout the Classic Period and tended to change through time at approximately the same rate. We do not find, for example, any single city preserving a particularly archaic form of the script by the Late Classic Period, and presumably any inscription could be read by any scribe anywhere in the Maya world. How scholars will resolve the issue of the language of the Maya script remains one of the more exciting challenges faced by epigraphers today.

For simplification, this dictionary lists entries in almost every instance by the Ch'olan form, unless the hieroglyph explicitly spells the word in Yucatec. Where appropriate—that is, where the situation appears equivocal—the dictionary lists double entries, with the Ch'olan form given first and the Yucatec second.

Pronunciation Guide

Glottal Stops

The various dialects of Mayan incorporate a distinctive sound that linguists call the "glottal stop," which sounds similar to the stoppage of air in English *uh-oh* or in *button* when spoken rapidly. Pronounced simultaneously with the vowel or consonant that it accompanies, the glottal stop gives the word a characteristic "pop." When transcribing Mayan into our modern English alphabet, an apostrophe (') represents the presence of a glottal stop.

Vowels and consonants that include the glottal stop can make a difference in the meaning of a word. For example, *kab'* means "bee," but the same sequence with glottalized *k'*, or *k'ab'*, means "manual labor"—not unlike the difference between *sweet* and *sweat* in English. Thus the glottal stop sometimes, but not always, changes the meaning of a word.

The presence of the glottal stop affects vowels and consonants in different ways. Theoretically, a glottal stop precedes every vowel that begins a word or stands alone—as in *'o*—but in such instances no change in meaning occurs, and writers of Mayan usually omit the prevocalic glottal stop, as does the present dictionary. In contrast, several, but not all, glottalized consonants do modify the meaning of a word. Mayan generally incorporates five such consonants.

Glottal stops occur in the hieroglyphic script and make a difference to the phonetic value of a sign, just as they change the meaning of a word in the language. Thus, in the hieroglyphs, **k'a** cannot be used to spell **ka**. Other consonantal signs take glottal stops, for example **b'a**, but the glottal stop can be included or omitted without difference in meaning. Out of the set of consonants where the glottal stop *does not* affect meaning, the present dictionary follows the currently widespread practice of adding the glottal stop only to signs that begin with the sound *b'* (thus *b'* instead of *b*).

VOWELS

Written transcriptions of both Maya hieroglyphs and the Mayan language use the same vowels as Spanish, but distinguish between long and short vowels. Lengthening the vowel can change meaning. The present book doubles the vowel when long, as in the example *chan* "snake" versus *chaan* "sky."

The following pronunciation should be used for short vowels, and long vowel sounds are simply a prolongation of these:

a   The sound of *a* in "father"

e   The sound of *a* in "fate"

i   The sound of *ee* in "feet"

o   The sound of *o* in "go"

u   The sound of *o* in "who"

CONSONANTS

The Mayan language employs nineteen consonants, including the five glottalized consonants that make a difference in meaning. Not every glottalized consonant has been identified in the hieroglyphic script, but at least three glottalized consonants do make an appearance. Note that Mayan dictionaries list words that begin with glottalized consonants separately from those without the glottal stop, so that *k'* follows *k*, *ch'* follows *ch*, and *tz'* follows *tz*. The reader should note that Mayan lacks *d*, *f*, or *v*, while making substitutions for *c, g, j, q,* and *z*. For the most part *r* in Mayan remains exceptionally rare.

The nineteen consonants are:

b'   The sound of *b* in "bed" but with the breath-stream stopped; the glottal stop in *b'* makes no difference to the meaning of a word

ch   The sound of *ch* in "church"

ch'   The sound of *ch* in "church" but with the breath-stream stopped; the glottal stop in *ch'* makes a difference to the meaning of a word

j	Sounds like English *h* in "house"; but unlike English it can occur before other consonants, as in *jmen* "shaman"
k	Sounds like English hard *c* in "caught" or "cat"
k'	Sounds like English hard *c* but with the breath-stream stopped; the glottal stop in *k'* makes a difference to the meaning of a word
l	Like Spanish or English *l*
m	Like Spanish or English *m*
n	Like Spanish or English *n*
p	Like Spanish or English *p*
p'	Like Spanish or English *p* but with the breath-stream stopped; as of this writing, no sure signs beginning with p' have been found in the hieroglyphic script
s	Like Spanish or English *s*
t	Like Spanish or English *t*
t'	Like Spanish or English *t* but with the breath-stream stopped; as of this writing, no sure signs beginning with t' have been found in the hieroglyphic script
tz	Sounds like *ts* in English "let's" or "toots"
tz'	Like *ts* in English "let's," but with the breath-stream stopped; the glottal stop in *tz'* makes a difference to the meaning of a word
x	Sounds like English *sh* in "shoe"
w	Like Spanish or English *w*
y	Sounds like English *y* in "yes"

ORTHOGRAPHY

Those who decipher hieroglyphs, called epigraphers, continue to argue over the spelling of Mayan words when transcribing them in our modern

English alphabet. For example, epigraphers lack consensus on when to use hard *j* and soft *h*, or whether vowels should include an initial glottal stop, which can have significant impact on certain words while having no effect on others. To complicate matters, epigraphers rarely apply orthographic conventions uniformly.

The present book adopts the conventions of the Academia de las Lenguas Mayas de Guatemala in an attempt to bring order and consistency, at least within these pages, to a needlessly chaotic situation. The chief significance of this decision is that the present dictionary makes no distinction between hard *j* and soft *h*, as in the difference between the phonetic sign *ja* and *ha'* "water." Current research indicates that the distinction between hard and soft *h* began to be lost by Late Classic times (after about A.D. 700). To avoid inconsistency and the logistical difficulties of distinguishing between early and late usage I have adopted the Academia's application of *j* for both consonants. Entries in the dictionary therefore use *j* for both *j* and *h*. Thus *jun* ("book") is given as an entry, rather than *hun*. In these cases the reader should remember that *j* is pronounced like Spanish *j*, which in turn sounds like *h* in English.

CONVENTIONS FOR TRANSCRIBING GLYPHS

I have tried to follow the conventions established by George Stuart in the *Research Reports* published by the Center for Maya Studies. In addition, James Fox and John Justeson's appendix to *Phoneticism in Mayan Hieroglyphic Writing* has proven invaluable. In actual practice, however, it became necessary to alter and expand these generally accepted rules, albeit very slightly. Consequently the following conventions apply.

SIGNS WRITTEN IN BOLDFACE

BOLD UPPERCASE: Distinguishes hieroglyphs that stand for logograms or complete words.

bold lowercase: Distinguishes hieroglyphs that function purely as phonetic syllables in the spelling of words and that generally have no meaning by themselves.

Example 1: **CHAAN-na**

CHAAN is rendered in bold uppercase because it denotes the logogram or word for "sky," while **-na** is given in bold lowercase because it functions as a phonetic sign or "complement" that clues the reader to the word's final sound.

Example 2: **AJ pi-tzi-la-wa**

AJ serves as the logogram for the male agentive prefix meaning "he" or "he of" and is therefore given in bold uppercase. The remaining **pi-tzi-la-wa** is given in bold lowercase because it spells out phonetically the word *pitzlaw* ("the youthful") with syllabic signs.

WORDS GIVEN IN *ITALICS*

Words given in *italics* correspond to words in the Mayan language, regardless of the specific dialect or language group. In order to avoid controversy concerning vowel complexity and disharmony, transcriptions of Mayan given in this book distinguish long and short vowels by doubling the vowel. Thus *chaan* ("sky") is used, and not *chan* and not *cha:n*.

ELEMENTS IN {}, [], ()

For purposes of the present dictionary, values within scroll-brackets {} indicate that the glyph corresponding to the enclosed element was left out by the scribe but should be pronounced, as for example **AJ k'u-{JUN}-na**, where **{JUN}** indicates a deleted but pronounced logogram. Straight brackets [] indicate a sign infixed within a glyph or within a word. Thus **CHUM-[mu]** denotes a logogram with infixed **-mu**, the latter functioning as a phonetic complement infixed inside the main sign **CHUM**, rather than serving as an element attached as a separate postfix.

In rendering glyphic transcriptions, hieroglyphic elements within parentheses () traditionally indicate unpronounced sounds. For example, in the transcription **CHAAN-(na)**, parentheses indicate that the final **na** remains silent and unpronounced. In this dictionary, however, the use of parentheses in transcriptions has been omitted, chiefly to maintain clarity and consistency within sometimes exceptionally complex entries and to avoid controversy over issues of spelling conventions and terminal endings on verbs.

T-NUMBERS

Entries throughout the dictionary make use of numbers preceded by a capital T. T-numbers correspond to glyphs identified in the catalog published in 1962 by J. Eric S. Thompson, which inventories all glyphs that were known at that time and organizes them according to whether they function as main signs or affixes. In Thompson's system a colon indicates that the glyph corresponding to the preceding number lies physically *above* the glyph that follows it. Glyphs after a period lie to the *right* of the glyph

corresponding to the previous number. For example, in T126.533:130, a compound transcribed in the dictionary as **ya-AJAW-wa** (*yajaw*), the affix that corresponds to number 126 is designated by the period as lying to the left of sign 533, whereas the colon indicates that the glyph corresponding to 130 lies below 533. Although not perfect (Thompson inevitably miscataloged or omitted various glyphs), the system serves as the standard reference to identify unequivocally individual signs.

Dictionary users should be aware that in each entry the sequence of Thompson numbers does not always correspond to the order of the phonetic elements. As an illustration of this, the several entries that begin with **K'AL** generally end with a word that is given first in the number sequence. When in doubt, a quick check in the dictionary of any element by its phonetic value or in the T-number index will indicate which glyph corresponds to which T-number.

Note also that T-numbers make use of lowercase letters to designate variations of the same glyph, for example a, b, c, and so on, as in 1030a, 1030b, and 1030c, all of which denote significant variations of the same glyph or similar glyphs. In addition, (v) serves in T-numbers as an abbreviation for "variant," (hv) indicates "head variant," and (ms) indicates "main sign." (Tnn) indicates that no T-number exists for that sign. The addition of abbreviations to T-numbers poses some confusion, but since entries in Thompson's catalog that go as high as (h) are confined to head variants, no inconsistencies actually arise. Finally, T-numbers incorporate Roman numerals to indicate numbers written in the Maya bar-and-dot or head variant mathematical system (for example I = 1 and X = 10).

GUIDE TO DICTIONARY ENTRIES

As in any dictionary, the order of information in each entry follows a formal sequence of presentation. Entries begin by offering *visual* examples of each hieroglyph or hieroglyphic compound. Immediately following the illustration comes the *phonetic spelling* of the entry, given in **bold**. All entries occur alphabetically in the *generally accepted order of their elements*. Symbolic versions of the glyph are given first and head variants last, beginning with glyphs that have the lowest T-number and proceeding to any higher numbers.

Each entry corresponds to an item's phonetic spelling, not to the transcription of the word or word sequence in Mayan. These entries, given in bold, can include alternative spellings, or Ch'olan versus Yucatec spellings (and vice versa), either back-to-back and separated by "/," or incorporated within parentheses, depending on the complexity of the entry. Whether or not an entry begins with its Ch'olan or Yucatec form depends on the general state of the glyph's decipherment, "prevailing" usage among epigraphers, or a lack of clear consensus concerning which language should be used. The present dictionary favors Ch'olan forms for initial entries, followed by their Yucatec equivalent. Note that especially complex entries include alternative decipherments in parentheses.

Following the phonetic reading comes the generally accepted transcription of the hieroglyph or glyph compound in the Mayan language, always indicated in *italics* within parentheses, followed by the T-number or Thompson catalog number, also given within parentheses. The part of speech comes next, then the most common and generally accepted definition, then additional definitions if warranted. Each definition follows in numerical sequence—1 ▶, 2 ▶, 3 ▶, and so on—with the most important and most securely identified generally coming first. The last items given in an entry, if called for, include pertinent information such as what the glyph represents graphically, its relationship to other glyphs, or any cross-references.

The following examples identify elements used in the dictionary entries.

SIMPLE ENTRY:

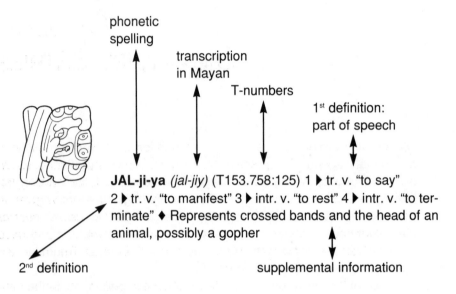

JAL-ji-ya *(jal-jiy)* (T153.758:125) 1 ▶ tr. v. "to say" 2 ▶ tr. v. "to manifest" 3 ▶ intr. v. "to rest" 4 ▶ intr. v. "to terminate" ◆ Represents crossed bands and the head of an animal, possibly a gopher

COMPLEX ENTRY:

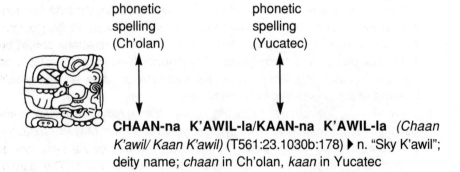

CHAAN-na K'AWIL-la/KAAN-na K'AWIL-la *(Chaan K'awil/ Kaan K'awil)* (T561:23.1030b:178) ▶ n. "Sky K'awil"; deity name; *chaan* in Ch'olan, *kaan* in Yucatec

GUIDE TO ABBREVIATIONS AND TERMS

adjective	adj.
adverb/adverbial	adv.
affix	af.
auxiliary	aux.
Calendar Round	CR
completive	com.
conjunction	conj.
declarative	decl.
demonstrative	dem.
Distance Number	DN
Distance Number Introductory Glyph	DNIG
Emblem Glyph	EG
ergative	erg.
feminine	fem.
first person	1st pers.
full figure	ff
head variant	hv
incompletive	incom.
Initial Series	IS
Initial Series Introductory Glyph	ISIG
intransitive	intr.
inverted	inv.
irregular	irreg.
locative/location	loc.
Long Count	LC
main sign	ms
masculine	masc.
no number	nn
noun	n.

numerical classifier	num. class.
particle	part.
passive	pass.
Period Ending	PE
person	pers.
phrase	phr.
plural	pl.
positional	pos.
possessive/possessed	poss.
prefix	pref.
preposition	prep.
prevocalic	prev.
Primary Standard Sequence	PSS
progressive	prog.
pronoun	pron.
quotative	quot.
reflexive	refl.
relationship glyph	relat.
second person	2nd pers.
singular	sing.
suffix	suf.
temporal	temp.
third person	3rd pers.
titular	tit.
transitive	tr.
variant	v
verb	v.

The following guide offers a convenient introduction to abbreviated terms used for grammatical elements and standard components of the Maya script.

adjective: modifies or describes a noun

adverb: modifies or describes a verb

affix: a comparatively small hieroglyphic sign attached to a larger main sign as a prefix, superfix, postfix, or subfix; a linguistic element added to the beginning or end of a word, often but not always serving a grammatical function

auxiliary: a "supplemental" element of verbs, as in the so-called **ti-**constructions that include an auxiliary and a main verb

Calendar Round: Mesoamerican calendar of fifty-two years that consists of the 260-day Tzolk'in calendar and 365-day Ja'ab' calendar; so-called because of its cyclical nature, where any given date repeats every fifty-two years

completive: refers to an action that has been completed or carried out to the point of being finished; an element of "aspect" that temporally contrasts actions or events as ongoing or completed

conjunction: a class of words that conjoin other words, clauses, phrases, or sentences, such as "and," "because," "but," "however," and so on

declarative: a word, phrase, or sentence that declares, makes known, or explains something

demonstrative: a word, phrase, or sentence that specifically indicates or singles out the object or person referred to: "*this* fellow smiles constantly"

Distance Number: a mathematical statement in the Maya calendar system that connects one date with another either by adding or subtracting so many periods of b'aktuns, k'atuns, tuns, winals, and k'ins

Distance Number Introductory Glyph: a specialized hieroglyph that generally, but not always, introduces Distance Numbers

Emblem Glyph: a distinct cluster of signs that together refer to a specific polity or town, or to the ruling elite of that locality; generally consists of one of the "blood group" or "water group" affixes (T32 through T41), the logogram **AJAW** (usually T168 or one of its allographs), and a variable main sign specific to the locality

ergative: a set of pronouns (usually called Set A) used in Mayan languages to highlight the agent or instrument of an action; more specifically, ergative pronouns indicate the subjects of transitive verbs and the possessors of nouns

feminine: refers to pronouns that highlight female objects and subjects

first person: the form used by a speaker when referring to him/herself: *I, me* (singular) and *we, us* (plural)

full figure: a class of hieroglyphs that depict the full figure of a human or creature (as opposed to head variant or symbolic forms)

head variant: a class of hieroglyphs that depict the head of a human or creature (as opposed to full figure and symbolic forms)

incompletive: refers to an action that remains unfinished and ongoing; an element of "aspect" that temporally contrasts actions or events as ongoing or completed

Initial Series: a calendrical statement in Maya hieroglyphic writing that incorporates the Long Count, Tzolk'in, and Ja'ab' calendars and often additional temporal information such as the Lords of the Night, Lunar, and Secondary Series; more or less a complete calendrical notation that is called the Initial Series because it usually occurs at the beginning of an inscription

Initial Series Introductory Glyph: a specialized hieroglyph that generally, but not always, introduces the Initial Series

intransitive: refers to verbs that occur with only a subject, and do not have a direct object: "John *runs*"

inverted: upside-down

irregular: refers to a word or glyph that does not conform to prevailing patterns of formation, inflection, or construction

locative/location: refers to position within space: "at," "on," "in," and so forth

Long Count: a calendrical statement in Maya hieroglyphic writing that identifies a specific year, using a system of periods of time—the k'in, winal, tun, k'atun, b'aktun, and so forth—added to the beginning date of the calendar, 3114 B.C.; makes use of a mathematical system based on bars and dots and a positional system incorporating the concept of zero

main sign: a comparatively large hieroglyphic sign to which other smaller signs, or affixes, are attached

masculine: refers to pronouns that highlight objects and subjects of masculine gender

no number: refers to hieroglyphic signs that lack T-numbers in the Thompson catalog

noun: the name of a person, place, or thing

numerical classifier: refers to linguistic elements that highlight specific classes of numbers, for example, cardinal versus ordinal numbers, or that highlight categories of counted things, for example, counted trees or animals

particle: a short word that has functional or relational use, such as an article, preposition, or conjunction

passive: refers to the "voice" of a sentence, which can be characterized as active or passive; presents an action in an indirect voice; for example, "John speaks" (active) versus "John is speaking" (passive)

Period Ending: a major calendrical "node" in the Maya calendar, equivalent in our own calendar to decades, centuries, and millenia; in Maya inscriptions, Period Endings most commonly consist of "end of tun," "end of k'atun," "end of half-k'atun," and "end of quarter-k'atun" statements

person: a linguistic element used to distinguish between a speaker and those to or about whom the speaker refers; usually a pronoun; "first person" (I, me, we, us), "second person" (you), and "third person" (he, she, it, they)

phrase: two or more words that act as a unit within a larger sentence

plural: more than one, as in "kiss" versus "kisses"

positional: refers to the location of an action in space, such as "lying down" or "stood upright"

possessive/possessed: refers to something that bears an intrinsic relationship to something else in the sense of "belonging to": "his shoes," "the belt of," "her house," and so forth

prefix: a comparatively small hieroglyphic sign attached to the left side of a larger main sign; a linguistic element added to the beginning of a word and usually having a grammatical function

preposition: a class of words used to modify verbs, nouns, or adjectives and that typically express a spatial or temporal relationship, as "in," "on," "by," "with," and so forth

prevocalic: occurring immediately *before* a vowel; in Mayan, usually refers to a pronoun or glottal stop that comes before a vowel

Primary Standard Sequence: a more or less regular sequence of hieroglyphs that is often written around the rims of Classic Period pottery vessels and that describes the type of vessel, what it was used for (its contents), and who its owner was; additional information expressed in the sequence includes a description of the surface treatment as either painted or carved

progressive: indicates a continuing or ongoing action in time: "he is doing it"

pronoun: a class of words used as replacements or substitutes for nouns: *you, he, it*, and so forth; pronouns can reflect qualities such as voice (first person, second person, third person) or possession (his, hers, its)

quotative: refers to something quoted, as verbatim speeches or utterances

reflexive: self-referential; refers to "self," "myself"

relationship glyph: a hieroglyph that expresses a relationship between two animate objects, usually human beings; for example, "the child of," "in the company of," "under the authority of"

second person: the form used by a speaker when talking to the person referred to: for example, *you*, as in "you can go now" (as opposed to *I, me* [first person] and *her, him* [third person])

singular: less than two, as in "one *kiss*" versus "many *kisses*"

suffix: a comparatively small element attached to the end of a word and usually having a grammatical function

temporal: refers to time

third person: the form used by a speaker when talking about something other than him/herself or the person addressed: for example, *he, her, it*, as in "he can go now" (as opposed to *I, me* [first person] and *you* [second person])

titular: refers to a title, generally an elite title, as in "titular phrase"

transitive: refers to verbs that have both a subject and an object: "John *loves* ice cream"

variant: an alternative element of the same meaning, use, or function

verb: a word that expresses action: *run, throw, eat*

DICTIONARY OF
MAYA HIEROGLYPHS

A

a/AJ *(a/aj)* (T12) 1 ▶ vowel *a* 2 ▶ masc. agentive pron. meaning "he" 3 ▶ agentive pref. "he of_____"; associates individuals with locations or qualities, as in *aj naab'* "he of water"

a/AJ *(a/aj)* (T228 and T229) 1 ▶ vowel *a* 2 ▶ masc. agentive pron. meaning "he" 3 ▶ agentive pref. "he of_____"; associates individuals with locations or qualities, as in *aj naab'* "he of water" 4 ▶ 2ⁿᵈ pers. poss. pron. of the ergative set, "your" and "you" when it marks the subject of the verb

a/AJ *(a/aj)* (T238) 1 ▶ vowel *a* 2 ▶ masc. agentive pron. meaning "he" 3 ▶ agentive pref. "he of_____"; associates individuals with locations or qualities, as in *aj Chaak* "he of Chaak" ♦ Represents the beak of a parrot or macaw. See also **MO'**.

a/AJ *(a/aj)* (T743) 1 ▶ vowel *a* 2 ▶ masc. agentive pron. meaning "he" 3 ▶ agentive pref. "he of_____"; associates individuals with locations or qualities, as in *aj naab'* "he of water" ♦ Represents the head of a turtle, macaw, or parrot

a-AK'OT-ta *(ak'ot)* (T228.516:103) ▶ n. "dance"

AB' *(ab')* (T548) 1 ▶ n. "year"; the year of 360 days; the **TUN** sign in IS and DN notations 2 ▶ n. part of the name of the ruler of Seibal, Aj B'olon Ab'taj (cf. Seibal Stelae 7, 9, 10, and 11) ♦ Represents the cross-section of a wooden drum, or *tunkul*. See also **JA'AB'** and **TUN**.

AB'-[b'i] *(ab')* (T548[585]) ▶ n. "year"; the **TUN** sign in IS and DN notations + infixed **b'i** ♦ Upper half represents the cross-section of a wooden drum, or *tunkul*. See **AB'**.

ACH-cha *(ach)* (T761b:520) ▶ n. "penis," with **cha** as phonetic complement to distinguish *ach* "penis" in Yucatec Mayan from *at* "penis" in
Ch'olan Mayan ♦ See **AT**.

AJAW *(ajaw)* (T168 or T584.687a) ▶ n. "lord"; royal title, office; designates
status of first-rank nobility of both sexes

AJAW *(ajaw)* (T168:518b) ▶ n. "lord"; royal title, office; designates status
of first-rank nobility of both sexes

AJAW *(ajaw)* (T364 or T774.584v) ▶ n. "lord"; royal title, office; designates
status of first-rank nobility of both sexes

AJAW *(Ajaw)* (T533) ▶ n. day sign; twentieth or last day of the Maya
Tzolk'in calendar; designates the Sun God ♦ Represents a face

AJAW *(ajaw)* (T747a) ▶ n. "lord"; royal title, office; designates first-rank nobility of both sexes ♦ Represents a vulture head with T533 **AJAW** over forehead

AJAW *(ajaw)* (Tnn) ▶ n. "lord"; royal title, office; designates first-rank nobility of both sexes ♦ Represents the head of a rodent with the so-called Jester God over forehead

AJAW *(ajaw)* (T1000d) ▶ n. "lord"; royal title, office; designates first-rank nobility of both sexes ♦ Represents the head of a young lord with T533 **AJAW** over forehead

a-ja-wa *(ajaw)* (T229.683b:130) ▶ n. "lord"; royal title, office; designates first-rank nobility of both sexes

AJAW-le-le *(ajawlel)* (T168:188:188) ▶ n. "rulership," "kingship," "lordship"

AJAW-wa *(ajaw)* (T168:130) ▶ n. "lord"; royal title, office; designates first-rank nobility of both sexes

AJAW-wa TE' *(ajaw te')* (T168:518:130) ▶ n. "tree lord"; royal title

a-ja-ya *(aya?)* (T228.683:137) ▶ v. phr. "[it] came into being"; introductory glyph of the PSS; actual reading uncertain ◆ See **a-li-ya**, **a-ya**, **a-ya-ya**.

AJ k'u-{JUN}-na *(aj k'ujun)* (T12.41:23) ▶ prep. phr. "he of the sacred books"; subordinate title, possibly an official title designating "royal librarian"; actual meaning unknown

AJ k'u-JUN-na *(aj k'ujun)* (T743:38 60:23) ▶ prep. phr. "he of the sacred books"; subordinate title, possibly an official title designating "royal librarian"; actual meaning unknown

AJ na-b'i *(aj naab')* (T228.23:585a) ▶ prep. phr. "he of the water" or "of the water"; subordinate title meaning roughly "artist"

AJ na-b'i *(aj naab')* (T238.23:585hv) ▶ prep. phr. "he of the water" or "of the water"; subordinate title meaning roughly "artist"

AJ pa-ya-la *(aj payal)* (T229.602:126:178) ▶ prep. phr. "he the leader"; elite title

AJ pi-tzi *(aj pitz)* (T12.177:507) 1 ▶ prep. phr. "he the youthful"; elite title 2 ▶ n. "ball player"; elite title

AJ pi-tzi-la-wa-{l} *(aj pitzlawal)* (T12:200:507 178:1000hv) 1 ▶ prep. phr. "he of the ball game"; elite title 2 ▶ n. "ball player"; elite title

AJ pi-tzi-la-wa-la *(aj pitzlawal)* (T12v:200:507 178:506:9) 1 ▶ prep. phr. "he of the ball game"; elite title 2 ▶ n. "ball player"; elite title

AJ su-lu *(aj sul)* (T12.216:568) ▶ prep. phr. "he the administrator," "administrator"; elite title

AJ tz'i-b'a *(aj tz'ib')* (T12.248:501) ▶ prep. phr. "he of the writing" or "scribe"; artist's title

AJ tz'i-b'a *(aj tz'ib')* (T12.nn:501:314) ▶ prep. phr. "he of the writing," or "scribe"; artist's title; designates the occupation of scribe, painter, or artist in general ♦ Tnn represents a hand holding a writing or painting instrument.

AJ u-xu-[lu] *(aj uxul)* (T12.13:756c) ▶ prep. phr. "he of the burnishing/scratching"; artist's title meaning roughly "he of the sculpture" or "sculptor"; designates the occupation of royal sculptor

AJ-wa-chi-NAL *(awa ichnal?)* (T228.78:78:671) ▶ decl. phr. "before you"

AJ-wi-na-{i} ke-na *(a winiken)* (T229.117:537 220v.23) ▶ decl. phr. "I am your servant" ◆ Includes the second-person possessive pronoun **AJ** "your"

AJ-wo-la *(awol)* (T229.67:534) ▶ poss. n. "your heart" ◆ Includes the second-person possessive pronoun **AJ** "your"

AJ-X-B'AK *(aj-X-b'ak)* (a. T12.II:570; b. T12.V:1045; c. T12.V:501.102; d. T12.683a:111) ▶ prep. phr. "Count of Captives" warrior title meaning "he of (x-number of) captives"; the "Count of Captives" epithet ▷ a. "he of two captives" ▷ b. "he of five captives" ▷ c. "he of five captives" ▷ d. "he of twenty captives"; denotes the number of individuals captured by a warrior in battle ◆ Usage confined largely if not exclusively to the Middle Usumacinta River Valley

AKB'AL *(Akb'al)* (T504) ▶ n. day sign; third day of the Maya Tzolk'in calendar ◆ Represents the quality of "darkness"; probably depicts the upper markings and belly-scales of a snake

a-ku *(ak)* (T228:528) ▶ n. "turtle"; title or personal name ◆ Especially common in royal names from the Usumacinta Valley and the Piedras Negras area

ak'/AK' *(ak')* (T504) 1 ▶ phonetic sign 2 ▶ n. "tongue" ◆ Probably represents the upper markings and belly-scales of a snake

ak'/AK'OT *(ak'/ak'ot)* (T516b) 1 ▸ phonetic sign 2 ▸ n. "dance" 3 ▸ tr. v. "to dance"

ak'/AK'OT *(ak'/ak'ot)* (T743[516b]) 1 ▸ phonetic sign 2 ▸ n. "dance" 3 ▸ tr. v. "to dance" ♦ Represents the head of a parrot, macaw or turtle

AK'AB' *(ak'ab')* (T504) ▸ n. "darkness" ♦ Probably represents the upper markings and belly-scales of a snake

AK'OT-ta *(ak'ot)* (T516b:103) 1 ▸ n. "dance" 2 ▸ tr. v. "to dance"

AK'OT-ta-ja *(ak'otaj)* (T743[516b]:102.181) ▸ pass. v. "was danced"

a-li-ya *(aliy?)* (T229.617:125v) ▶ intr. v. "to say," "it is said"; introductory glyph of the PSS; actual reading uncertain ♦ See alternative spellings **a-ya**, **a-ja-ya**, **a-ya-ya**.

am *(am)* (Tnn) ▶ phonetic sign ♦ Represents the head of a bird

am *(am)* (T1047a) ▶ phonetic sign ♦ Represents the head of a bird

at *(at)* (T552) ▶ phonetic sign ♦ Represents crossed bands

AT *(at)* (T761b) ▶ n. "penis" (Yucatec Mayan) ♦ Represents a human penis and scrotum. See **ACH-cha**.

AT-ti *(at)* (T761b:59) ▶ n. "penis" (Yucatec Mayan) ◆ Phonetic complement distinguishes Yucatec *at* from Ch'olan *ach*; tabs at top may represent incisions inflicted during self-sacrifice, and may clue a reading of
XAT "scarred penis."

a-ya *(aya)* (T238.1011) ▶ v. phr. "came into being"; introductory glyph
of the PSS; actual reading uncertain ◆ See alternative spellings **a-li-ya**,
a-ja-ya, **a-ya-ya**.

a-ya-ya *(aya)* (T229.617:125v) ▶ v. phr. "came into being"; introductory
glyph of the PSS; actual reading uncertain ◆ See alternative spellings
a-li-ya, **a-ja-ya**, **a-ya**.

AYIN *(ayin)* (T844) 1 ▶ n. "crocodile" 2 ▶ n. "lizard"; occurs especially
in the names of the Early and Late Classic Tikal rulers Yax Nuun Ayin I
and II ◆ Represents the head of a crocodile or lizard. Also spelled **AIN**
and **AYIIN**.

B'

b'a *(b'a)* (T138) ▶ phonetic sign

b'a/B'A *(b'a)* (T501) 1 ▶ phonetic sign 2 ▶ n. "head" 3 ▶ adj. "first" 4 ▶ refl. suf. "self," "thing" 5 ▶ n. "image," "being," "self" ◆ Represents a water lily

b'a/B'A *(b'a)* (T757) 1 ▶ phonetic sign 2 ▶ n. "head" 3 ▶ adj. "first" 4 ▶ refl. suf. "self," "thing" 5 ▶ n. "image," "being," "self" ◆ Represents the head of a rodent, possibly a gopher

B'A AJAW *(b'a ajaw)* (T168:757) ▶ adj. + n. "first lord"; elite title

B'A ch'o-ko *(b'a ch'ok)* (T501.758b:110) 1 ▶ adj. + n. "first sprout" 2 ▶ adj. + n. "first young person," "first youth" 3 ▶ adj. + n. "first lineage member"; elite title

b'a-ja *(b'aj)* (T60:757.181) ▶ n. "image," as in *u b'a* "(is) his/her image"; formerly "doing," "going," as in *u b'a* "he/she did it," "his/her doing"

b'a-ji-ni *(b'ajin)* (T501:314.116) ▶ adv. "indeed"

B'AK *(b'ak)* (T570 and T111) 1 ▶ n. "bone," as in *u b'ak* "his/her bone," "the bone of" 2 ▶ n. "captive," as in *u b'ak* "his/her captive," "the captive of" ♦ Represents a human bone

B'AK *(b'ak)* (T1045) 1 ▶ n. "bone," as in *u b'ak* "his/her bone," "the bone of" 2 ▶ n. "captive," as in *u b'ak* "his/her captive," "the captive of" ♦ Represents an animal's skull

b'a-ka-b'a *(b'akab')* (T501.25:501) 1 ▶ n. "standing one" 2 ▶ n. "first in the world"; royal/elite title

b'a-ki *(b'ak)* (T501:102) 1 ▶ n. "bone," as in *u b'ak* "his/her bone," "the bone of" 2 ▶ n. "captive," as in *u b'ak* "his/her captive," "the captive of" ♦ Without the third-person possessive pronoun *u* this signifies "it is a bone," "it is a captive."

B'AKTUN   See **pi/PI**, **pi-ji**, **PI-ya**.

B'ALAM *(b'alam)* (T751) ▶ n. "jaguar" ♦ Represents the head of a jaguar

b'a-na *(b'an)* (T501:23) ▶ tr. v. "to scatter"

b'a-te' *(b'ate')* (T501:87) ▶ n. "warrior"; elite title

b'a-tz'u *(b'atz')* (T501.203v) ▶ n. "monkey," "howler monkey," *saraguate*

B'A u-xu-[lu] *(b'a uxul)* (T501.1:756c) ▶ adj. + n. "first sculptor"; elite title

B'A YAL *(b'a yal)* (T501.19:670) ▶ adj. + n. "first born"; elite title

b'e/B'E *(b'e)* (T301) 1 ▶ phonetic sign 2 ▶ n. "road" ♦ Represents a human footprint on the surface of a road

b'e/B'E *(b'e)* (T301v) 1 ▶ phonetic sign 2 ▶ n. "road" ♦ Represents a human footprint

B'EN *(B'en)* (T584) ▶ n. day sign; thirteenth day of the Maya Tzolk'in calendar

b'i/B'I *(b'i)* (T585) 1 ▶ phonetic sign 2 ▶ n. "road" ♦ The "quincunx" glyph

b'i/B'l *(b'i)* (T1029) 1 ▶ phonetic sign 2 ▶ n. "road" ◆ Depicts a zoomorphic head with T585 infixed

B'IXAN-na *(b'ixan)* (T95[585]:23) 1 ▶ incom. irreg. v. "goes" 2 ▶ incom. irreg. v. "walks" 3 ▶ incom. irreg. v. "travels" 4 ▶ com. irreg. v. "went"

B'IXAN-ni-ya *(b'ixaniy)* (T95[585]:116:126) ▶ com. irreg. v. "went"

b'o *(b'o)* (T519v) ▶ phonetic sign

B'OLON *(b'olon)* (TIX) 1 ▶ n. "nine"; cardinal number 2 ▶ adj. "many"

B'OLON *(b'olon)* (TIXhv) 1 ▶ n. "nine"; cardinal number 2 ▶ adj. "many"
♦ Represents a human head with beard

B'OLON i-pi-[la]-ja *(b'olon iplaj)* (TIX.679.177:683[534]) ▶ adj. + n. "many
strengths," "many deaths"?

b'u *(b'u)* (T21) ▶ phonetic sign

b'u *(b'u)* (T21.741v) ▶ phonetic sign ♦ The head component represents a
frog, iguana, or other reptile.

b'u-ku *(b'uk)* (T21:528) ▶ pl. n. "clothes"

b'u-la *(b'ul)* (T21:534) ▶ n. "bean," "beans"

B'ULUK *(b'uluk)* (TXI) ▶ n. "eleven"; cardinal number

B'ULUK *(b'uluk)* (TXIhv) ▶ n. "eleven"; cardinal number ♦ Represents a head infixed with T526 "earth"

B'UTZ' *(b'utz')* (T122:563a) ▶ n. "smoke" ♦ See also **K'AK'**.

B'UTZ' *(b'utz')* (T1035a) ▶ n. "smoke" ♦ See also **K'AK'**.

CH

cha/ka *(cha/ka)* (T108) ▶ phonetic sign

cha/ka *(cha/ka)* (T135) ▶ phonetic sign

cha/ka *(cha/ka)* (T228) ▶ phonetic sign

cha/ka *(cha/ka)* (T520) ▶ phonetic sign

cha/ka *(cha/ka)* (T520v) ▶ phonetic sign

CHA/KA *(cha/ka)* (TII) ▶ n. "two"; cardinal number

CHA/KA *(cha/ka)* (TIIhv) ▶ n. "two"; cardinal number ◆ Represents a human head surmounted by a human hand

CHAAK *(Chaak)* (T1011) ▶ n. "Chaak"; deity name, the Maya rain god ◆ Represents a portrait of the Rain God

CHAAK *(Chaak)* (T1011) ▶ n. "Chaak"; deity name, the Maya rain god ◆ Represents a portrait of the Rain God

CHAAK *(Chaak)* (T1011) ▶ n. "Chaak"; deity name, the Maya rain god ♦ Represents a portrait of the Rain God

CHAAK-ki *(Chaak)* (T1011.102) ▶ n. "Chaak"; deity name, the Maya rain god ♦ Represents a portrait of the Rain God

CHAAN/KAAN *(chaan/kaan)* (T561c) 1 ▶ n. "sky"; *chaan* in Ch'olan, *kaan* in Yucatec 2 ▶ n. "captor" ♦ Homophonous or semi-homophonous with *chan/kan* "four" and "snake"

CHAAN/KAAN *(chaan/kaan)* (T746) ▶ n. "sky"; *chaan* in Ch'olan, *kaan* in Yucatec ♦ Homophonous or semi-homophonous with *chan/kan* "four" and "snake." Represents the head of a bird. See also **B'AKTUN** and **pi/PI/PIJ**.

CHAAN/KAAN *(chaan/kaan)* (T746ff) ▶ n. "sky"; *chaan* in Ch'olan, *kaan* in Yucatec ♦ Homophonous or semi-homophonous with *chan/kan* "four" and "snake." Represents the full figure of a bird. See also **B'AKTUN** and **pi/PI/PIJ**.

CHAAN CH'EN-na/KAAN CH'EN-na *(chaan ch'en/kaan ch'en)* (T561. 571:23) ▶ n. "sky cave"

CHAAN-na/KAAN-na *(chaan/kaan)* (T561:23) 1 ▶ n. "sky"; *chaan* in Ch'olan, *kaan* in Yucatec 2 ▶ n. "captor" ♦ Homophonous or semi-homophonous with *chan/kan* "four" and "snake"

CHAAN-na CH'EN-na/KAAN-na CH'EN-na *(chaan ch'en/kaan ch'en)* (T561:23.598:23) ▶ n. "sky cave"; *chaan* in Ch'olan, *kaan* in Yucatec

CHAAN-na CH'UL/KAAN-na K'UL *(chaan ch'ul/kaan k'ul)* (T561:23.36)
▶ adj. + pl. n. "the heavenly gods"; *chaan* in Ch'olan, *kaan* in Yucatec.
Alternatively **CHAAN-na-CH'UJUL/KAAN-na K'UJUL** *(chaan ch'ujul/kaan k'ujul)*.

CHAAN-na K'AWIL-la/KAAN-na K'AWIL-la *(Chaan K'awil/Kaan K'awil)*
(T561:23.1030b.178) ▶ n. "Sky K'awil"; deity name; *chaan* in Ch'olan,
kaan in Yucatec

[CHAAN]-NAL K'U/[KAAN]-NAL K'U *(chaanal k'u/kaanal k'u)* (T86:1016
[561]) ▶ adj. + pl. n. "the heavenly gods"; *chaan* in Ch'olan, *kaan* in Yucatec

CHAAN-na-NAL/KAAN-na-NAL *(chaanal/kaanal)* (T86:325?[561]:23)
▶ adj. "heavenly"; *chaan* in Ch'olan, *kaan* in Yucatec

cha-CHAN/ka-KAN *(chan/kan)* (T108:764) 1 ▶ n."snake," "serpent" 2 ▶ n. "captor" ♦ Homophonous or semi-homophonous with *chaan/kaan* "sky" and *chan/kan* "four." Depicts the head of a snake.

CHAK *(chak)* (T109) 1 ▶ adj. "red" 2 ▶ adj. "great"

CHAK *(chak)* (T109) 1 ▶ adj. "red" 2 ▶ adj. "great"

CHAK *(chak)* (T109) 1 ▶ adj. "red" 2 ▶ adj. "great"

CHAK *(chak)* (T590v) 1 ▶ adj. "red" 2 ▶ adj. "great" ♦ Represents a human mandible

CHAK *(chak)* (T590v) 1 ▶ adj. "red" 2 ▶ adj. "great" ◆ Represents a human mandible

CHAK CH'UL AJAW/CHAK K'UL AJAW *(chak ch'ul ajaw/chak k'ul ajaw)* (T109.168:41) 1 ▶ adj. + n. "great holy lord" 2 ▶ adj. + n. "red holy lord" ◆ Functions as the Emblem Glyph of Chinikihá, Chiapas. Alternatively **CHAK CH'UJUL AJAW/CHAK K'UJUL AJAW**.

CHAK EK' *(chak ek')* (T109:510v) ▶ adj. + n. "great star"; proper name of the planet Venus

cha-ki *(Chaak)* (T520:102) ▶ n. "Chaak"; deity name, the Maya rain god

cha-ki *(Chaak)* (T520v.102) ▶ n. "Chaak"; deity name, the Maya rain god

cha-ki CHAAN-na/cha-ki KAAN-na *(Chaak Chaan/Chaak Kaan)* (T520hv. 561hv:23) ▶ n. "Rain God Sky"; deity name

CHAK-ka-ta   See **SIP**.

CHAK K'AT *(chak'at)* (T109:552) 1 ▶ n. name of the "basket staff" dance object 2 ▶ n. month sign; third month of the Maya Ja'ab' calendar; the month of **SIP** ♦ Depicted at Yaxchilán as an object held in "dance" scenes; in this context it follows the verb **AK'OT** and its variants.

CHAK XIB' cha-ki *(Chak Xib' Chaak)* (T109.1008 520v:102) ▶ n. "Red Man Rain God"?; deity name

CHALAJUN/KALAJUN *(chalajun/kalajun)* (TXII) ▶ n. "twelve"; cardinal number

CHALAJUN/KALAJUN *(chalajun/kalajun)* (TXIIhv) ▶ n. "twelve"; cardinal number ♦ Depicts a human head with T561 **CHAAN/KAAN** "sky" as a headdress

CHAM *(cham)* (T736v) ▶ intr. v. "to die"; generally "death" ♦ Depicts a human skull

CHAM *(cham)* (T736v) ▶ intr. v. "to die"; generally "death" ♦ Depicts a human skull

CHAM-li *(chamil)* (T736v:24) ▶ intr. v. "to die"; generally "death"

CHAM-mi *(cham)* (T736v:173) ▶ intr. v. "to die"; generally "death"

CHAM-mi-ya *(chamiy)* (T736v.173:126) ▶ intr. incom. v. "dies"; generally "death"

●
●
●
●

CHAN/KAN *(chan/kan)* (TIV) ▶ n. "four"; cardinal number ♦ Homophonous or semi-homophonous with *chaan/kaan* "sky" and *chan/kan* "snake"

CHAN/KAN *(chan/kan)* (T206) ▶ n. "four"; cardinal number ♦ Homophonous or semi-homophonous with *chaan/kaan* "sky" and *chan/kan* "snake." Depicts a snake.

CHAN/KAN *(chan/kan)* (T764) 1 ▶ n. "snake," "serpent" 2 ▶ n. "captor" ♦ Homophonous or semi-homophonous with *chaan/kaan* "sky" and *chan/kan* "four." Main sign of Emblem Glyph of Calakmul, Campeche, Mexico. Depicts the head of a snake.

CHAN/KAN *(chan/kan)* (T764) 1 ▶ n. "snake," "serpent" 2 ▶ n. "captor" ♦ Homophonous or semi-homophonous with *chaan/kaan* "sky" and *chan/kan* "four." Main sign of the Calakmul Emblem Glyph. Depicts the head of a snake.

CHAN/KAN *(chan/kan)* (T1010) ▶ n. "four"; cardinal number ♦ Homophonous or semi-homophonous with *chaan/kaan* "sky" and *chan/kan* "snake." Represents a portrait of the Sun God, with infix T544 **K'IN**.

cha-nu/ka-nu *(chan/kan)* (T135:592) ▶ n. "captor" ♦ Homophonous or semi-homophonous with *chaan/kaan* "sky," *chan/kan* "four," and *chan/kan* "snake"

CHAPAT *(chapat)* (Tnn) ▶ n. "centipede" ♦ Represents the head of a monstrous centipede

cha-TAN-na *(chatan)* (T299:520.606:23) ▶ prep. phr. "in the center"? ♦ Possibly a surname or location?

cha-te' K'AB'A *(chat k'ab'a)* (T187:520:87) ▶ n. phr. "*chat* 'name'"; *chat* of unknown meaning; refers to a type of name

CHAY/KAY *(chay/kay)* (T738) ▶ n. "fish" ◆ Represents the full figure of a fish. See also **ka**.

cha-ya *(chay/kay)* (T520.126) ▶ n. "fish"

che *(che)* (T145) ▶ phonetic sign ◆ Represents a knot or hank of hair

che *(che)* (T145) ▶ phonetic sign ◆ Represents a knot or hank of hair

che *(che)* (T145) ▶ phonetic sign ◆ Represents a knot or hank of hair

che *(che)* (T148) ▶ phonetic sign ◆ Represents a knot or hank of hair

che-b'u *(cheb')* (T148.21:741v) ▶ n. "quill pen"

che-e-na *(che'en)* (T148.741a:23) ▶ quot. part. "so he/she/they/it says"
♦ Common in Ch'ol and Ch'orti stories

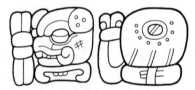

che-e-na TU b'a-ki *(che'en tu b'ak)* (T148.741a:23 89.501:102) ▶ v. phr.
"so it says on his/her/its bone" ♦ Includes the quotative particle *che'en*

che-je-na *(che'en)* (T148.574:23) ▶ quot. part. "so he/she/they/it says"
♦ Common in Ch'ol and Ch'orti stories

chi/CHI *(chi)* (T671) 1 ▶ phonetic sign 2 ▶ n. "mouth"; *chi* means "mouth" in almost all Mayan languages ◆ Represents the back of an upright human hand

CHIJ *(chij)* (T291.nn) ▶ n. "deer"; "white-tailed deer" ◆ Represents the head of a deer with an antler on the forehead

chi-ji-la-ma *(chi'lam)* (T671:314 534:142) 1 ▶ n. "interpreter" 2 ▶ n. "speaker"

CHIKCHAN *(Chicchan)* (T508) ▶ n. day sign; fifth day of the Maya Tzolk'in calendar

CHIKCHAN *(Chicchan)* (T764) ▶ n. day sign; fifth day of the Maya Tzolk'in calendar ♦ Represents the head of a snake

chi-[K'IN]-li *(chik'inil)* (T671[544]:82) ▶ prep. phr. "in the west"; cardinal direction ♦ Alternatively **[K'IN]-chi-li** or *k'inichil* "the sun-face of"

chi-K'IN-ni   See **OCH-K'IN**.

CHIT *(chit)* (T580) ▶ n. "father"; relationship glyph ♦ Phonetic **lo**. See also **lo**.

CHITAM *(chitam)* (T753v) ▶ n. "peccary" ♦ Represents the head of a peccary

CHIT-ti *(chit)* (T580:59) ▶ n. "father"; relationship glyph

cho *(cho)* (T590) ▶ phonetic sign ◆ Represents a human mandible

CHOK *(chok)* (T33v.710v) 1 ▶ tr. v. "to scatter" 2 ▶ tr. v. "to throw" ◆ Represents a hand scattering droplets

CHOK-ji *(chokij)* (T33v.710v:136) 1 ▶ tr. v. phr. "to scatter drops" 2 ▶ tr. v. phr. "to throw drops" ◆ General verb for "bloodletting" and "scattering" rites

CHOK-ko-wa CH'A-ji *(chokaw ch'aj)* (T590:110:130.93:136) 1 ▶ tr. v. phr. "to scatter drops of liquid" 2 ▶ tr. v. phr. "to throw drops of liquid" ♦ General verb for "bloodletting" and "scattering" rites

CHOK-wa CH'A-ji *(chokaw ch'aj)* (T33v.710v:130.93:136) 1 ▶ tr. v. phr. "to scatter drops of liquid" 2 ▶ tr. v. phr. "to throw drops of liquid" ♦ General verb for "bloodletting" and "scattering" rites

chu *(chu)* (T87.515a) ▶ phonetic sign

chu *(chu)* (T515a) ▶ phonetic sign

chu *(chu)* (T601) ▶ phonetic sign

chu-ka *(chuk)* (T87.515a:25) 1 ▶ tr. v. "to seize" 2 ▶ tr. v. "to capture"
◆ General verb meaning "capture"

chu-ka-ja *(chukaj)* (T87.515a:25.181) ▶ pass. v. "was captured"; general
verb meaning "capture"

chu-[ku] *(chuk)* (T87.515a[528]) 1 ▶ tr. v. "to seize" 2 ▶ tr. v. "to capture"
◆ General verb meaning "capture"

chu-[ku]-ja *(chukaj)* (T87.515a[528].181) ▶ pass. v. "was captured"; general verb meaning "capture"

chu-[ku]-ji-ya *(chukjiy)* (T87.515a[528]:17.126) ▶ intr. com. v. "(was) captured"; general verb meaning "capture"

CHUM *(chum)* (T644) ▶ pos. v. "to be seated"; general verb meaning "accession" ◆ Represents the lower half of a human body seated in profile

CHUM (?) *(chum?)* (T700) ▶ pos. v. "to be seated"; general verb meaning "accession" ◆ Represents the lower half of a crouching human body

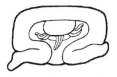

CHUM (?) *(chum?)* (T702v) ▶ pos. v. "to be seated"; general verb meaning "accession" ♦ Represents the lower half of a crouching human body

CHUM-la-ji-ya *(chumlajiy)* (T644a:178.88:126) ▶ pos. com. v. "seated"; general verb meaning "accession"

CHUM-[mu] *(chum)* (T644b) ▶ pos. v. "to be seated"; general verb meaning "accession" ♦ Represents the lower half of a human body seated in profile

CHUM-[mu]-la-ji-ya *(chumlajiy)* (T644b:88.178.126) ▶ pos. com. v. "seated"; general verb meaning "accession"

CHUM-[mu] TUN-ni *(chum tun)* (T644b.528:116) ▶ v. phr. "seating of the *tun*," "seating of the stone"; PE calendrical glyph for *tun* endings

CHUM-[mu]-wa-ni-ya *(chumwaniy)* (T644b:130.116:126) ▶ pos. com. v. "seated"; general verb meaning "accession"

[CHUM] TUN-ni *(chum tun)* (T528[644a]:116) ▶ v. phr. "seating of the *tun*," "seating of the stone"; PE calendrical glyph for *tun* endings

CHUM-wa-ni TI AJAW-le-{l} *(chumwan ti ajawlel)* (T644[584]:116:130 59.168:188) ▶ *ti*-construction v. phr. "seated in lordship"; primary and complete statement of "accession"

CHUWEN *(Chuwen)* (T520) ▶ n. day sign; eleventh day of the Maya Tzolk'in calendar

CHUWEN *(chuwen)* (Tnn:520) ▶ n. "artist"; artist's title

CH'

ch'a/CH'A *(ch'a)* (T93) 1 ▶ phonetic sign 2 ▶ n. "drops" 3 ▶ n. "drop of water, urine, or other liquid"

ch'a/CH'A *(ch'a)* (T93) 1 ▶ phonetic sign 2 ▶ n. "drops," "droplet" 3 ▶ n. "drop of water, urine, or other liquid"

ch'a *(ch'a)* (Tnn) ▶ phonetic sign ◆ Represents the head of an unidentified animal

CH'AB' *(ch'ab')* (T712) 1 ▶ intr. v. "do penance, sacrifice" 2 ▶ intr. v. "to pierce with a lance," "lancing"; when used in parentage relationship statements may have the meaning "to create" ◆ Represents an obsidian lancet

CH'AB' *(ch'ab')* (T712:116v) 1 ▶ intr. v. "do penance, sacrifice" 2 ▶ intr. v. "to pierce with a lance," "lancing"; when used in parentage relationship statements may have the meaning "to create" ◆ Represents an obsidian lancet

ch'a-b'a *(ch'ab')* (T89:501) 1 ▶ intr. v. "do penance, sacrifice" 2 ▶ intr. v. "to pierce with a lance," "lancing"; when used in parentage relationship statements may have the meaning "to create"

ch'a-ja-{l}-te' *(ch'ajalte')* (T93:683:87) ▶ n. type of drink

ch'a-ji *(ch'aj)* (T93:758b) 1 ▶ n. "drops," "droplet" 2 ▶ n. "drop of water, urine, or other liquid"

ch'a-JOM *(ch'ajom)* (T93.672hv) ▶ n. "dripper," "scatterer"; elite title; the "shell-fist" title

ch'a-jo-ma *(ch'ajom)* (T93:672.142) ▶ n. "dripper," "scatterer"; elite title; the "shell-fist" title

ch'a-jo-ma *(ch'ajom)* (T93.607v:74) ▶ n. "dripper," "scatterer"; elite title; the "shell-fist" title

CH'AK *(ch'ak)* (T190) 1 ▶ tr. v. "to chop" 2 ▶ tr. v. "to decapitate" 3 ▶ tr. v. "to chop with a blow" ♦ General war-related verb, the "axe verb." Possibly related specifically to wars against armies or individuals as opposed to those against sites or locations. Represents an axe.

ch'a-ka-ja *(ch'akaj)* (T93.25:683) 1 ▶ pass. v. "it was axed," "it was chopped" 2 ▶ pass. v. "it was decapitated" ♦ General war-related verb; phonetic spelling of the "axe verb." Possibly related specifically to wars against armies or individuals as opposed to those against sites or locations.

CH'AK-ka *(ch'ak)* (T333) 1 ▶ tr. v. "to chop" 2 ▶ tr. v. "to decapitate" 3 ▶ tr. v. "to chop with a blow" ♦ General war-related verb, the "axe verb." Possibly related specifically to wars against armies or individuals as opposed to those against sites or locations.

CH'AK-ka-b'a *(ch'akab')* (T333.501) 1 ▶ intr. v. "to self-decapitate" 2 ▶ intr. v. "to self-axe" ♦ Can function as the reflexive form of *ch'ak*. General verb meaning "self-sacrifice."

CH'AK-ka-b'a *(ch'akab')* (T333.757:60) 1 ▶ intr. v. "to self-decapitate" 2 ▶ intr. v. "to self-axe" ♦ Can function as the reflexive form of *ch'ak*. General verb meaning "self-sacrifice."

CH'AM *(ch'am)* (T670) 1 ▶ tr. v. "to receive" 2 ▶ tr. v. "to harvest" 3 ▶ n. "harvest" ♦ Represents an outstretched human hand

CH'AM *(ch'am)* (T533:670) 1 ▶ tr. v. "to receive" 2 ▶ tr. v. "to harvest" 3 ▶ n. "harvest" ♦ Represents an outstretched human hand holding T533

CH'AM K'AWIL-la *(ch'am K'awil)* (T533:670.1030dv) 1 ▶ tr. v. "to receive K'awil" 2 ▶ tr. v. "to harvest K'awil"

CH'AM-ma *(ch'am)* (T670:142) 1 ▶ tr. v. "to receive" 2 ▶ tr. v. "to harvest" 3 ▶ n. "harvest" ♦ Represents an outstretched human hand

CH'AM-ma *(ch'am)* (T508:670:142) 1 ▶ tr. v. "to receive" 2 ▶ tr. v. "to harvest" 3 ▶ n. "harvest" ♦ Represents an outstretched human hand holding T508

CH'AM-ma K'AWIL-la *(ch'am K'awil)* (T508:670:142.1030dv:178) 1 ▶ tr. v. "to receive K'awil" 2 ▶ tr. v. "to harvest K'awil"

ch'a-ti *(ch'at)* (T93.59) 1 ▶ n. "dwarf" 2 ▶ n. "hunchback"

ch'a-ti *(ch'at)* (Tnn:59) 1 ▶ n. "dwarf" 2 ▶ n. "hunchback"

CH'EN *(Ch'en)* (T95.528:74) ▶ n. month sign; ninth month of the Maya Ja'ab' calendar

CH'EN *(ch'en)* (T571) ▶ n. "cave"; the "impinged bone" glyph

CH'EN *(ch'en)* (T598v) ▶ n. "cave"; the "impinged bone" glyph

CH'EN *(ch'en)* (T598v) ▶ n. "cave"; the "impinged eye" glyph

CH'EN *(ch'en)* (Tnn) ▶ n. "cave"; the "impinged **K'IN**" glyph

CH'EN *(ch'en)* (T598hv) ▶ n. "cave" ♦ Represents the head of a bird with trifoliate eye

CH'EN *(ch'en)* (Tnn.598hv) ▶ n. "cave" ♦ Represents the head of a bird with trifoliate eye

CH'EN-na *(ch'en)* (T571:23) ▶ n. "cave"

CH'EN-na *(ch'en)* (T598v:23) ▶ n. "cave"

ch'o *(ch'o)* (T287) ▶ phonetic sign ♦ Represents a pair of eyes

ch'o *(ch'o)* (T287) ▶ phonetic sign ♦ Represents a pair of eyes

ch'o *(ch'o)* (T758) ▶ phonetic sign ♦ Represents the head of a rodent

ch'o-ko *(ch'ok)* (T287:nn) 1 ▶ n. "youth" 2 ▶ n. "youngster," "young one" 3 ▶ adj. "young" 4 ▶ adj. "unripe" ♦ Elite title. Variant of the "Rodent Bone" title.

ch'o-ko *(ch'ok)* (T757v:110) 1 ▶ n. "youth" 2 ▶ n. "youngster," "young one" 3 ▶ adj. "young" 4 ▶ adj. "unripe" ♦ Elite title. The "Rodent Bone" title.

ch'o-[ko] *(ch'ok)* (T758) 1 ▶ n. "youth" 2 ▶ n. "youngster," "young one" 3 ▶ adj. "young" 4 ▶ adj. "unripe" ♦ Elite title. The "Rodent Bone" title.

ch'o-[ko] K'AB'A *(ch'ok k'ab'a)* (T187:758) ▶ adj. + n. "youthful name"

CH'OK TE' NA *(ch'ok te' na)* (T600:87.4) ▶ n. "sprout tree house"; the "founder" glyph; the "crossed batons" glyph; reference to the founder's house?

CH'UL/K'UL (CH'UJUL/K'UJUL) *(ch'ul/k'ul, ch'ujul/k'ujul)* (T32) ▶ adj. "sacred," "holy," "divine"; incorporates a visual and conceptual analogy between blood and the soul; derives from the word *ch'ulel* in several Mayan languages, meaning "soul," "holiness," "divinity," "spirituality" ♦ Depicts drops of liquid, most likely blood, although other suggestions include drops of water and pellets of incense

CH'UL/K'UL (CH'UJUL/K'UJUL) *(ch'ul/k'ul, ch'ujul/k'ujul)* (T36) ▶ adj. "sacred," "holy," "divine"; incorporates a visual and conceptual analogy between blood and the soul; derives from the word *ch'ulel* in several Mayan languages, meaning "soul," "holiness," "divinity," "spirituality" ♦ Depicts drops of liquid, most likely blood, and the **K'AN** glyph

CH'UL/K'UL (CH'UJUL/K'UJUL) *(ch'ul/k'ul, ch'ujul/k'ujul)* (T37) ▶ adj. "sacred," "holy," "divine"; incorporates a visual and conceptual analogy between blood and the soul; derives from the word *ch'ulel* in several Mayan languages, meaning "soul," "holiness," "divinity," "spirituality" ♦ Depicts drops of liquid, most likely blood, and the **YAX** glyph

CH'UL/K'UL (CH'UJUL/K'UJUL) *(ch'ul/k'ul, ch'ujul/k'ujul)* (T38) ▶ adj. "sacred," "holy," "divine"; incorporates a visual and conceptual analogy between blood and the soul; derives from the word *ch'ulel* in several Mayan languages, meaning "soul," "holiness," "divinity," "spirituality" ♦ Depicts drops of liquid, most likely blood, and a shell ear ornament

CH'UL/K'UL (CH'UJUL/K'UJUL) *(ch'ul/k'ul, ch'ujul/k'ujul)* (T38) ▶ adj. "sacred," "holy," "divine"; incorporates a visual and conceptual analogy between blood and the soul; derives from the word *ch'ulel* in several Mayan languages, meaning "soul," "holiness," "divinity," "spirituality" ♦ Depicts drops of liquid, most likely blood, and a shell ear ornament

CH'UL/K'UL (CH'UJUL/K'UJUL) *(ch'ul/k'ul, ch'ujul/k'ujul)* (T40) ▶ adj. "sacred," "holy," "divine"; incorporates a visual and conceptual analogy between blood and the soul; derives from the word *ch'ulel* in several Mayan languages, meaning "soul," "holiness," "divinity," "spirituality" ◆ Depicts drops of liquid, most likely blood, and an "upside-down Ajaw" glyph (**Ia**)

CH'UL/K'UL (CH'UJUL/K'UJUL) *(ch'ul/k'ul, ch'ujul/k'ujul)* (T41) ▶ adj. "sacred," "holy," "divine"; incorporates a visual and conceptual analogy between blood and the soul; derives from the word *ch'ulel* in several Mayan languages, meaning "soul," "holiness," "divinity," "spirituality" ◆ Depicts drops of liquid, most likely blood, and the **K'U** glyph

CH'UL/K'UL (CH'UJUL/K'UJUL) *(ch'ul/k'ul, ch'ujul/k'ujul)* (T32:683v) ▶ adj. "sacred," "holy," "divine"; incorporates a visual and conceptual analogy between blood and the soul; derives from the word *ch'ulel* in several Mayan languages, meaning "soul," "holiness," "divinity," "spirituality" ◆ Depicts drops of liquid, most likely blood, and the "moon sign" **JUL** variant infixed with an eye

CH'UL AJAW-wa/K'UL AJAW-wa (CH'UJUL AJAW-wa/K'UJUL AJAW-wa) *(ch'ul ajaw/k'ul ajaw, ch'ujul ajaw/k'ujul ajaw)* (T37.168:518:130) ▶ adj. + n. "sacred/holy/divine lord"; royal title

CH'UL CHAAN CH'UL KAB'/K'UL KAAN K'UL KAB' (CH'UJUL CHAAN CH'UJUL KAB'/K'UJUL KAAN K'UJUL KAB') *(ch'ul chaan ch'ul kab'/ k'ul kaan k'ul kab', ch'ujul chaan ch'ujul kab'/k'ujul kaan k'ujul kab')* (T35.561hv 35.526hv) ▶ tit. phr. "heavenly god, earthly god"

CH'UL cha-TAN-na wi-WINIK-ki/K'UL cha-TAN-na wi-WINIK-ki (CH'UJUL cha-TAN-na wi-WINIK-ki/K'UJUL cha-TAN-na wi-WINIK-ki) *(ch'ul chatan winik/k'ul chatan winik, ch'ujul chatan winik/k'ujul chatan winik)* (T41 299:520.606:23 117.741v:102) ▶ tit. phr. "sacred Chatan person"; resembles an EG but with "person" rather than "lord": *ch'ul . . . winik/ch'ul . . . ajaw*; refers to someone from "Chatan"

CH'UL cha-TAN WINIK/K'UL cha-TAN WINIK (CH'UJUL cha-TAN WINIK/K'UJUL cha-TAN WINIK) *(ch'ul chatan winik/k'ul chatan winik, ch'ujul chatan winik/k'ujul chatan winik)* (T33:520.606:521) ▶ tit. phr. "sacred Chatan person"; resembles an EG but with "person" rather than "lord": *ch'ul . . . winik/ch'ul . . . ajaw*; refers to someone from "Chatan"

CH'UL IXIK-ki/K'UL IXIK-ki (CH'UJUL IXIK-ki/K'UJUL IXIK-ki) *(ch'ul ixik/k'ul ixik, ch'ujul ixik/k'ujul ixik)* (T36.1002a:102) ▶ adj. + n. "sacred/holy/divine woman"

CH'UL K'AB'A/K'UL K'AB'A *(ch'ul k'ab'a/k'ul k'ab'a)* (T187:1016) ▶ adj. + n. "sacred/holy/divine name"

CH'UL-lu/K'UL-lu (CH'UJUL-lu/K'UJUL-lu) *(ch'ul/k'ul, ch'ujul/k'ujul)* (T32:568v) ▶ adj. "sacred," "holy," "divine" ◆ Represents drops of liquid, most likely blood—the essence of the spirit—with the **lu** glyph

CH'UL-lu to-k'a/K'UL-lu to-k'a (CH'UJUL-lu to-k'a/K'UJUL-lu to-k'a)
(ch'ul tok'/k'ul tok', ch'ujul tok'/k'ujul tok') (T38.568.44:669) ▶ adj. + n. "sacred/holy/divine flint"

CH'UL to-{k} TAN AJAW/K'UL to-{k} TAN AJAW (CH'UJUL to-{k} TAN AJAW/K'UJUL to-{k} TAN AJAW) *(Ch'ul Tok Tan Ajaw/K'ul Tok Tan Ajaw, Ch'ujul Tok Tan Ajaw/K'ujul Tok Tan Ajaw)* (T40.168:44:606v) ▶ adj. + n. "Sacred/Holy/Divine Cloud Center Lord," "Sacred/Holy/Divine Cloud Place Lord"; elite title

CH'UL WINIK-ki/K'UL WINIK-ki (CH'UJUL WINIK-ki/K'UJUL WINIK-ki)
(ch'ul winik/k'ul winik, ch'ujul winik/k'ujul winik) (T33:520.60) 1 ▶ adj. + n. "sacred/holy/divine man" 2 ▶ adj. + n. "sacred/holy/divine person"

E

e *(e)* (T542a) ▶ vowel *e*

e *(e)* (T542a) ▶ vowel *e*

e *(e)* (T741v) ▶ vowel *e*

e *(e)* (T741v) ▶ vowel *e*

EB' *(Eb')* (T1045v[528]) ▶ n. day sign; twelfth day of the Maya Tzolk'in calendar ♦ Represents a skull with T528 **KAWAK** infix

EB'-[b'u] *(eb')* (T843[21.741]) ▶ n. "stairway," "staircase" ♦ Represents a staircase in profile with phonetic **b'u** infix

e-b'u *(eb')* (T741v:21.741v) ▶ n. "stairway," "staircase"

EK' *(ek')* (T89) ▶ adj. "black"

EK' *(ek')* (T89) ▶ adj. "black"

EK' *(ek')* (T89) ▶ adj. "black"

EK' *(ek'/Ek')* (T510af) 1 ▶ n. "star"; represents one-half of the full "star" glyph 2 ▶ n. "Venus"? ♦ Half of the complete "star" glyph

EK' *(ek'/Ek')* (T510) 1 ▶ n. "star" 2 ▶ n. "Venus"? ♦ The complete "star" glyph

EK' JUN *(ek' jun)* (T89ms:60) ▶ adj. + n. "black headband"

EK'-ka-ta See **WO**.

EK' WAY-NAL *(ek' waynal)* (T89.86:769:140) 1 ▶ adj. + n. "black hole"
2 ▶ n. "Black Hole Place"

EM *(em)* (T227) ▶ intr. v. "to descend"

ETZ'NAB' *(Etz'nab')* (T527) ▶ n. day sign; eighteenth day of the Maya
Tzolk'in calendar ♦ Represents the surface pattern of a pressure-flaked
flint blade

I

i/I *(i)* (T679) 1 ▶ vowel *i* 2 ▶ part. "and then," "then"; the "Posterior Date Indicator" (PDI)

i/I *(i)* (T679) 1 ▶ vowel *i* 2 ▶ part. "and then," "then"; the "Posterior Date Indicator" (PDI)

i/I *(i)* (T87?.512[679]) 1 ▶ vowel *i* 2 ▶ part. "and then," "then"; the "Posterior Date Indicator" (PDI)

i *(i)* (T237v) ▶ vowel *i* ♦ Represents a bird plucking the eye of a dog or other animal

i *(i)* (T237v) ▶ vowel *i* ♦ Represents a bird plucking the eye of a dog or other animal

i-b'a-k'a *(ib'ak')* (T679.501:669a) ▶ n. "armadillo"

ICH'AK *(ich'ak)* (T5) 1 ▶ n. "jaguar claw" 2 ▶ n. "jaguar paw"; possible alternative reading: **MOL** (specifically "paw," as opposed to "claw") ♦ Represents a jaguar's paw. See also **MOL**.

ICH'AK-ki *(ich'ak)* (Tnn:102) ▶ n. "claw" ◆ Represents a jaguar's paw, together with the phonetic complement **ki**

ICH'AK TUN-ni *(ich'ak tun)* (T5:528:116) ▶ n. "jaguar claw stone," "jaguar paw stone"

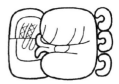

I-IL-ji *(ilij)* (T679.618v.136) ▶ part. + tr. v. "and then he/she saw it," "and then he/she witnessed it"

i-ka-tzi *(ikatz)* (T679.25:507) ▶ n. "burden," "load," "tribute"

i-ka-tzi *(ikatz)* (T679:25:124) ▶ n. "burden," "load," "tribute"

i-ki-tzi *(ikitz)* (T679.102:507) ▶ n. "burden," "load," "tribute"; evidently an alternative spelling of **i-ka-tzi**

IK' *(Ik')* (T23) ▶ n. day sign; second day of the Maya Tzolk'in calendar; a rare **IK'** logogram; found especially in early texts from Uaxactun

IK' *(Ik')* (T503) ▶ n. day sign; second day of the Maya Tzolk'in calendar; the "T" sign associated with "wind," "breath," and the Wind God

IK' *(Ik')* (T503hv) ▶ n. day sign; second day of the Maya Tzolk'in calendar; the "T" sign associated with "wind," "breath," and the Wind God

IK' K'U *(Ik' K'u)* (T23:503.36?) ▶ n. "Wind God"; proper name of the Classic Maya wind god?; T23 **na** functions as part of the Ik' sign logogram

-il *(-il)* (T24) ▶ part. suf. indicating possession ♦ Represents a mirror. See also **li**.

-il *(-il)* (T24) ▶ part. suf. indicating possession ♦ Represents a mirror. See also **li**.

-il *(-il)* (T82) ▶ part. suf. indicating possession ♦ See also **li**.

-il *(-il)* (T82) ▶ part. suf. indicating possession ♦ See also **li**.

-il *(-il)* (T83) ▶ part. suf. indicating possession ◆ See also **li**.

-il *(-il)* (T360) ▶ part. suf. indicating possession ◆ See also **li**.

-il *(-il)* (Tnn) ▶ part. suf. indicating possession ◆ See also **li**. The "worm-bird" glyph.

-il *(-il)* (Tnn) ▶ part. suf. indicating possession ◆ See also **li**. The "worm-bird" glyph.

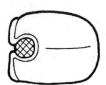

IL *(il)* (T618v) ▶ tr. v. "to see"

IL-ja *(ilaj)* (T618v) ▶ pass. v. "was seen"

IMIX *(Imix)* (T501) ▶ n. day sign; first day of the Maya Tzolk'in calendar
♦ Represents a water lily blossom

IMIX *(Imix)* (T501) ▶ n. day sign; first day of the Maya Tzolk'in calendar
♦ Represents a water lily blossom

IMIX *(Imix)* (T501hv) ▶ n. day sign; first day of the Maya Tzolk'in calendar
♦ Represents the saurian Water Lily Monster

IN *(in)* (T116) 1 ▶ 1ˢᵗ pers. pron. "I"; marks the subject of transitive verbs 2 ▶ 1ˢᵗ pers. poss. pron. "my"; when attached to a noun, the noun becomes possessed ◆ May represent a tail

IN-b'u-ku *(in b'uk)* (T116.21:528) ▶ poss. n. "my clothes"; includes the first-person possessive pronoun *in-* "my"

IN CH'EN *(in ch'en)* (T116.598v:?) ▶ poss. n. "my cave"; includes the first-person possessive pronoun *in-* "my"

IN KAB' *(in kab')* (T116.526) ▶ poss. n. "my earth," "my land"; includes the first-person possessive pronoun *in-* "my"

IN pa-ta *(in pat)* (T116.586:103?) ▶ poss. n. "my tribute"; includes the first-person possessive pronoun *in-* "my"

IN tu-pa *(in tup)* (T116.92:586) ▶ poss. n. "my earspool"; includes the first-person possessive pronoun *in-* "my"

ITZ' *(itz')* (T152) 1 ▶ n. "essence" 2 ▶ n. "sweat" 3 ▶ n. "resin" 4 ▶ n. "flower nectar" ♦ Related to the concept of the soul and "sacred essence." Represents a flower with stamen drooping from its blossom.

itz'-am-{na} *(Itz'amná)* (T152.nn) ▶ n. deity name; proper name of the god Itz'amná, principal god of the Maya pantheon; incorporates the **itz'** sign, but *itz'am* can mean "crocodile" or "lizard," with the whole possibly meaning "lizard house"

ITZ'AM ye-ji *(Itz'am Yej)* (T152.nn 512:136) ▶ n. deity name; proper name of the Principal Bird Deity

ITZ'AT *(itz'at)* (Tnn) ▶ n. "sage," "wise man," "learned one"; in general, "artist"

ITZ'AT *(itz'at)* (Tnn) ▶ n. "sage," "wise man," "learned one"; in general, "artist"

i-tz'a-ta *(itz'at)* (T58[679]:103) ▶ n. "sage," "wise man," "learned one"; in general, "artist"

ITZ'AT-ta *(itz'at)* (Tnn.102) ▶ n. "sage," "wise man," "learned one"; in general, "artist"

i-tz'i-{n} *(itz'in)* (T237v:752) ▶ n. "younger brother"

i-tz'i-{n} WINIK *(itz'in winik)* (T237v:752.248:521) ▶ adj. + n. "younger brother person"

i-tz'i-{n} wi-WINIK-ki *(itz'in winik)* (T679.248:521:103.117) ▶ adj. + n. "younger brother person"

i-u-ti *(i-ut)* (T679.513:59) ▶ part. + intr. v. "and then it happened," "and then it occurred"; the "Posterior Date Indicator" (PDI)

i-u-ti *(i-ut)* (T679.738:59) ▶ part. + intr. v. "and then it happened," "and then it occurred"; the "Posterior Date Indicator" (PDI)

IX *(Ix/ix)* (T524) 1 ▶ n. day sign; fourteenth day of the Maya Tzolk'in calendar 2 ▶ n. "jaguar" ◆ Depicts three glints within an eye (below the eyelid), with the glints possibly doubling as jaguar spots

IX *(Ix/ix)* (T524) 1 ▶ n. day sign; fourteenth day of the Maya Tzolk'in calendar 2 ▶ n. "jaguar" ◆ Depicts three glints within an eye (below the eyelid), with the glints represented as jaguar spots

IX/IXIK *(ix/ixik)* (T1000b) ▶ feminine agentive prefix; "woman"

IXIK-ki *(ixik)* (T1000b:102) ▶ feminine agentive prefix; "woman"

IX TZ'AM(?) *(ix tz'am?)* (T524:150) ▶ n. "jaguar throne"

IX TZ'AM(?) ku-aj *(Ix Tz'am? Ku-aj)* (T524:150.528:12) ▶ n. "Jaguar Throne Stone Place"

i-yu-wa-la *(i-yuwal)* (T679:61:177) ▶ progressive aspect marker; refers to ongoing action

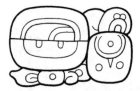

i-yu-wa-la *(i-yuwal)* (T679:62.130:534) ▶ progressive aspect marker; refers to ongoing action

J

ja *(ja)* (T181) ▶ phonetic sign; the "moon" sign

ja *(ja)* (T181) ▶ phonetic sign; the "moon" sign

ja *(ja)* (T683) ▶ phonetic sign; the "moon" sign

ja *(ja)* (T683) ▶ phonetic sign; the "moon" sign

JAL *(jal)* (T153) 1 ▶ tr. v. "to say" 2 ▶ tr. v. "to manifest" 3 ▶ intr. v. "to rest" 4 ▶ intr. v. "to terminate" ♦ Represents crossed bands

JAL-ji-ya *(jal-jiy)* (T153.758:125) 1 ▶ tr. v. "to say" 2 ▶ tr. v. "to manifest" 3 ▶ intr. v. "to rest" 4 ▶ intr. v. "to terminate" ♦ Represents crossed bands and the head of an animal, possibly a gopher

JANAAB' *(janaab')* (T624v) ▶ n. "flower"; occurs in the names of several Palenque Classic Period kings, including Janaab' Pakal the Great (ruled A.D. 615–683) ♦ Differs from **PAKAL** "shield" in that it has a dotted outline, rather than a cross-hatched outer perimeter, and has the "propeller" sign infixed within the center. See also **AJ na-b'i**, **NIKTE'**, and **PAKAL**.

JANAAB' *(janaab')* (T624hv) ▶ n. "flower"; occurs in the names of several Palenque Classic Period kings, including Janaab' Pakal the Great (ruled A.D. 615–683) ♦ Represents the head of a bird with a "flower-shield" sign infixed within the eye. See also **AJ na-b'i**, **NIKTE'**, and **PAKAL**.

JANAAB' *(janaab')* (T624ff) ▶ n. "flower"; occurs in the names of several Palenque Classic Period kings, including Janaab' Pakal the Great (ruled A.D. 615–683) ♦ Represents the full figure of a bird with a "flower-shield" sign infixed within the eye. See also **AJ na-b'i**, **NIKTE'**, and **PAKAL**.

[JANAAB'] PAKAL *(janaab' pakal)* (T624) 1 ▶ n. "flower-shield" 2 ▶ n. the name of several Palenque Classic Period kings, including Janaab' Pakal the Great (ruled A.D. 615–683) ♦ Represents a shield with the "propeller" glyph infix. See also **AJ na-b'i**, **NIKTE'**, and **PAKAL**.

[JANAAB'] PAKAL-la *(janaab' pakal)* (T624b:178) 1 ▶ n. "flower-shield" 2 ▶ n. the name of several Palenque Classic Period kings, including Pakal the Great (ruled A.D. 615–683)

ja-na-b'i *(janaab')* (T181.23:585hv) ▶ n. "flower" ♦ See also **AJ na-b'i** and **NIKTE'**.

ja-sa-wa *(jasaw)* (T683:130.630af) ▶ n. "banner," "flap-staff"; proper name of object held in dances; figures in the name of Jasaw Chaan K'awil, twenty-seventh (Late Classic) ruler of Tikal

ja-sa-wa *(jasaw)* (T181.630:130) ▶ n. "banner," "flap-staff"; proper name of object held in dances; figures in the name of Jasaw Chaan K'awil, twenty-seventh (Late Classic) ruler of Tikal

ja-tz'a-yi *(jatz'ay)* (T181:366v.17) 1 ▶ tr. v. "to strike" 2 ▶ tr. v. "to split" 3 ▶ tr. v. "to wound"

ja-wa-te' *(jawte')* (T181:130.87) ▶ n. "ceramic tripod plate"; used in the PSS to designate a specific type of vessel

ja-wa-te' *(jawte')* (T181:130.87hv) ▶ n. "ceramic tripod plate"; used in the PSS to designate a specific type of vessel

ja-yi *(jay)* (T681:17) ▶ n. "thin-walled vessel," "ceramic bowl"

ja-yi *(jay)* (T681hv nn.17ms) ▶ n. "thin-walled vessel," "ceramic bowl"

ja' *(ja')* (T60.1042) ▶ phonetic sign ♦ Spelled alternatively **ha'**

JA' *(ja')* (T501v) ▶ n. "water" ♦ Represents the blossom of a water lily

JA' *(ja')* (T501v) ▶ n. "water" ♦ Represents the blossom of a water lily

JA' *(ja')* (T1031a) ▶ n. "water" ♦ Represents the head of a zoomorphic monster surmounted by a water lily blossom

JA'AB' *(ja'ab')* (T548) ▶ n. "year"; the year of 365 days as used in the 52-Year Cycle or Calendar Round ♦ Represents the cross-section of a cylindrical wooden drum, or *tunkul*. See also **AB'** and **TUN**.

JA'AB' *(ja'ab')* (T548) ▶ n. "year"; the year of 365 days as used in the 52-Year Cycle or Calendar Round ♦ Represents the cross-section of a cylindrical wooden drum, or *tunkul*. See also **AB'** and **TUN**.

ja'-i *(ja'-i)* (T60.1041) ▶ dem. pron. "this," "that," "that one"; focus marker

ja'-li *(jal)* (T60.1042:24) 1 ▶ tr. v. "to say" 2 ▶ tr. v. "to manifest" 3 ▶ intr. v. "to rest" 4 ▶ intr. v. "to terminate"

ja'-o-b'a *(ja'ob')* (T60.1042:279.501:314) ▶ dem. pl. pron. "they," "these," "they are," "these are"; the plural form of **ja'-i**; ex.: "these are the so-and-so"

je *(je)* (T69) ▶ phonetic sign; the "down balls" glyph

je *(je)* (T514) ▶ phonetic sign

je *(je)* (T574) ▶ phonetic sign ◆ Represents a univalve shell

JEM *(jem)* (T69:610) ▶ n. "valley"

JEM NA *(jem na)* (T69:610:23) ▶ n. "valley house"?

JEM-NAL *(jemnal)* (T86:69:610) ▶ n. "valley place"

ji *(ji)* (T60) ▶ phonetic sign ◆ Represents a knot of cloth or hair. Spelled alternatively **hi**.

ji *(ji)* (T60) ▶ phonetic sign ◆ Represents a knot of cloth or hair

ji *(ji)* (T88) ▶ phonetic sign

ji *(ji)* (T88) ▶ phonetic sign

ji *(ji)* (T136) ▶ phonetic sign

ji *(ji)* (T136) ▶ phonetic sign

ji *(ji)* (T136) ▶ phonetic sign

ji *(ji)* (T136) ▶ phonetic sign

ji *(ji)* (T758b) ▶ phonetic sign ♦ Represents the head of a rodent

ji *(ji)* (T60:528) ▶ phonetic sign ♦ Spelled alternatively **hi**

ji-chi *(jich)* (T18.671) ▶ n. "surface [for writing]"

ji-chi *(jich)* (T18.671hv) ▶ n. "surface [for writing]"

ji-IX *(jix)* (T60:524) ▶ n. "jaguar" ♦ Represents the head of a jaguar. See also **B'ALAM** and **IX**.

ji-JIX *(jix)* (T60:762v) ▶ n. "jaguar" ♦ Represents the head of a jaguar with phonetic complement. See also **B'ALAM**.

ji-li *(jil)* (T60:528.24) 1 ▶ intr. v. "to rest" 2 ▶ intr. v. "to end"

JIX *(jix)* (T762v) ▶ n. "jaguar" ♦ Represents the head of a jaguar. See also **B'ALAM**.

-ji-ya *(-jiy)* (T88.126) ▶ intransitive completive verbal suffix pattern

-ji-ya *(-jiy)* (T246) ▶ intransitive completive verbal suffix pattern

jo *(jo)* (T589) ▶ phonetic sign ◆ May represent the cross-section of a shell

jo *(jo)* (T607) ▶ phonetic sign ◆ May represent the cross-section of a shell

jo *(jo)* (T607) ▶ phonetic sign ◆ May represent the cross-section of a shell

jo *(jo)* (T672[552]) ▶ phonetic sign ◆ Represents a human fist. Spelled alternatively **ho**.

JO *(jo)* (TV) ▶ n. "five"; cardinal number

JO *(jo)* (TVhv) ▶ number "five" head variant ♦ Represents the head of an elderly man surmounted by the sign for **TUN**

jo-JOY *(joy)* (Tnn:607v) 1 ▶ tr. v. "to accede" 2 ▶ tr. v. "to emerge," "to come out"; general "accession" verb; the "toothache" glyph; first part of the "affix cluster"

jo-JOY-ja *(joyaj)* (T607v.684a) 1 ▶ pass. v. "was put in office," "accession" 2 ▶ pass. v. "was emergent," "was come out"; general "accession" verb incorporating the "toothache" glyph; first part of the "affix cluster"

jo-JOY-ja TI AJAW-le-{l} *(joyaj ti ajawlel)* (T607v.684a 59.168:188) ▶ pass. v. phr. "(did) accede in lordship," "(did) accede as ruler," "was emergent in lordship"; general "accession" phrase; the "affix cluster"

JOL *(jol)* (T1040) ▶ n. "head" ♦ Represents a skull

JOL-lo *(jol)* (T1040[580]) ▶ n. "head" ♦ Represents a skull with infixed T580 **lo**

JOM *(jom)* (T218) ▶ tr. v. "to end" ♦ Represents an outstretched human hand and bauble. Spelled alternatively **HOM**. Possibly polyvalent **TZUTZ**.

JOM *(jom)* (T672) 1 ▶ tr. v. "to throw down" 2 ▶ tr. v. "to destroy," "to demolish" 3 ▶ tr. v. "to end" ♦ Represents a human fist. Spelled alternatively **HOM**.

JOM *(jom)* (Tnn) 1 ▶ tr. v. "to throw down" 2 ▶ tr. v. "to destroy," "to demolish" 3 ▶ tr. v. "to end" ♦ Represents a "blindfolded" human head. Spelled alternatively **HOM**.

JOM *(jom)* (Tnn) 1 ▶ tr. v. "to throw down" 2 ▶ tr. v. "to destroy," "to demolish" 3 ▶ tr. v. "to end" ♦ Represents the head of an unidentified animal. Spelled alternatively **HOM**.

JOY *(joy)* (Tnn) 1 ▶ tr. v. "to accede" 2 ▶ tr. v. "to emerge," "to come out"; general "accession" verb; the "toothache" glyph; major component of the "affix cluster" ♦ Represents the cloth knot binding on a bundle. Read alternatively **JOK'**.

JOY-ja *(joyaj)* (T684a) 1 ▶ pass. v. "was put in office," "accession" 2 ▶ pass. v. "was emergent," "was come out"; general "accession" verb incorporating the "toothache" glyph; first part of the "affix cluster"

JOY-[ja]-ji-ya *(joyajiy)* (T684hv.88:126v) 1 ▶ intr. com. v.? "acceded" 2 ▶ tr. v. "to emerge," "to come out"; general "accession" verb; the "toothache" glyph; first part of the "affix cluster"

ju *(ju)* (T45 and T46) ▶ phonetic sign

ju *(ju)* (T45v) ▶ phonetic sign

ju *(ju)* (T740) ▶ phonetic sign ◆ Represents the "upended" head of a frog, lizard or other reptile. Spelled alternatively **hu**.

ju *(ju)* (T1030o) ▶ phonetic sign ◆ Represents the head of the so-called Jester God who symbolizes divine kingship. Spelled alternatively **hu**.

JUB' *(jub')* (T579v) 1 ▶ n. "shell" 2 ▶ n. "shell trumpet" ◆ May represent the cross-section of a shell

JUB' (?) *(jub')* (T510af:325[526]) 1 ▶ intr. v. "to take down" 2 ▶ intr. v. "to bring down"; general "war" verb; "Star-Over-Earth" ◆ Although its function as a verb for "war" has long been established, its actual reading remains uncertain; the phonetic reading given here is suggested by its apparent substitution for **ju-b'u-yi**; see below.

JUB'-b'a *(jub')* (T579v:501) 1 ▶ n. "shell" 2 ▶ n. "shell trumpet"

JUB'-EMBLEM GLYPH *(jub'-Emblem Glyph)* (T510af:325[528:?.528.528]) ▶ intr. v. "to bring down [a site/location/polity]"; general "war" verb, called "Star-Over-Emblem Glyph" ◆ Although its function as a verb for "war" has long been established, its actual reading remains uncertain; the phonetic reading given here is suggested by its apparent substitution for **ju-b'u-yi**; see below.

ju-b'u-yi *(jub'uy)* (T45v.21:575) 1 ▶ intr. v. "taken down" 2 ▶ intr. v. "brought down"; general "war" verb

ju-b'u-yi *(jub'uy)* (T45v.21.741v:17) 1 ▶ intr. v. "taken down" 2 ▶ intr. v. "brought down"; general "war" verb

JUB'(?)-yi *(jub'uy?)* (T510af:325[575]) ▶ intr. v. "taken down," "brought down"; general "war" verb; "Star-Over-Shell" ♦ Although its function as a verb for "war" has long been established, its actual reading remains uncertain; the phonetic reading given here is suggested by its apparent substitution for **ju-b'u-yi**; see above.

JUB'(?)-yi-ya *(jub'uy?)* (T325[510af:526]:17:125) ▶ intr. v. "taken down," "brought down"; general "war" verb; "Star-Over-Shell" ♦ Although its function as a verb for "war" has long been established, its actual reading remains uncertain; the phonetic reading given here is suggested by its apparent substitution for **ju-b'u-yi**; see above.

JUL *(jul)* (T220v) ▶ intr. v. "to arrive" ♦ Represents the back of an upright human hand. Spelled alternatively **HUL**.

JUL *(jul)* (T653) 1 ▶ n. "engraving" 2 ▶ tr. v. "to throw" 3 ▶ tr. v. "to shoot" 4 ▶ tr. v. "to spear" 5 ▶ tr. v. "to pierce"

JUL *(jul)* (T683v) ▶ intr. v. "to arrive"; specifically the variant of T683 with an eye; the "moon" sign ♦ Spelled alternatively **HUL**

ju-li *(jul)* (T45:82ms) 1 ▶ intr. v. "to arrive" 2 ▶ tr. v. "to throw" 3 ▶ tr. v. "to shoot" 4 ▶ tr. v. "to spear" 5 ▶ tr. v. "to pierce"

JUL-li *(jul)* (T683v:24) 1 ▶ intr. v. "to arrive" 2 ▶ tr. v. "to throw" 3 ▶ tr. v. "to shoot" 4 ▶ tr. v. "to spear" 5 ▶ tr. v. "to pierce"

JUL-li-ja *(julaj)* (T220:24.181) 1 ▶ pass. v. "was arrived" 2 ▶ pass. v. "was thrown" 3 ▶ pass. v. "was shot" 4 ▶ pass. v. "was speared"

JUL-li-ja *(julaj)* (T220:82.181) 1 ▶ pass. v. "was arrived" 2 ▶ pass. v. "was thrown" 3 ▶ pass. v. "was shot" 4 ▶ pass. v. "was speared"

ju-li-OB' *(julob')* (T45:82:142) 1 ▶ intr. pl. v. "they arrived" 2 ▶ intr. pl. v. "they threw" 3 ▶ intr. pl. v. "they shot" ◆ All three definitions include the possible plural ending *-ob'*.

ju-li-ya *(juliy)* (T740:24.125) ▶ intr. com. v. "arrived"

JUN *(jun)* (TI) ▶ n. "one"; cardinal number

JUN *(jun)* (T60) 1 ▶ n. "paper" 2 ▶ n. "book" 3 ▶ adj. + n. "paper headband"
♦ Represents a tied headband

JUN *(jun)* (T329) ▶ n. "one"; cardinal number ♦ Represents a human fore-finger

JUN *(jun)* (T609) ▶ n. "book" ♦ Represents a screen-fold codex or book with jaguar pelt covers

JUN *(jun)* (T1000a) ▶ n. "one"; cardinal number ◆ Represents the head of a woman. See also **NA** and **IX/IXIK**.

ju-na *(jun)* (T740:23) 1 ▶ n. "paper" 2 ▶ n. "book" 3 ▶ adj. + n. "paper headband"

ju-na *(jun)* (T1030o:23) 1 ▶ n. "paper" 2 ▶ n. "book" 3 ▶ adj. + n. "paper headband"

ju-na-la *(junal)* (T740:23:178) ▶ n. "headband"

JUN NAL YE *(Jun Nal Ye)* (TI.84:512a) ▶ n. deity name; proper name of the Maize God

JUN TAN-na *(jun tan)* (TI:606:23) ▶ adj. "beloved," "cherished"; part of the "child of mother" sequence

K

ka *(ka)* (T25) ▶ phonetic sign ♦ Represents the fin of a fish?

ka *(ka)* (T203) ▶ phonetic sign ♦ Represents the full figure of a fish

ka *(ka)* (T738) ▶ phonetic sign ♦ Represents the head of a fish

KAAN See **CHAAN**.

KAB' *(kab')* (T758c) ▶ n. "earth" ♦ Represents the head of a rodent with T526 **KAB'AN** infix

KAB' *(kab')* (T526) ▶ n. "earth" ♦ Represents the sign for "earth"

KAB'AN *(Kab'an)* (T526) ▶ n. day sign; seventeenth day of the Maya Tzolk'in calendar ♦ Represents the sign for "earth"

KAB'-ji *(kab'ij)* (T526:136) 1 ▶ relat. "under the auspices," "under the authority" 2 ▶ tr. v. "did it"

KAB'-ji *(kab'ij)* (T526:88) 1 ▶ relat. "under the auspices," "under the authority" 2 ▶ tr. v. "did it"

KAB'-ji-ya *(kab'jiy)* (T526:246) 1 ▶ relat. "under the auspices," "under the authority" 2 ▶ tr. v. "did it"

KAB'-la K'U *(kab'al k'u)* (T526:178.38) ▶ adj. + pl. n. "earthly gods" ♦ Pluralization questionable

KAB'-la K'U *(kab'al k'u)* (T38.1016[526]:178v) ▶ adj. + pl. n. "earthly gods" ♦ Pluralization questionable

KAB'-ya *(kab'iy)* (T526:126) 1 ▶ relat. "under the auspices," "under the authority" 2 ▶ tr. v. "did it"

ka-KALOMTE'-te' *(kalomte')* (T25:74:528.513v:87) ▶ n. elite and/or royal title of unknown meaning; formerly known as the "Makuch," "Batab," and "Chak Te'" title; frequently preceded by the directional glyph for "west," **OCH K'IN**

ka-ka-wa *(kakaw)* (T25.25.738c:130) ▶ n. "cacao," "chocolate"

ka-{ka}-wa *(kakaw)* (T738{738}:130) ▶ n. "cacao," "chocolate" ◆ Represents the head of a fish with phonetic **-wa**. The two dots on the forehead, referred to as "doubler dots," double the value of the **ka** sign.

ka-{ka}-wa *(kakaw)* (T738:130) ▶ n. "cacao," "chocolate"

ka-lo-ma-te' *(kalomte')* (T25.580:74.87) ▶ n. elite and/or royal title of unknown meaning; formerly known as the "Makuch," "Batab," and "Chak Te'" title; frequently preceded by the directional glyph for "west," **OCH K'IN**

KALOMTE' *(kalomte')* (T74:528.518c:87) ▶ n. elite and/or royal title of unknown meaning; formerly known as the "Makuch," "Batab," and "Chak Te'" title; frequently preceded by the directional glyph for "west," **OCH K'IN**

KALOMTE'-te' *(kalomte')* (T1030mv) ▶ n. elite and/or royal title of unknown meaning; formerly known as the "Makuch," "Batab," and "Chak Te'" title; frequently preceded by the directional glyph for "west," **OCH K'IN**

KAN See **CHAN**.

KAWAK *(Kawak)* (T528) ▶ n. day sign; nineteenth day of the Maya Tzolk'in calendar ♦ May represent rain clouds (the so-called bunched grapes) and the rainbow

ke *(ke)* (T220) ▶ phonetic sign ◆ Represents an upright human hand

KEJ *(Kej)* (T109:528:142) ▶ n. month sign; twelfth month of the Maya Ja'ab' calendar

ke-KELEM *(kelem)* (T220.??) 1 ▶ n. "youth" 2 ▶ adj. "strong"

ke-le-ma *(kelem)* (T220:136.188) 1 ▶ n. "youth" 2 ▶ adj. "strong"

ki *(ki)* (T100v) ▶ phonetic sign

ki *(ki)* (T102) ▶ phonetic sign

ki *(ki)* (T100hv) ▶ phonetic sign

KIB' *(Kib')* (T525) ▶ n. day sign; sixteenth day of the Maya Tzolk'in calendar

KIMI *(Kimi)* (T1045v) ▶ n. day sign; sixth day of the Maya Tzolk'in calendar
♦ Represents a human skull

KIX (?) *(kix?)* (T212) ▶ n. "stingray spine" ♦ Represents a stingray spine

KIX (?) *(kix?)* (T212) ▶ n. "stingray spine" ♦ Represents a stingray spine

KIX (?) *(kix?)* (T212) ▶ n. "stingray spine" ♦ Represents a stingray spine

ko *(ko)* (T110) ▶ phonetic sign

KOJAW *(kojaw)* (T678) 1 ▶ n. "helmet" 2 ▶ n. "headdress" ♦ Represents a scaled helmet

ko-ja-wa *(kojaw)* (T110:1042:130) 1 ▶ n. "helmet" 2 ▶ n. "headdress"

KOJAW-wa *(kojaw)* (T678.130) 1 ▶ n. "helmet" 2 ▶ n. "headdress" ♦ Represents a scaled helmet

ko-jo-yi *(kojoy)* (T110:607:24) ▶ intr. v. "to go down"

ko-ko-no-OB' *(kokonob')* (T110.110:134[595]:142) ▶ pl. n. "guardians"; includes the possible plural suffix *-ob'*

ko-tz'o *(kotz')* (T110.nn) ▶ tr. v. "to roll up"

ku *(ku)* (T528) ▶ phonetic sign ♦ May represent rain clouds (the so-called bunched grapes) and the rainbow (the arch in lower right corner)

KUCH *(kuch)* (T174) 1 ▶ n. "burden," "cargo," "load" 2 ▶ tr. v. "to carry"

KUCH AB'AK *(kuch ab'ak)* (T174:709v) ▶ n. "inkpot"

KUCH-ta-ja *(kuch-taj)* (T174:709v.181) ▶ pass. v. "it was carried"

KUCH TUN *(kuch tun)* (T174:528) ▶ adj. + n. "burden stone"

ku-chu *(kuch)* (T87.528v:601) 1 ▶ n. "burden," "cargo," "load" 2 ▶ tr. v. "to carry"

KUMK'U *(Kumk'u)* (T155:506:142) ▶ n. month sign; eighteenth month of the Maya Ja'ab' calendar

ku-tz'u *(kutz')* (T528.560v) ▶ n. "turkey," "ocellated turkey"

K'

k'a/ch'a *(k'a/ch'a)* (T76 and T77) ▶ phonetic sign ♦ Represents a bird's wing

k'a/ch'a (K'A/CH'A?) *(k'a/ch'a)* (T128) 1 ▶ phonetic sign 2 ▶ pos. "lying down" 3 ▶ pos. "horizontal"?

k'a/ch'a *(k'a/ch'a)* (T516b) ▶ phonetic sign; polyvalent **AK'OT** "dance"

k'a/ch'a *(k'a/ch'a)* (T669a) ▶ phonetic sign ♦ Combines the form of a human fist with a human head

k'a/ch'a *(k'a/ch'a)* (T669b) ▶ phonetic sign ♦ Represents a human fist

K'AB' *(k'ab')* (T671) ▶ n. "hand" ♦ Represents a human hand

K'AB'A *(k'ab'a)* (T187) ▶ n. "name"

k'a-[b'a] *(k'ab')* (T669[501]) 1 ▶ n. "hand" 2 ▶ n. "arm" ♦ Combines the form of a water lily (T501) with a human fist

K'A CHAAN-na *(k'a chaan)* (T128:561:23) ▶ pos. + n. "lying down sky"?

K'AK' *(k'ak')* (T122) ▶ n. "fire" ♦ Represents smoke or tongues of flame

K'AK' *(k'ak')* (T122) ▶ n. "fire" ♦ Represents smoke or tongues of flame

k'a-K'AK' *(k'ak')* (T669.122) ▶ n. "fire"

k'a-K'AWIL *(K'awil)* (T1030f) ▶ n. deity name; proper name of the god K'awil, god of generations, royal lineage bloodlines; GII of the Palenque Triad ♦ The reclining position with umbilical cord-like scroll emerging may indicate the god is "newborn."

K'AK'-k'a *(k'ak')* (T122:669v) ▶ n. "fire"

K'AK'-k'a B'UTZ'-tz'i *(k'ak' b'utz')* (T122:669.122:563) ▶ n. "fire [and] smoke"

K'AK' NAAB' *(k'ak' naab')* (T122.86[527]:521v[188]) ▶ adj. + n. "fire sea," "primordial sea," "fiery water place"

K'AL *(k'al)* (T683a) ▶ n. "twenty"; cardinal number; the "moon" sign

K'AL *(k'al)* (T713a) 1 ▶ tr. v. "to bind/tie/wrap" 2 ▶ tr. v. "to close" 3 ▶ tr. v. "to set" 4 ▶ n. "completion" ◆ Represents the back of an extended human hand

k'a-li *(k'al)* (T669b:24) ▶ tr. incom. v. "closing"

K'AL-ja *(k'alaj)* (T24:713a.181) 1 ▶ pass. v. "was bound/tied/wrapped" 2 ▶ pass. v. "was closed" 3 ▶ pass. v. "was set"

K'AL-ja MAY(?)-ji *(k'alaj mayij?)* (Tnn:713a:136.181) ▶ pass. v. phr. "was bound/tied/wrapped the deer hoof"; phonetic value **MAY** uncertain; general verb possibly meaning "heir apparency"

K'AL-ji-ya SAK JUN *(k'al-jiy sak jun)* (T58.60:713a:246) 1 ▶ tr. v. phr. "bound/tied/wrapped the white headband" 2 ▶ tr. v. phr. "closed the white headband"; general "accession" verb

K'AL JUN-na *(k'al jun)* (T740.23:713a) 1 ▶ tr. v. phr. "bound/tied/wrapped the headband" 2 ▶ tr. v. phr. "closed the headband"; general "accession" verb

K'AL JUN NA *(k'al jun na)* (T60:713a:?.4) ▶ adj. + n. "accession house"

K'AL SAK JUN *(k'al sak jun)* (T60.522:713a) 1 ▶ v. phr. "bound/tied/ wrapped the white headband" 2 ▶ v. phr. "closed the white headband"; general "accession" verb

K'AL SAK ju-na *(k'al sak jun)* (T58.1030a.23:713a) 1 ▶ v. phr. "bound/ tied/wrapped the white headband" 2 ▶ v. phr. "closed the white headband"; general "accession" verb

K'AL TUN-ni *(k'al tun)* (T528.116:713a) 1 ▶ intr. v. phr. "stone-binding" 2 ▶ pass. v. phr. "was closed the stone" 3 ▶ pass. v. phr. "was set the stone"; general PE glyph for *tun*-ending dates

K'AN *(k'an)* (T281ms) 1 ▶ adj. "yellow" 2 ▶ adj. "precious" ♦ The "K'an Cross" glyph

K'AN *(K'an)* (T506) ▶ n. day sign; fourth day of the Maya Tzolk'in calendar ♦ Probably represents a grain of maize

[K'AN]-a-si-ya   See **K'AYAB'**.

K'ANK'IN *(K'ank'in)* (T559.117) ▶ n. month sign; fourteenth month of the Maya Ja'ab' calendar

K'AN-na *(k'an)* (T281ms:23) 1 ▶ adj. "yellow" 2 ▶ adj. "precious"

K'AN-NAL-la e-b'u *(K'anal Eb')* (T86:281:178.741a:21) ▶ adj. + n. "Precious Stair Place"

K'AN TUN-ni *(k'an tun)* (T528[281]:116) 1 ▶ adj. + n. "yellow stone" 2 ▶ adj. + n. "precious stone"

K'ATUN *(k'atun)* (T25.528.25:548) ▶ n. period of twenty years of 360 days each; used in the Maya Long Count calendar; actual Classic Period name unknown ♦ Main sign represents the **TUN** sign

K'ATUN *(k'atun)* (T1034v) ▶ n. period of twenty years of 360 days each; used in the Long Count; actual Classic Period name unknown ♦ Represents a bird

K'AWIL *(K'awil)* (T1030b) ▶ n. deity name; proper name of the god K'awil, god of generations, royal lineage bloodlines; GII of the Palenque Triad ♦ Represents the head of the god with infixed forehead mirror and "smoking axe"

K'AWIL-la *(K'awil)* (T1030b:178) ▶ n. deity name; proper name of the god K'awil, god of generations, royal lineage bloodlines; GII of the Palenque Triad ♦ Represents the head of the god with infixed forehead mirror and "smoking axe"

K'AWIL-li *(K'awil)* (T122.617v:82) ▶ n. deity name; proper name of the god K'awil, god of generations, royal lineage bloodlines; GII of the Palenque Triad ♦ Represents the god's forehead mirror and smoke or flames

K'AWIL-NAL-OB' *(K'awilnalob')* (T84:325?[1030d]) ▶ pl. n. "K'awilnals"; includes the possible plural suffix *-ob'* ♦ Represents the god's forehead mirror and smoke or flames

K'AWIL-OB' *(K'awilob')* (T1030b:142) ▶ pl. n. "K'awils"; includes the possible plural suffix *-ob'* ♦ Represents the head of the god, with infixed forehead mirror and "smoking axe"

k'a-wi-NAL WINIK *(K'awinal winik)* (T669:117.86:521) ▶ adj. + n. "K'awilnal person"

K'AYAB' *(K'ayab')* (T743[281]:57:125) ▶ n. month sign; seventeenth month of the Maya Ja'ab' calendar; components spell **[K'AN]-a-si-ya** or *K'anasiy*, the name of the seventeenth month in Ch'olan

k'a-yi/ch'a-yi *(k'ay/ch'ay)* (T76:575) 1 ▶ intr. incom. v. "it terminates" 2 ▶ intr. incom. v. "it flies" ♦ Portion of the "death" verb *k'ay u sak nik nal*. **K'AY** in Yucatec, **CH'AY** in Ch'olan.

k'a-yi U SAK NIK IK'-li/ch'a-yi U SAK NICH IK'-li *(k'ay u sak nik ik'il/ch'ay u sak nich ik'il)* (T76:575 1:179.1082:82) ▶ intr. incom. v. phr. "it terminates, his/her resplendent soul," "it terminated, his/her white flowery soul"; general verb meaning "death" ♦ **K'AY** in Yucatec, **CH'AY** in Ch'olan

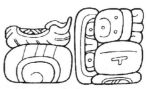

k'a-yi U SAK NIK IK'-li/ch'a-yi U SAK NICH IK'-li *(k'ay u sak nik ik'il/ch'ay u sak nich ik'il)* (T204:575 1.179:503:24) ▶ intr. incom. v. phr. "it terminates, his/his resplendent soul," "it terminated, his/her white flowery soul"; general verb meaning "death" ♦ **K'AY** in Yucatec, **CH'AY** in Ch'olan

K'IN *(k'in)* (T544) 1 ▶ n. "day" 2 ▶ n. "sun" 3 ▶ n. period of one day, used in the Maya LC calendar and DNs ♦ Represents a four-petaled flower, possibly a plumeria flower, which symbolizes the sun and thus the "day"

K'IN (?) *(k'in?)* (T574) ▶ n. "day"; used in DNs for the period of one day ♦ May represent a grain of maize or a bivalve shell

K'IN *(k'in)* (T544hv) 1 ▶ n. "day" 2 ▶ n. "sun" 3 ▶ n. period of one day, used in the Maya Long Count calendar ♦ Represents the humanized head of an animal

K'INA/K'INICH *(k'ina/k'inich)* (T74.184) 1 ▶ adj. "sun-eyed" 2 ▶ adj. "sun-faced"

K'INICH *(k'inich)* (T1010a.184.74) 1 ▶ adj. "sun-eyed" 2 ▶ adj. "sun-faced"

K'INICH-ni *(k'inich)* (T671[544]:116) 1 ▶ adj. "sun-eyed" 2 ▶ adj. "sun-faced"

K'IN-ni *(k'in)* (T544:116) 1 ▶ n. "day" 2 ▶ n. "sun" 3 ▶ n. period of one day; used in the Maya Long Count calendar

K'IN-ni *(k'in)* (T1010:116) 1 ▶ n. "day" 2 ▶ n. "sun" 3 ▶ n. period of one day; used in the Maya Long Count calendar

K'IN-ni AJAW *(K'in Ajaw)* (T168:544:116) ▶ adj. + n. "Sun Lord"; royal/elite title

K'IN-ni-chi TZAM(?) TUN-ni *(K'inich Tzam? Tun)* (T671[544]:116 150.528:116) ▶ adj. + n. "Sun-faced Throne Stone"

K'IN-ni JA'-NAL *(K'in Ja'nal)* (T544:116.86:1031a) ▶ adj. + n. "Sun Water Place"

k'o *(k'o)* (T220) ▶ phonetic sign

k'o-b'a *(k'ob'a)* (T217:501:314) 1 ▶ n. "image" 2 ▶ n. "mask" 3 ▶ n. "statue"

k'o-jo *(k'oj)* (T220:607) 1 ▶ n. "image" 2 ▶ n. "mask" 3 ▶ n. "statue"

k'u/K'U *(k'u)* (T41) 1 ▶ phonetic sign 2 ▶ n. "god," "divinity" 3 ▶ adj. "divine," "sacred"

k'u *(k'u)* (T604) ▶ phonetic sign

k'u/K'U *(k'u)* (T1016) 1 ▶ phonetic sign 2 ▶ n. "god," "divinity" 3 ▶ adj. "divine," "sacred" ♦ May represent a monkey's face

k'u-ju *(k'uj)* (T604v:740v) ▶ n. "god," "divinity"

k'u-ju *(k'uj)* (T604v.740v) ▶ n. "god," "divinity"

K'UK' *(k'uk')* (T744a) ▶ n. "quetzal bird" ♦ Represents the head of the quetzal bird

K'UL/K'UJUL   See **CH'UL/CH'UJUL**.

k'u-xa-ja *(k'uxaj)* (T603:114.181) 1 ▶ pass. v. "was eaten" 2 ▶ pass. v. "was ground" 3 ▶ pass. v. "was hurt" ♦ Accompanies representations of captives and may refer to "torture" or "cannibalism"

k'u-xa-ji-ya *(k'uxajiy)* (T604:136.114:126v) 1 ▶ tr. com. v. "ate" 2 ▶ tr. v. "to grind" 3 ▶ tr. v. "to hurt" ♦ Accompanies representations of captives and may refer to "torture" or "cannibalism"

k'u-yu NIK-ki AJAW *(K'uy Nik Ajaw)* (T604:61 168:533.102) ▶ adj. + n. "Bird Flower Lord"; royal title used especially at Copán

L

la *(la)* (T178 and T534) ▶ phonetic sign

la *(la)* (T178) ▶ phonetic sign

-la-ja *(-laj)* (T178.181) ▶ positional completive verbal suffix pattern

-la-ja *(-laj/laj)* (T534.181) 1 ▶ positional completive verbal suffix pattern
2 ▶ tr. v. "to end," "to finish"

-[la]-ja *(-laj)* (T181[178]) ▶ positional completive verbal suffix pattern

-[la]-ja *(-laj)* (T683[178]) ▶ positional completive verbal suffix pattern

-la-ji *(-laj)* (T178.88) ▶ positional completive verbal suffix pattern

LAJUN *(lajun)* (TX) ▶ n. "ten"; cardinal number

LAJUN *(lajun)* (TXhv) ▶ n. "ten"; cardinal number ◆ Represents a human skull

LAK *(lak)* (T183) ▶ n. "plate"; includes an infixed **K'IN** sign (T544) ♦ Represents a bowl or plate with infixed **K'IN** sign

la-ka *(lak)* (T534:25.25) ▶ n. "plate," "bowl"

LAKAM *(lakam)* (T767) 1 ▶ adj. "large," "big" 2 ▶ adj. "great" 3 ▶ n. "banner"

LAKAM *(lakam)* (T767) 1 ▶ adj. "large," "big" 2 ▶ adj. "great" 3 ▶ n. "banner"

la-ka-ma *(lakam)* (T178:738:74) 1 ▶ adj. "large," "big" 2 ▶ adj. "great" 3 ▶ n. "banner"

LAKAM JA' *(lakam ja')* (T767af.501v:314) 1 ▶ adj. + n. "wide water" 2 ▶ adj. + n. "great water"

LAKAM TUN *(lakam tun)* (T767b:528) 1 ▶ adj. + n. "large, big stone" 2 ▶ adj. + n. "great stone" 3 ▶ adj. + n. "banner stone"

LAKAM TUN-ni *(lakam tun)* (T767b:528:116) 1 ▶ adj. + n. "large, big stone" 2 ▶ adj. + n. "great stone" 3 ▶ adj. + n. "banner stone"

LAK-K'IN-ni *(lak'in)* (T183:544.116) ▶ n. "east"; cardinal direction

LAMAT *(Lamat)* (T510) ▶ n. day sign; eighth day of the Maya Tzolk'in calendar; the symbol for "star," or **EK'**

la-ta *(-lat/lat)* (T534:103) 1 ▶ temp. suf. "X-number of days later" 2 ▶ n. "day"; period of time representing a day in DNs

le *(le)* (T188) ▶ phonetic sign

li *(li)* (T24) ▶ phonetic sign ♦ Represents a mirror. See also **-il**.

li *(li)* (T24) ▶ phonetic sign ♦ Represents a mirror. See also **-il**.

li *(li)* (T82) ▶ phonetic sign ♦ See also **-il**.

li *(li)* (T82) ▶ phonetic sign ♦ See also **-il**.

li *(li)* (T83) ▶ phonetic sign ♦ See also **-il**.

li *(li)* (T360) ▶ phonetic sign ♦ See also **-il**.

li *(li)* (Tnn) ▶ phonetic sign; the "worm-bird" glyph ♦ See also **-il**.

li *(li)* (Tnn) ▶ phonetic sign; the "worm-bird" glyph ♦ See also **-il**.

lo *(lo)* (T580) ▶ phonetic sign ◆ Logographic **CHIT**?

lo-k'u-ta *(lok'-ta)* (T580:1016:565) 1 ▶ intr. v. "came out from" 2 ▶ intr. v. "emerged from"

LOK'-yi *(lok'iy)* (T327:575) 1 ▶ intr. com. v. "came out" 2 ▶ intr. com. v. "emerged" 3 ▶ intr. com. v. "escaped" ◆ Represents a serpent-like form emerging from the sign for **yi**

lo-mu *(lom)* (T580:19.741v) 1 ▶ n. "lance" 2 ▶ n. "staff"

lu *(lu)* (T568) ▶ phonetic sign

lu *(lu)* (T568) ▶ phonetic sign

lu-k'u *(luk')* (T568:604) 1 ▶ n. "mud" 2 ▶ n. "clay"

lu-mi *(lum)* (T568:173) ▶ n. "earth"

M

ma/MA *(ma)* (T74) 1 ▶ phonetic sign 2 ▶ negative marker 3 ▶ adv. "not"

ma/MA *(ma)* (T74) 1 ▶ phonetic sign 2 ▶ negative marker 3 ▶ adv. "not"

ma *(ma)* (T140) ▶ phonetic sign

ma *(ma)* (T140) ▶ phonetic sign

ma *(ma)* (T142) ▶ phonetic sign

ma/MA *(ma)* (T502) 1 ▶ phonetic sign 2 ▶ negative marker 3 ▶ adv. "not" ◆ Represents a water lily with infixed **AJAW**

ma *(ma)* (T566) ▶ phonetic sign ◆ Probably represents the upper markings and belly-scales of a snake

ma *(ma)* (T566) ▶ phonetic sign ◆ Probably represents the upper markings and belly-scales of a snake

ma/MA *(ma)* (T74:501:142) 1 ▶ phonetic sign 2 ▶ negative marker 3 ▶ adv. "not"

MA-[IL]-aj *(ma ilaj)* (T74.743) ▶ pass. v. "was not seen"

MAK *(Mak)* (T74:501v:25) ▶ n. month sign; thirteenth month of the Maya Ja'ab' calendar

ma-ka *(mak/Mak)* (T502:314.25) 1 ▶ tr. v. "to close" 2 ▶ tr. v. "to cover" 3 ▶ tr. v. "to betroth" 4 ▶ n. "cover," "lid" 5 ▶ n. "capstone" 6 ▶ n. month sign; thirteenth month of the Maya Ja'ab' calendar

ma-ka-ja *(makaj)* (T502:25.25.181) 1 ▶ pass. v. "was closed" 2 ▶ pass. v. "was covered" 3 ▶ pass. v. "was betrothed"

ma-ka-xa *(makax)* (T502:25.25.114) 1 ▶ tr. v. "to close" 2 ▶ tr. v. "to cover" 3 ▶ tr. v. "to betroth"

ma-ko-ma *(makom)* (T74:110:74) ▶ n. "calabash tree"

MAM *(mam)* (T1014v) 1 ▶ relat. "maternal grandfather" 2 ▶ relat. "ancestor"

MANIK' *(Manik')* (T671) ▶ n. day sign; seventh day of the Maya Tzolk'in calendar ♦ Represents a human hand

ma-ta-wi-la *(matawil)* (T74:565a:178.117) ▶ n. divinity title; specific meaning unknown; probably related to a geographical or other specific location

ma-xi *(max)* (T74:736v) ▶ n. "monkey," "spider monkey"

ma-xi *(max)* (T74:736v) ▶ n. "monkey," "spider monkey"

ma-xi *(max)* (T502:142 736v) ▶ n. "monkey," "spider monkey"

MAY (?) *(may?)* (Tnn) 1 ▶ n. "deer hoof" 2 ▶ n. "tobacco" 3 ▶ "fawn"? ◆ Phonetic value uncertain. Represents the hoof of a deer.

MEN *(Men)* (T1017v?) ▶ n. day sign; fifteenth day of the Maya Tzolk'in calendar ◆ Represents a zoomorphic head tentatively identified as an eagle or other bird

mi/MI *(mi)* (T173) 1 ▶ phonetic sign 2 ▶ n. "nothing," "zero"; negative marker

mi/MI *(mi)* (T217v) 1 ▶ phonetic sign 2 ▶ n. "nothing," "zero"; negative marker

mi/MI *(mi)* (T217v) 1 ▶ phonetic sign 2 ▶ n. "nothing," "zero"; negative marker

mi/MI *(mi)* (Tnn) ▶ n. "nothing," "zero"; negative marker ◆ Represents a human head with hand over lower jaw

MI OL-la *(mi ol)* (T173.506:178) ▶ negative marker + n. "no heart"

mo *(mo)* (T582) ▶ phonetic sign

mo/MO' *(mo/mo')* (T743v) 1 ▶ phonetic sign 2 ▶ n. "macaw" ♦ Represents the head of a macaw

mo-ko-chi *(mokoch)* (T582.110 671) ▶ n. "Knot-Mouth"; proper name of a lesser god

MOL *(Mol)* (T581) ▶ n. month sign; eighth month of the Maya Ja'ab' calendar

MOL (?) *(mol?)* (T5) ▶ n. "jaguar paw" ♦ Represents the jaguar's paw as opposed to its claws or the paw with extended claws? Alternative reading: **ICH'AK** (specifically "claw," as opposed to "paw"). See also **ICH'AK**.

MOL(?) TUN-ni *(mol tun?)* (T5:528:116) ▶ n. "jaguar paw stone"? ♦ See **MOL**, **ICH'AK**, and **ICH'AK TUN-ni**.

mo-o WITZ AJAW *(Mo' Witz Ajaw)* (T582:279.168:529) ▶ n. "Macaw Mountain Lord"

mo-o wi-tzi AJAW *(Mo' Witz Ajaw)* (T582:279 117.168:507) ▶ n. "Macaw Mountain Lord"

MO' *(mo')* (T238) ▶ n. "macaw" ♦ Represents the beak of a parrot or macaw. See also **a/AJ**.

MO' WITZ *(Mo' Witz)* (T743v:1030p) ▶ n. "Macaw Mountain"

mu *(mu)* (T19) ▶ phonetic sign

mu *(mu)* (T19.741v) ▶ phonetic sign ♦ The head component represents a frog, iguana, or other reptile.

mu-ka *(muk)* (T19.741v:25) ▶ tr. v. "to bury"

mu-ka-ja *(mukaj)* (T19.741v:25.181) ▶ pass. v. "was buried"

mu-ka-ja *(mukaj)* (T19.25:1000a[181]) ▶ pass. v. "was buried"

mu-ka-ja *(mukaj)* (T19:738c.181) ▶ pass. v. "was buried"

mu-ku-yi *(mukuy)* (T19.528:17) 1 ▶ n. "dove" 2 ▶ n. "pigeon"

MULUK *(Muluk)* (T513) ▶ n. day sign; ninth day of the Maya Tzolk'in calendar

mu-ti *(mut)* (T19:59) 1 ▶ n. "bird," species unknown 2 ▶ n. "omen"

mu-ti *(mut)* (T19:741v:59) 1 ▶ n. "bird," species unknown 2 ▶ n. "omen"

MUTUL *(mutul)* (T569) ▶ n. "bird," species unknown; main sign of the Tikal EG ♦ Represents bound hair

MUTUL *(mutul)* (T778) ▶ n. "bird," species unknown; main sign of the Tikal EG ◆ Represents bound hair?

MUTUL *(mutul)* (T778hv) ▶ n. "bird," species unknown; main sign of the Tikal EG

MUTUL AJAW-TAK *(mutul ajaw-tak)* (T569.168:559[544]) ▶ pl. n. "Mutul lords"; includes the plural suffix *-tak*

mu-wa-ni *(muwan)* (T19.741v:130:116) 1 ▶ n. "bird" 2 ▶ n. month sign; fifteenth month of the Maya Ja'ab' calendar ◆ Denotes a mythological bird; type of sparrow hawk?

MUWAN-na *(muwan)* (T744:23) 1 ▶ n. "bird" 2 ▶ n. month sign; fifteenth month of the Maya Ja'ab' calendar ♦ Represents the head of the mythological Muwan bird; type of sparrow hawk?

MUWAN-ni *(muwan)* (T744:116) 1 ▶ n. "bird" 2 ▶ n. month sign; fifteenth month of the Maya Ja'ab' calendar ♦ Represents the head of the mythological Muwan bird

MUYAL *(muyal)* (T632v) ▶ n. "cloud"

MUYAL *(muyal)* (T632v) ▶ n. "cloud"

N

na/NA/NAJ *(na/naj)* (T4) 1 ▶ phonetic sign 2 ▶ n. "house" 3 ▶ adj. "first"; ordinal number

na/NA/NAJ *(na/naj)* (T4) 1 ▶ phonetic sign 2 ▶ n. "house" 3 ▶ adj. "first"; ordinal number

na/NA/NAJ *(na/naj)* (T4) 1 ▶ phonetic sign 2 ▶ n. "house" 3 ▶ adj. "first"; ordinal number

na/NA/NAJ *(na/naj)* (T23) 1 ▶ phonetic sign 2 ▶ adj. "first"; ordinal number

na/NA/NAJ *(na/naj)* (T48) ▶ n. "house"

na/NA/NAJ *(na/naj)* (T537) ▶ n. "house"

na/NA/NAJ *(na/naj)* (T4.1008) ▶ n. "house"

na/NA/NAJ *(na/naj)* (T1000a) 1 ▶ phonetic sign 2 ▶ adj. "first"; ordinal number 3 ▶ n. "lady" 4 ▶ n. "mother" ♦ Represents the head of a woman. See also **IX/IXIK**.

NAAB' *(naab')* (T501v) 1 ▶ n. "water" 2 ▶ n. "sea" 3 ▶ n. "plaza" 4 ▶ n. "water lily"? ♦ Represents the blossom of a water lily

NAAB' *(naab')* (T86[527]:521[188]) 1 ▶ n. "water" 2 ▶ n. "sea" 3 ▶ n. "plaza" 4 ▶ n. "water lily"?

NAAB' TUN-chi *(naab' tunich)* (T86[527]:671[528]) ▶ adj. + n. "watery stone" ♦ Location associated with Calakmul

na-b'i *(naab')* (T23:585a) 1 ▶ n. "water" 2 ▶ n. "sea" 3 ▶ n. "plaza" 4 ▶ n. "water lily"?

na-ja *(-naj)* (T1000a.181) ▶ part of the PSS dedication phrase; possibly a verbal ending

na-ja-yi *(najiy)* (T1000a.681:17) ▶ tr. incom. v. "fills up"

NA ka-KAN *(Na Kan)* (T4.25.25:764a) ▶ n. deity name; serves as part of the name of one of the Vision Serpents conjured during bloodletting rites

na-ku *(nak)* (T4:528) 1 ▶ numerical classifier for counts with titles, as in *ka nak te'* "second tree" 2 ▶ tr. v. "to conquer" 3 ▶ intr. v. "to ascend," "to rise," "to elevate" 4 ▶ n. "crown," "diadem" 5 ▶ n. "face" 6 ▶ n. "mask"

NAL *(nal)* (T84) 1 ▶ n. "maize," "maize curl" 2 ▶ n. part of the proper name of the Maize God 3 ▶ locative determinative suffix meaning "place"

NAL *(nal)* (T86) 1 ▶ n. "maize," "maize curl" 2 ▶ n. part of the proper name of the Maize God 3 ▶ locative determinative suffix meaning "place"

NAL *(nal)* (T86) 1 ▶ n. "maize," "maize curl" 2 ▶ n. part of the proper name of the Maize God 3 ▶ locative determinative suffix meaning "place"

NAL (?) *(nal)* (T1008) ▶ n. "north"; cardinal direction

na-NAL (?) *(nal)* (T4.1008) ▶ n. "north"; cardinal direction

NA OTOT-ja *(na otot)* (T4.614:115.515.181) ▶ n. "house"

na-wa-ja *(nawaj)* (T23:130:683) ▶ pass. v. "was adorned"; refers to the act of "dressing" prisoners destined for sacrifice but also of idols, ritual images, and individuals in ceremonies

ne/NE *(ne)* (T120) 1 ▶ phonetic sign 2 ▶ n. "tail"

ne/NE *(ne)* (T120) 1 ▶ phonetic sign 2 ▶ n. "tail"

ne/NE *(ne)* (T856v) 1 ▶ phonetic sign 2 ▶ n. "tail" ♦ Probably represents a curled-up jaguar's tail

ne/NE *(ne)* (Tnn) 1 ▶ phonetic sign 2 ▶ n. "tail" ♦ Represents a jaguar's tail

ni *(ni)* (T116) ▶ phonetic sign

ni *(ni)* (T1019) ▶ phonetic sign

NICH/NIK *(nich/nik)* (T533v) 1 ▶ n. "flower" 2 ▶ relat. "son" ♦ The "capped **AJAW**" glyph

NICH/NIK *(nich/nik)* (T535) 1 ▶ n. "flower" 2 ▶ relat. "son"

ni-chi-{m} *(nichim)* (T116:671) 1 ▶ n. "flower" 2 ▶ relat. "son"

NICH-li/NIK-li *(nichil/nikil)* (T533v:24) 1 ▶ n. "flower" 2 ▶ relat. "son"

NICH-li/NIK-li *(nichil/nikil)* (Tnn:24v) 1 ▶ n. "flower" 2 ▶ relat. "son"

NIKTE' *(nikte')* (T646) ▶ n. "flower"; possibly the mayflower

NIKTE' *(nikte')* (T646v) ▶ n. "flower"; possibly the mayflower

NIKTE'-te' *(nikte')* (T299:646v:87) ▶ n. "flower"; possibly the mayflower

no *(no)* (T134[595]) ▶ phonetic sign

NOJ *(noj)* (T4) ▶ adj. "great"?; value uncertain ♦ See **na/NA/NAJ** for alternative reading.

NOJ *(noj)* (T4) ▶ adj. "great"?; value uncertain ♦ See **na/NA/NAJ** for alternative reading.

NOJ *(noj)* (T4) ▶ adj. "great"?; value uncertain ♦ See **na/NA/NAJ** for alternative reading.

NOJ *(noj)* (T48) ▶ adj. "great"?; value uncertain ◆ See **na/NA/NAJ** for alternative reading.

NOJOL *(nojol)* (T74:134[856v]:178) ▶ n. "north"; cardinal direction ◆ See also **NAL**.

nu *(nu)* (T106) ▶ phonetic sign

nu *(nu)* (T106) ▶ phonetic sign

nu *(nu)* (T149) ▶ phonetic sign

nu *(nu)* (T151) ▶ phonetic sign

nu *(nu)* (T151) ▶ phonetic sign

nu *(nu)* (T264 and T592) ▶ phonetic sign

nu *(nu)* (T282) ▶ phonetic sign

nu *(nu)* (T608) ▶ phonetic sign

nu-ku *(nuk)* (T151:528) 1 ▶ adj. "great" 2 ▶ adj. "large" 3 ▶ adj. "wide"

NUUN *(nuun)* (T60) ▶ presumably a noun; meaning unknown; apparently polyvalent ◆ See also **ji**, **JUN**, and **TAJ**.

o *(o)* (T99) ▶ vowel *o* ♦ Represents a feather

o *(o)* (T99) ▶ vowel *o* ♦ Represents a feather

o *(o)* (T99) ▶ vowel *o* ♦ Represents a feather

o *(o)* (T134) ▶ vowel *o*

o *(o)* (T155) ▶ vowel *o*

o *(o)* (T155) ▶ vowel *o*

o *(o)* (T155v) ▶ vowel *o*

o *(o)* (T279) ▶ vowel *o* ◆ Represents a feather

o *(o)* (T279) ▶ vowel *o* ◆ Represents a feather

o *(o)* (Tnn) ▶ vowel *o*

o *(o)* (T694) ▶ vowel *o*

o *(o)* (T1034v?) ▶ vowel *o* ♦ Represents a bird

OCH *(och)* (T207v) ▶ intr. v. "to enter" ♦ Represents the rattles of a rattlesnake

OCH *(och)* (T207v) ▶ intr. v. "to enter" ♦ Represents the rattles of a rattlesnake

OCH *(och)* (T213v) ▶ intr. v. "to enter" ♦ Represents a leaf

OCH *(och)* (T361) ▶ intr. v. "to enter" ♦ Represents a human hand holding a celt

OCH/OK *(och/ok)* (T765) 1 ▶ intr. v. "to enter" 2 ▶ n. "foot" ♦ Represents an animal, probably a dog

OCH/OK *(och/ok)* (T765v) 1 ▶ intr. v. "to enter" 2 ▶ n. "foot" ♦ Represents an animal, probably a dog

OCH B'I *(och b'i)* (T207v.585a) ▶ tr. v. phr. "entered the road"; general "death" verb

OCH B'I-ja *(och b'i-aj)* (T361:585a.181) ▶ pass. v. phr. "was entered the road"; general "death" verb

OCH B'I-ji-ji-ya *(och b'ij-jiy)* (T207v:585a:136.88:246v) ▶ tr. v. phr. "road-entered"; general "death" verb

OCH-chi *(och)* (T207v:671) ▶ intr. v. "to enter"

OCH-chi K'AK' *(och k'ak')* (T207v:671.122) ▶ tr. v. phr. "entered the fire," "fire-entered"; general "dedication" verb; probably refers to ritual cleansing by burning incense

OCH-chi K'AK' *(och k'ak')* (T207v:671.122:563) ▶ tr. v. phr. "entered the fire," "fire-entered"; general "dedication" verb; probably refers to ritual cleansing by burning incense

OCH-ja/OK-ja *(ochaj/okaj)* (T764v:683a) ▶ pass. v. "was entered"

OCH JA' *(och ja')* (T361:501) ▶ tr. v. phr. "entered the water," "water-entered"; general "death" verb

OCH JA'-ja *(och ja'-aj)* (T361:501.181) ▶ pass. v. phr. "was entered, the water"; general "death" verb

OCH K'AK' *(och k'ak')* (T99v.671:122) ▶ tr. v. phr. "entered the fire," "fire-entered"; general "dedication" verb; probably refers to ritual cleansing by burning incense

OCH K'IN *(och k'in)* (T361:544) ▶ n. "west"; cardinal direction

OCH TA CHAAN-na/OK TA KAAN-na *(och ta chaan/ok ta kaan)* (T758.113v:561:23) ▶ tr. v. phr. "entered into the sky," "became the sky," "sky-entered"

OCH TE'/OK TE' *(och te'/ok te')* (T764b:87) ▶ tr. v. phr. "entered the tree"

OK *(Ok)* (T765a) ▶ n. day sign; tenth day of the Maya Tzolk'in calendar
♦ Represents a dog or other canine

OL *(ol)* (T506) 1 ▶ n. "middle," "center" 2 ▶ n. "heart"

OL *(ol)* (T774) 1 ▶ n. "middle," "center" 2 ▶ n. "heart"

o-la-si *(olas)* (T99.534:57) 1 ▶ n. phr. "the whole" 2 ▶ adj. + n. "the whole set"?

o-la-si K'U *(olas k'u)* (T99.534:57 38.1016) ▶ n. phr. "the whole set of gods"?, "all the gods"

o-OL-si *(olis)* (Tnn:774:57) 1 ▶ n. phr. "the whole" 2 ▶ adj. + n. "the whole set"?

o-OL-si *(olis)* (T99.506:57) 1 ▶ n. phr. "the whole" 2 ▶ adj. + n. "the whole set"?

o-OL-si K'U *(olis k'u)* (T99.506:57 36.1016) ▶ n. phr. "the whole set of gods"?, "all the gods"

OTOT *(otot)* (T614:514v:59) ▶ n. "house" ♦ Represents a house in profile

OTOT-ja *(ototaj)* (T221:115v:514v.181) ▶ pass. v. "was housed"

OX *(ox)* (TIII) 1 ▶ n. "three"; cardinal number 2 ▶ adj. "many"

OX *(ox)* (TIIIhv) 1 ▶ n. "three"; cardinal number 2 ▶ adj. "many" ♦ Represents a human head with distinctive headaddress

OX aj-ja-li *(ox ajal)* (TIII.228.60.1042v:24) 1 ▶ v. phr. "thrice said" 2 ▶ v. phr. "thrice manifested"

OX B'OLON CHAAK *(Ox B'olon Chaak)* (TIII.IX:1010) ▶ n. deity name; proper name of deity; possibly GI of the Palenque Triad

P

pa/PAJ *(pa/paj)* (T586) 1 ▶ phonetic sign 2 ▶ n. "wall" 3 ▶ tr. v. "to choose"

pa/PAJ *(pa/paj)* (T586) 1 ▶ phonetic sign 2 ▶ n. "wall" 3 ▶ tr. v. "to choose"

pa/PAJ *(pa/paj)* (T602) 1 ▶ phonetic sign 2 ▶ n. "wall" 3 ▶ tr. v. "to choose"

pa/PAJ *(pa/paj)* (T586hv) 1 ▶ phonetic sign 2 ▶ n. "wall" 3 ▶ tr. v. "to choose" ♦ Represents a human head with cross-hatching

pa-ka-b'a *(pakab')* (T586:25:501) ▶ n. "lintel"

PAKAL *(pakal)* (T624v) 1 ▶ n. "shield" 2 ▶ n. the name of several Palenque Classic Period kings, including Pakal the Great (ruled A.D. 615–683) ♦ Represents a specific type of shield

pa-ka-la *(pakal)* (T586.25:178) 1 ▶ n. "shield" 2 ▶ n. the name of several Palenque Classic Period kings, including Pakal the Great (ruled A.D. 615–683)

pa-ka-la-ja *(paklaj)* (T586:25.178:181) 1 ▶ pos. v. "was faced down" 2 ▶ pos. v. "was doubled over"

pa-ka-xa *(pakax)* (T586.25:114) ▶ v. phr. reference to "someone coming back"

pa-ka-xa *(pakax)* (T586:25.736v) ▶ v. phr. reference to "someone coming back"

pa-k'a *(pak')* (T586.669) 1 ▶ tr. v. "to mold" 2 ▶ tr. v. "to form in clay" 3 ▶ tr. v. "to plant" 4 ▶ tr. v. "to hoist"

pa-k'a-ji-ya *(pak'ajiy)* (T586.669:136:126) 1 ▶ intr. com. v. "molded" 2 ▶ intr. com. v. phr. "formed in clay" 3 ▶ intr. com. v. "planted" 4 ▶ intr. com. v. "hoisted"

PAS/PASAJ *(pas/pasaj)* (T561:544:526) 1 ▶ tr. v. "to open" 2 ▶ n. "dawn"

PAS/PASAJ *(pas/pasaj)* (T222:561) 1 ▶ tr. v. "to open" 2 ▶ n. "dawn"

pa-sa *(pas)* (T602:630) 1 ▶ tr. v. "to open" 2 ▶ n. "dawn"

pa-si-li *(pasil)* (T586:57:82) 1 ▶ n. "opening" 2 ▶ n. "doorway"

PAT *(pat)* (T80) 1 ▶ tr. v. "to form"; general "dedication" verb 2 ▶ tr. v. "to make"; general "dedication" verb 3 ▶ n. "back" 4 ▶ n. "shoulders" 5 ▶ n. "tribute"

PAT *(pat)* (T80) 1 ▶ tr. v. "to form"; general "dedication" verb 2 ▶ tr. v. "to make"; general "dedication" verb 3 ▶ n. "back" 4 ▶ n. "shoulders" 5 ▶ n. "tribute"

PAT *(pat)* (T80) 1 ▶ tr. v. "to form"; general "dedication" verb 2 ▶ tr. v. "to make"; general "dedication" verb 3 ▶ n. "back" 4 ▶ n. "shoulders" 5 ▶ n. "tribute"

PAT *(pat)* (T80:614) 1 ▶ tr. v. "to form"; general "dedication" verb 2 ▶ tr. v. "to make"; general "dedication" verb 3 ▶ n. "back" 4 ▶ n. "shoulders" 5 ▶ n. "tribute"

pa-ta-{n} *(patan)* (T586:103) ▶ n. "tribute"

pa-ta-na *(patan)* (T586:565.23) ▶ n. "tribute"

PAT-b'u-ya *(pat b'uy)* (T80:21.741v:126) ▶ tr. com. v. "formed," "made"; general "dedication" verb

pa-ti *(pat)* (T602:59) 1 ▶ tr. v. "to form"; general "dedication" verb 2 ▶ tr. v. "to make"; general "dedication" verb 3 ▶ n. "back" 4 ▶ n. "shoulders" 5 ▶ n. "tribute"

PAT-[la]-ja *(patlaj)* (T79:683[178]) ▶ pos. com. v. "formed," "made"; general "dedication" verb

PAT-ta *(pat)* (T80:565a) 1 ▶ tr. v. "to form"; general "dedication" verb 2 ▶ tr. v. "to make"; general "dedication" verb 3 ▶ n. "back" 4 ▶ n. "shoulders" 5 ▶ n. "tribute"

PAT-ta-b'u-ji *(pat b'uj)* (T80:113:21:136) ▶ tr. com. v. "made," "formed"; general "dedication" verb

PAT-ta-wa-ni *(patwan)* (T80:565a:130.116) ▶ com. v. "made," "formed"; general "dedication" verb

PAT-wa-ni *(patwan)* (T80:614:130.116) ▶ com. v. "made," "formed"; general "dedication" verb

PAX *(Pax)* (T549:142) ▶ n. month sign; sixteenth month of the Maya Ja'ab' calendar ◆ Represents a "sprout" emerging from the **TUN** sign

PAX *(Pax)* (T549hv) ▶ n. month sign; sixteenth month of the Maya Ja'ab' calendar ◆ Represents a "sprout" emerging from the head of a frog, lizard, or other reptile

PET *(pet)* (T511v) 1 ▶ intr. v. "to turn," "to rotate" 2 ▶ n. "jewel" 3 ▶ n. "island"

PET-ji-ya *(petjiy)* (T511v:88.126) ▶ intr. com. v. "turned," "rotated"

pi *(pi)* (T177) ▶ phonetic sign

pi/PI/PIJ *(pi/pij)* (T528.528) 1 ▶ phonetic sign 2 ▶ n. "bundle" 3 ▶ n. period of 400 years of 360 days each; used in the Maya LC calendar; the "B'aktun" glyph

pi/PI/PIJ *(pi/pij)* (T1033v) 1 ▶ phonetic sign 2 ▶ n. "bundle" 3 ▶ n. period of 400 years of 360 days each; used in the Maya LC calendar; the "B'aktun" glyph ◆ Represents the head of a bird

pi-b'i NA-aj *(pib' naj)* (T177.585:4:12) ▶ n. "sweat bath," *temescal*

pi-b'i-NA-li *(pib'nal)* (T177:585hv:24.48) ▶ n. "sweat bath," *temescal*

pi-ji *(pij)* (T528.528:60) ▶ n. period of 400 years of 360 days each; used in the Maya LC calendar; the "B'aktun" glyph

PIK *(pik)* (T528.528) ▶ num. class. for units/groups of 8,000; ex.: *jo pik kakaw* "five units of 8,000 cacao {beans}"

pi-si *(pis)* (T177v:57) ▶ num. class. for "measured" or counts of periods of time; ex.: *jun pis tun* "first measured year"

pi-tzi *(pitz)* (T177:507) 1 ▶ adj. "youthful" 2 ▶ n. "ball game" 3 ▶ n. "ball player"

pi-tzi-la *(pitzal)* (T177.507hv:178) 1 ▶ adj. "youthful" 2 ▶ intr. v. "play ball"

pi-tzi-la-ja *(pitzalaj)* (T200:507hv:178.181) 1 ▶ adj. "youthful" 2 ▶ pos. com. v. "played ball"

pi-xo-ma *(pixom)* (T177.536:142) 1 ▶ n. "headdress" 2 ▶ tr. v. "to wrap"

PI-ya *(pi-i/piy)* (T528.528:126) 1 ▶ n. "bundle" 2 ▶ n. period of 400 years of 360 days each; used in the Maya LC calendar; the "B'aktun" glyph

po *(po)* (T687a) ▶ phonetic sign ◆ May represent an earflare

POP *(Pop)* (T551:130) ▶ n. month sign; first month of the Maya Ja'ab' calendar

pu/PU/PUJ *(pu/puj)* (T854) 1 ▶ phonetic sign 2 ▶ n. "reed," "cattail reed" 3 ▶ n. "bullrush" 4 ▶ n. proper name of "Tollan"? ◆ An inverted "sky" sign (**CHAAN/KAAN**) (T561)

pu-lu-yi *(puliy)* (T854.568:17) 1 ▶ intr. com. v. "burned" 2 ▶ intr. com. v. "sprinkled"

PUL-[yi] *(puliy)* (T122:1010c[17]) 1 ▶ intr. com. v. "burned" 2 ▶ intr. com. v. "sprinkled" ◆ Represents a human head with infixed **K'IN** sign and surmounted by smoke or flame

S

sa/SA *(sa)* (T278) 1 ▶ phonetic sign 2 ▶ n. "corn/maize gruel," *atole*

sa/SA *(sa)* (Tnn) 1 ▶ phonetic sign 2 ▶ n. "corn/maize gruel," *atole*

sa *(sa)* (T630) ▶ phonetic sign

sa *(sa)* (T630v) ▶ phonetic sign

sa *(sa)* (T1004v) ▶ phonetic sign ◆ Depicts a human head with T526 **KAB'AN** superimposed over the mouth

sa/SA *(sa)* (T278:552) ▶ phonetic sign

sa/SA *(sa)* (T278:552) ▶ phonetic sign

sa-aj-mi-ya *(sajmiy)* (T1004v:173.743:126v) ▶ temp. phr. "earlier today" ◆ See **sa-mi-ya**.

sa-ja-la *(sajal)* (T630.181:178) 1 ▶ n. elite title of unknown specific meaning but generally signifying "subordinate lord" 2 ▶ n. "one who fears"?; generally "underlord"

sa-ja-la *(sajal)* (T1004v:178) 1 ▶ n. elite title of unknown specific meaning but generally signifying "subordinate lord" 2 ▶ n. "one who fears"?; generally "underlord"

SAK *(sak)* (T58) 1 ▶ adj. "white" 2 ▶ adj. "resplendent" 3 ▶ adj. "pure"

SAK *(Sak)* (T58:528.142) ▶ n. month sign; eleventh month of the Maya Ja'ab' calendar

SAK CHUWEN *(sak chuwen)* (T58.nn:520) ▶ adj. + n. "pure, resplendent artist"; elite title

SAK IK' EK' *(sak ik' ek')* (T58.503v 510a) ▶ n. deity name; proper name of god with "wind" manifestations; "Resplendent Wind God Star"?

SAK la-ka-TUN *(sak lak tun)* (T58:534:25.25.528) ▶ n. "incensario"; proper name of the class of object "incensario"; literally "white stone plate"

SAK la-ka-TUN-ni *(sak lak tun)* (T58:534.25:528:116) ▶ n. "incensario"; proper name of the class of object "incensario"; literally "white stone plate"

SAK NIK *(sak nik)* (T179) ▶ adj. "white flowery"; used in the general "death" verbal phrase *u k'ay sak nik ik'il*, which broadly means "diminished its white flowery soul"

SAK NIK *(sak nik)* (T179) ▶ adj. "white flowery"; used in the general "death" verbal phrase *u k'ay sak nik ik'il*, which broadly means "diminished its white flowery soul"

SAK nu-ku NAJ *(Sak Nuk Naj)* (T58.151:528.4) ▶ adj. + n. "White Great House"; proper name of building/house

SAK TE' AJAW-wa *(Sak Te' Ajaw)* (T58:168:513:130) ▶ adj. + n. "White Tree Lord"; elite/royal title

sa-mi-ya *(samiy)* (T630v.1000h[713]:126) ▶ temp. phr. "earlier today" ◆ See **sa-aj-mi-ya**.

sa-ta *(sat)* (T1004:103) 1 ▶ tr. v. "to destroy" 2 ▶ tr. v. "to lose"

sa-ta-yi *(satay)* (T1004:103.17) 1 ▶ intr. com. v. "destroyed" 2 ▶ intr. com. v. "lost"

se *(se)* (T520) ▶ phonetic sign

SEK *(Sek)* (T25:520:130) ▶ n. month sign; fifth month of the Maya Ja'ab' calendar

si *(si)* (T57) ▶ phonetic sign

si *(si)* (T57) ▶ phonetic sign

si *(si)* (T146) ▶ phonetic sign

SI *(si)* (T740) ▶ intr. v. "to be born"; general "birth" glyph; the "upended frog" glyph

SI-ji-ya *(sij-ya)* (T740:246) 1 ▶ intr. com. v. "born"; general "birth" verb 2 ▶ n. "birth" ◆ The "upended frog" glyph

SIP *(Sip)* (T109:552) ▶ n. month sign; third month of the Maya Ja'ab' calendar; sometimes spelled phonetically **CHAK-ka-ta** for *Chak'at*

si-tzi WINIK-ki *(sitz winik)* (T57:248 521:102) ▶ n. "glutton"

SI-ya-ja *(siyaj)* (T740:126.181) ▶ pass. v. "was born"; general "birth" verb
♦ The "upended frog" glyph

SOTZ' *(Sotz')* (T756) ▶ n. month sign; fourth month of the Maya Ja'ab' calendar ♦ Represents the head of a leaf-nosed bat. See also **tz'i** and **xu**.

su *(su)* (T216) ▶ phonetic sign

su-ku-{n} *(sukun)* (T216:528) ▶ n. "older brother"

su-ku-{n} WINIK-ki *(sukun winik)* (T216:528.521:102) ▶ adj. + n. "older brother person"

su-sa-ja *(susaj)* (T216.630af:1025v) 1 ▶ pass. v. "was cut up" 2 ▶ pass. v. "was rasped"

su-tz'i *(sutz')* (T216:563a) ▶ n. "bat"

T

ta/TA *(ta)* (T51 and T53) 1 ▶ phonetic sign 2 ▶ prep. "in," "at," "with," "to"

ta/TA *(ta)* (T103) 1 ▶ phonetic sign 2 ▶ prep. "in," "at," "with," "to"

ta/TA *(ta)* (T113) 1 ▶ phonetic sign 2 ▶ prep. "in," "at," "with," "to"

ta/TA *(ta)* (T122:150) 1 ▶ phonetic sign 2 ▶ prep. "in," "at," "with," "to" ♦ See also **TAJ**.

ta/TA *(ta)* (T552v) 1 ▶ phonetic sign 2 ▶ prep. "in," "at," "with," "to"

ta/TA *(ta)* (T565) 1 ▶ phonetic sign 2 ▶ prep. "in," "at," "with," "to"

ta/TA *(ta)* (T565) 1 ▶ phonetic sign 2 ▶ prep. "in," "at," "with," "to"

ta/TA *(ta)* (T565) 1 ▶ phonetic sign 2 ▶ prep. "in," "at," "with," "to"

ta/TA *(ta)* (T645) 1 ▶ phonetic sign 2 ▶ prep. "in," "at," "with," "to"

ta/TA *(ta)* (T776.776) 1 ▶ phonetic sign 2 ▶ prep. "in," "at," "with," "to"

TAB' *(tab')* (T32:843v) 1 ▶ tr. v. "to ascend," "to rise up," "to go up" 2 ▶ tr. v. "to present" ♦ General "dedication" verb. The "footprint on staircase" glyph. Formerly **JOY**.

TAB'-[yi] *(tab'iy)* (T32:843v[17]) 1 ▶ intr. com. v. "ascended," "rose up," "went up" 2 ▶ intr. com. v. "presented" ♦ General "dedication" verb. The "footprint on staircase" glyph. Formerly **JOY**.

TAB'-[yi] *(tab'iy)* (T1014a[17]) 1 ▶ intr. com. v. "ascended," "rose up," "went up" 2 ▶ intr. com. v. "presented" ♦ General "dedication" verb. Represents God N with his diagnostic "net" headdress, probably a manifestation of the Pawatun gods. Formerly **JOY**.

TAB'-[yi] *(tab'iy)* (T45.843[17]) 1 ▶ intr. com. v. "ascended," "rose up," "went up" 2 ▶ intr. com. v. "presented" ♦ General "dedication" verb. Variant of the "footprint on staircase" glyph with **yi** as verbal inflection. Formerly **JOY**.

TAB'-[yi] *(tab'iy)* (T46.843[17]) 1 ▶ intr. com. v. "ascended," "rose up," "went up" 2 ▶ intr. com. v. "presented" ◆ General "dedication" verb. Variant of the "footprint on staircase" glyph with **yi** as verbal inflection. Formerly **JOY**.

TAB'-[yi] *(tab'iy)* (T46.1014a[17]) 1 ▶ intr. com. v. "ascended," "rose up," "went up" 2 ▶ intr. com. v. "presented" ◆ General "dedication" verb. Represents God N with his diagnostic "net" headdress, probably a manifestation of the Pawatun gods. Formerly **JOY**.

TAJ *(taj)* (T60) ▶ n. "torch" ◆ Represents a tied cloth knot or headband. Apparently polyvalent: see also **ji**.

TAJ *(taj)* (T122:150) ▶ n. "torch," "pine torch"

ta-ji *(taj)* (T565v:136) ▶ n. "obsidian"

TAJ TUN *(taj tun)* (T122.150:528) ▶ n. "torch stone" ◆ Alternatively **ta-ku**

TAK *(-tak)* (T559[544]) ▶ plural suffix

ta-ki *(-tak)* (T565v.102) ▶ plural suffix

ta-ki-ja *(takaj)* (T565:102.181) ▶ pass. v. "was come," "to have come"

TAK-ki *(-tak)* (T559[544]:102) ▶ plural suffix with phonetic complement

TAL *(tal)* (T676) 1 ▶ intr. v. " to come," "to arrive" 2 ▶ numerical classifier for ordinal numbers, ex.: "first," "second"

ta-li *(tal)* (T113.82) 1 ▶ intr. v. " to come," "to arrive" 2 ▶ numerical classifier for ordinal numbers, ex.: "first," "second"

TAN *(tan)* (T606) 1 ▶ loc. prep. "in" 2 ▶ prep. phr. "in the center of," "in the middle of" 3 ▶ prep. phr. "in front of"

TAN *(tan)* (T606) 1 ▶ loc. prep. "in" 2 ▶ prep. phr. "in the center of," "in the middle of" 3 ▶ prep. phr. "in front of"

TAN *(tan)* (T606v) 1 ▶ loc. prep. "in" 2 ▶ prep. phr. "in the center of," "in the middle of" 3 ▶ prep. phr. "in front of"

TAN CH'EN-na *(tan ch'en)* (T606.598v:23) 1 ▶ double loc. phr. "in front of the cave" 2 ▶ double loc. phr. "within the cave" ♦ "Introductory" phrase for locations

TAN CH'EN OX WITZ-aj *(tan ch'en ox witzaj)* (T606.571v:III.528hv.228) 1 ▶ double loc. phr. + n. "in front of the cave Three Hill Water" 2 ▶ double loc. phr. + n. "within the cave Three Hill Water" ♦ Proper name of a location

[TAN] LAM *(tan lam)* (T699v) ▶ adj. "half diminished" ♦ The "half period" glyph. Used for PEs of the Maya LC calendar.

[TAN] LAM-ja *(tan lamaj)* (T699v.181) ▶ pass. v. "was half diminished" ♦ The "half period" glyph. Used for PEs of the Maya LC calendar.

TAN-na *(tan)* (T606:23) 1 ▶ loc. prep. "in" 2 ▶ prep. phr. "in the center of," "in the middle of" 3 ▶ prep. phr. "in front of"

TA OCH-le-{l} *(ta ochlel)* (T102.765:188) 1 ▶ prep. phr. "at the foot of" 2 ▶ prep. phr. "at the enter-treeship," "in enter-treeship"; general reference to "heir designation"

TA yu-ta-{l} *(ta yutal)* (T51.61:565) 1 ▶ prep. phr. "for his/her fruited" 2 ▶ prep. phr. "for his/her seeds/beans" ♦ Final *lv* (the consonant *l* + vowel) optional. Part of the PSS "contents" phrase.

te'/TE' (che'/CHE') *(te'/che')* (T87) 1 ▶ phonetic sign 2 ▶ n. "tree" 3 ▶ n. "wood"

te'/TE' (che'/CHE') *(te'/che')* (T350) 1 ▶ phonetic sign 2 ▶ n. "tree" 3 ▶ n. "wood"

te'/TE' (che'/CHE') *(te'/che')* (T513) 1 ▶ phonetic sign 2 ▶ n. "tree" 3 ▶ n. "wood"

te'/TE' (che'/CHE') *(te'/che')* (T514) 1 ▶ phonetic sign 2 ▶ n. "tree" 3 ▶ n. "wood"

te'/TE' (che'/CHE') *(te'/che')* (T514v) 1 ▶ phonetic sign 2 ▶ n. "tree" 3 ▶ n. "wood"

te'/TE' (che'/CHE') *(te'/che')* (T514v) 1 ▶ phonetic sign 2 ▶ n. "tree" 3 ▶ n. "wood"

te'/TE' (che'/CHE') *(te'/che')* (T580[646]) 1 ▶ phonetic sign 2 ▶ n. "tree" 3 ▶ n. "wood"

te'/TE' (che'/CHE') *(te'/che')* (T78:514v) 1 ▶ phonetic sign 2 ▶ n. "tree" 3 ▶ n. "wood"

te'/TE' (che'/CHE') *(te'/che')* (T87hv) 1 ▶ phonetic sign 2 ▶ n. "tree" 3 ▶ n. "wood" ♦ Represents the "Pax" god (god of the month of Pax)

te'-k'a *(tek')* (T580:669b) ▶ tr. v. phr. "to step on"

te'-k'a-ja *(tek'aj)* (T580:669b.181) ▶ pass. v. phr. "was stepped on"

te'-TE'-le *(te'el)* (T87:513.188) ▶ adj. "tree-fresh" ♦ Functions as part of a compound adjective in the "contents" phrase of the PSS: *ta itz' te'el kakaw* "for tree-fresh kakaw"

ti/TI *(ti)* (T59) 1 ▶ phonetic sign 2 ▶ prep. "on," "to," "with," "from," "in," "at"

ti/TI *(ti)* (T747) 1 ▶ phonetic sign 2 ▶ prep. "on," "to," "with," "from," "in," "at"

TI AJAW le-{l} *(ti ajawlel)* (T59.168:188) ▶ prep. phr. "in rulership," "in lordship," "in kingship" ♦ Final component of the "affix cluster." Part of the general "accession" verbs *joy ti ajawlel* and *chumwan ti ajawlel*.

ti-ka-la *(tikal)* (T59.25:534) ▶ tr. v. phr. "to get drunk on"

ti-ki-li *(tikil)* (T59:102:24) ▶ prep. phr. "as the . . ."

TIL *(til)* (T758v) ▶ n. "tapir" ♦ Represents the head of a tapir

ti-xu-[ku]-pi *(ti xukpi)* (T59:756[528].177) ▶ prep. phr. "with a bird" ♦ Refers to the dance object held on lintels at Yaxchilán. *Xukpi* may refer to the "mot mot" bird. Preceded by **AK'OT** "dance."

TI ya-AK'-il *(ti yak'il?)* (T59.126:504v:24) ▶ prep. phr. "in the tongue"

to *(to)* (T44) ▶ phonetic sign

to *(to)* (T44) ▶ phonetic sign

to *(to)* (T44:563b) ▶ phonetic sign

to-jo-li *(tojol)* (T44:607:24v) ▶ n. "payment," "tribute"

to-jo-li *(tojol)* (T44:695:24) ▶ n. "payment," "tribute"

to-ko *(tok)* (T44:110) ▶ n. "cloud"

to-ko TAN AJAW *(Tok Tan Ajaw)* (T110.168:44:606) ▶ n. "Cloud Center Lord"; elite/royal title associated with a location at Palenque

to-ko-TAN-na *(tok tan/Tok Tan)* (T44:110.606:23) 1 ▶ n. "cloud center" 2 ▶ n. "Cloud Center"; proper name of location at Palenque

to-ko TAN WINIK-ki *(Tok Tan Winik)* (T44:110:606.521:102) ▶ n. "Cloud Center Person"; elite/royal title associated with a location at Palenque

TOK' *(tok')* (T257) ▶ n. "flint" ♦ Represents a flint blade

TOK' *(tok')* (T257) ▶ n. "flint" ♦ Represents a flint blade

TOK' *(tok')* (T257) ▶ n. "flint" ◆ Represents a flint blade

to-k'a *(tok')* (T44:669) ▶ n. "flint"

to-k'a pa-ka-la *(tok' pakal)* (T44:669.586b:25:178) ▶ n. "flint-shield"; general war-related epithet; metaphor for "war"

TOK' PAKAL *(tok' pakal)* (T257:624) ▶ n. "flint-shield"; general war-related epithet; metaphor for "war"

to-[xa]-AT-ti *(toxat)* (T44:691v:59) ▶ n. "bled penis"

to-XAT *(toxat)* (T1030j) ▶ n. "bled penis"

TU *(tu)* (T89, T90, and T92) ▶ prep. + 3ʳᵈ pers. poss. pron. "in his/her/its . . ."; contraction of the preposition *ti* (**TI**) and the third-person possessive pronoun *u* (**U**)

tu-ku-nu *(tukun)* (T89.528:592v) ▶ n. "dove"

TU K'U-li *(tuk'ul)* (T89.1016:24) ▶ prep. phr. "in his/her/its divinity"

TUL *(tul)* (T758v) ▶ n. "rabbit" ◆ Represents the head of a rabbit. See **tz'o**.

TUN *(tun)* (T528) 1 ▶ n. "stone" 2 ▶ n. "year"; primarily used with this meaning in PE glyphs ♦ May represent rain clouds (the so-called bunched grapes) and the rainbow. See **KAWAK** and **ku**.

TUN *(tun)* (T528hv) 1 ▶ n. "stone" 2 ▶ n. "year"; primarily used with this meaning in PE glyphs ♦ Represents a zoomorphic head with possible infixed rain clouds (the so-called bunched grapes) and the rainbow. See **KAWAK** and **ku**.

TUN *(tun)* (T548) ▶ n. "year"; year of 360 days used in the Maya LC calendar and DNs ♦ Thought to represent a cylindrical wooden drum, or *tunkul*, in cross-section

TUN *(tun)* (T548) ▶ n. "year"; year of 360 days used in the Maya LC calendar and DNs ♦ Thought to represent a cylindrical wooden drum, or *tunkul*, in cross-section

TUN *(tun)* (T1034) ▶ n. "year"; year of 360 days used in the Maya LC calendar and DNs ◆ Represents the head of a bird

TU na-ja *(tu naj)* (T89.5.683) 1 ▶ prep. phr. "in his/her/its structure" 2 ▶ prep. phr. "in his/her/its house"

TUN-ni *(tun)* (T528:116) 1 ▶ n. "stone" 2 ▶ n. "year"; primarily used with this meaning in PE glyphs ◆ See **KAWAK** and **ku**.

tu-pa *(tup)* (T89:586) ▶ n. "earflare"

tu-pa-ja *(tupaj)* (T89.586:683) ▶ pass. v. "was ear-flared"; metaphorically "was adorned"

TU WAY-[b'i]-li *(tu wayb'il)* (T89.539[585]:82) ▶ prep. phr. "in his/her/its sleeping place," "in his/her/its dreaming place"

TZ

tza *(tza)* (T699v) ▶ phonetic sign

tza *(tza)* (T714v) ▶ phonetic sign ♦ Represents an upright human hand

tza-[ka] *(tzak)* (T714) 1 ▶ tr. v. "to grasp," "to grab" 2 ▶ tr. v. "to conjure" 3 ▶ intr. v. "to appear" ♦ General verb meaning "blood sacrifice," especially "self-sacrifice." The "hand-grasping-fish" verb.

tza-[ka] *(tzak)* (T714) 1 ▶ tr. v. "to grasp," "to grab" 2 ▶ tr. v. "to conjure" 3 ▶ intr. v. "to appear" ♦ General verb meaning "blood sacrifice," especially "self-sacrifice." The "hand-grasping-fish" verb.

tza-[ka]-wa *(tzakaw)* (T714:130) 1 ▶ tr. v. "to grasp," "to grab" 2 ▶ tr. v. "to conjure" 3 ▶ tr. v. "to make appear" ♦ General verb meaning "blood sacrifice," especially "self-sacrifice." The "hand-grasping-fish" verb.

tza-[ka]-wa CH'UL/tza-[ka]-wa K'UL *(tzakaw ch'ul/tzakaw k'ul)* (T714:130.35) ▶ tr. v. phr. "to conjure/manifest/make appear god/divinity/holiness" ♦ The **tza-[ka]-wa** portion of this phrase can be followed by **CH'UL/K'UL**, **K'AWIL**, or the name of one of the Vision Serpents as the thing conjured.

tzi *(tzi)* (T124) ▶ phonetic sign ♦ The uppermost element of the ISIG. Value uncertain. See also **tzo**.

tzi *(tzi)* (T507b) ▸ phonetic sign

tzi *(tzi)* (T507hv) ▸ phonetic sign

tzi/TZI *(tzi)* (T1000v) 1 ▸ phonetic sign 2 ▸ adj. "fresh," "new" 3 ▸ adj. "seasoned" ◆ Represents a human head

tzi-ka JA'AB' (?)/tzi-ka AB' (?) *(tzik ja'ab'?/tzik ab'?)* (T124:25:548:142) ▸ intr. v. phr. "the count of years"?; the Initial Series Introductory Glyph ◆ The central element rendered in outline varies depending on the Ja'ab' month of the Calendar Round.

tzo *(tzo)* (T124) ▸ phonetic sign ◆ The uppermost element of the ISIG. Value uncertain. See also **tzi**.

tzo *(tzo)* (T299:683) ▶ phonetic sign ♦ Represents a sprout emerging from the "moon" sign (T683)

tzu/TZU *(tzu)* (T559) 1 ▶ phonetic sign 2 ▶ n. "gourd"

tzu *(tzu)* (T560v) ▶ phonetic sign ♦ Probably represents the ribs of a dog

tzu-lu *(tzul)* (T560v.568) ▶ n. "dog"

TZUTZ *(tzutz)* (T218) 1 ▶ tr. v. "to end," "to terminate," "to expire" 2 ▶ tr. v. "to join" ♦ Possibly polyvalent **JOM** with approximately the same meaning. Represents the back of a human hand and bauble.

TZUTZ *(tzutz)* (T756inv) 1 ▶ tr. v. "to end," "to terminate," "to expire" 2 ▶ tr. v. "to join" ♦ Represents an upside-down bat head

TZUTZ *(tzutz)* (T756inv) 1 ▶ tr. v. "to end," "to terminate," "to expire" 2 ▶ tr. v. "to join" ♦ Represents an upside-down bat head

TZUTZ-ja *(tzutzaj)* (T756inv.181) ▶ pass. v. "was ended," "was terminated," "was expired"

tzu-tzu-ja *(tzutzaj)* (T559.559.181) ▶ pass. v. "was ended," "was termi-nated," "was expired" ♦ The two dots on the upper left edge of T559 **tzu** double the phonetic value, yielding **tzu-tzu**.

TZUTZ-yi *(tzutziy)* (T218:17) ▶ intr. com. v. "ended," "terminated," "expired"
♦ Alternate spelling: **JOM-yi**

TZUTZ-yi *(tzutziy)* (T756inv.181) ▶ intr. com. v. "ended," "terminated," "expired"

TZ'

tz'a/TZ'A *(tz'a)* (T366v) 1 ▶ phonetic sign 2 ▶ tr. v. "to give"

TZ'AK *(tz'ak)* (T573) 1 ▶ tr. v. "to put in order" 2 ▶ tr. v. "to count," "to increase" 3 ▶ adj. "whole"

TZ'AK-aj *(tz'akaj)* (T573:12) 1 ▶ pass. v. "was put in order" 2 ▶ pass. v. "was counted," "was increased" ♦ The DNIG and "Successor" glyph

TZ'AK b'u-li *(tz'ak b'ul)* (T573.21:83) 1 ▶ tr. v. "to put in order" 2 ▶ tr. v. "to count," "to increase"

TZ'AM (?) *(tz'am?)* (T150) ▶ n. "throne"

tz'a-[pa] *(tz'ap)* (T68:586) 1 ▶ pos. v. "to plant upright" 2 ▶ pos. v. "to hoist" 3 ▶ tr. v. "to stack," "to pile up"; general "dedication" verb for monuments

tz'a-pa-ja *(tz'apaj)* (T366:586hv.181) 1 ▶ pass. v. "was planted upright" 2 ▶ pass. v. "was hoisted" 3 ▶ pass. v. "was stacked," "was piled up"; general "dedication" verb for monuments

tz'a-[pa]-ja *(tz'apaj)* (T68:586:1025v) 1 ▶ pass. v. "was planted upright" 2 ▶ pass. v. "was hoisted" 3 ▶ pass. v. "was stacked," "was piled up"; general "dedication" verb for monuments

tz'a-pa-ji-ya *(tz'apajiy)* (T366v.586hv:246) 1 ▶ intr. com. v. "planted upright" 2 ▶ intr. com. v. "hoisted" 3 ▶ intr. com. v. "stacked," "piled up"; general "dedication" verb for monuments

tz'a-[pa]-wa *(tz'apwa)* (T68:586:130) 1 ▶ pos. v. "to plant upright" 2 ▶ pos. v. "to hoist" 3 ▶ pos. v. "to stack," "to pile up"; general "dedication" verb for monuments

tz'i *(tz'i)* (T248) ▶ phonetic sign

tz'i *(tz'i)* (Tnn) ▶ phonetic sign ♦ Represents a hand grasping a writing instrument

tz'i *(tz'i)* (T563a) ▶ phonetic sign

tz'i *(tz'i)* (T563b) ▶ phonetic sign

TZ'I *(tz'i)* (T752) ▶ n. "dog" ♦ Represents the head of a dog

TZ'I *(tz'i)* (T753) ▶ n. "dog" ♦ Represents the head of a dog

tz'i *(tz'i)* (T756b) ▶ phonetic sign ♦ Represents the head of a leaf-nosed bat. See also **xu**.

tz'i-b'a *(tz'ib')* (T243:501) 1 ▶ n. "writing" 2 ▶ n. "painting"

tz'i-b'a *(tz'ib')* (T243.501hv:314) 1 ▶ n. "writing" 2 ▶ n. "painting"

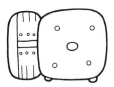

tz'i-b'i *(tz'ib')* (T243.585) 1 ▶ n. "writing" 2 ▶ n. "painting"

tz'i-b'i *(tz'ib')* (T243.585hv) 1 ▶ n. "writing" 2 ▶ n. "painting"

tz'i-i *(tz'i)* (T243:679a) ▶ n. "dog"

tz'o *(tz'o)* (T758v) ▶ phonetic sign ◆ Represents the head of a rabbit? See **TUL**.

tz'u *(tz'u)* (T203v) ▶ phonetic sign

tz'u *(tz'u)* (T608) ▶ phonetic sign

tz'u-nu-{n} *(tz'unun)* (T203v.592) ▶ n. "hummingbird"

U

u/U *(u)* (T1) 1 ▶ vowel *u* 2 ▶ 3ʳᵈ pers. pron. "he," "she," "it" 3 ▶ 3ʳᵈ pers. poss. pron. "his," "hers," "its"

u/U *(u)* (T1) 1 ▶ vowel *u* 2 ▶ 3ʳᵈ pers. pron. "he," "she," "it" 3 ▶ 3ʳᵈ pers. poss. pron. "his," "hers," "its"

u/U *(u)* (T3) 1 ▶ vowel *u* 2 ▶ 3ʳᵈ pers. pron. "he," "she," "it" 3 ▶ 3ʳᵈ pers. poss. pron. "his," "hers," "its"

u/U *(u)* (T13) 1 ▶ vowel *u* 2 ▶ 3ʳᵈ pers. pron. "he," "she," "it" 3 ▶ 3ʳᵈ pers. poss. pron. "his," "hers," "its"

u/U *(u)* (T191) 1 ▶ vowel *u* 2 ▶ 3ʳᵈ pers. pron. "he," "she," "it" 3 ▶ 3ʳᵈ pers. poss. pron. "his," "hers," "its"

u/U *(u)* (T204) 1 ▶ vowel *u* 2 ▶ 3ʳᵈ pers. pron. "he," "she," "it" 3 ▶ 3ʳᵈ pers. poss. pron. "his," "hers," "its"

u/U *(u)* (T231) 1 ▶ vowel *u* 2 ▶ 3ʳᵈ pers. pron. "he," "she," "it" 3 ▶ 3ʳᵈ pers. poss. pron. "his," "hers," "its" ♦ Represents a human head with prominent lips

u/U *(u)* (T232) 1 ▶ vowel *u* 2 ▶ 3ʳᵈ pers. pron. "he," "she," "it" 3 ▶ 3ʳᵈ pers. poss. pron. "his," "hers," "its"

u/U *(u)* (T513) 1 ▶ vowel *u* 2 ▶ 3rd pers. pron. "he," "she," "it" 3 ▶ 3rd pers. poss. pron. "his," "hers," "its"

u/U *(u)* (T738v) 1 ▶ vowel *u* 2 ▶ 3rd pers. pron. "he," "she," "it" 3 ▶ 3rd pers. poss. pron. "his," "hers," "its" ◆ Represents the head of a fish

u/U *(u)* (T1008v) 1 ▶ vowel *u* 2 ▶ 3rd pers. pron. "he," "she," "it" 3 ▶ 3rd pers. poss. pron. "his," "hers," "its" ◆ Represents a human head with closed eye

U B'A *(u b'a)* (T1:60:757:314) 1 ▶ poss. n. "his/her/its image," "the image of" 2 ▶ poss. n. "his/her/its doing," "the doing of"

U B'A *(u b'a)* (T13v.60:757) 1 ▶ poss. n. "his/her/its image," "the image of" 2 ▶ poss. n. "his/her/its doing," "the doing of"

UCH' *(uch')* (Tnn[501]) 1 ▶ n. "drink" 2 ▶ intr. v. "to drink"

u-lu *(ul)* (T738v:568) ▶ n. "maize gruel," *atole*; used in the "contents" prepositional phrase of the PSS

u-ne-{n} *(unen)* (T511:856) ▶ relat. "child [of father]"

u-ti *(ut)* (T513:59) ▶ intr. v. "to happen," "to occur," "to come to pass"

u-ti *(ut)* (T738:59) ▶ intr. v. "to happen," "to occur," "to come to pass"

u-ti-ji-ya *(utjiy)* (T513v:59:126) 1 ▶ intr. com. v. "since it happened," "since it occurred," "since it came to pass"; the "Anterior Date Indicator" (ADI); T126 used as a "background marker" with the meaning "since" 2 ▶ prep. phr. "it happened at"; used in place name sequences

u-ti-ya *(utiy)* (T513.59:126) 1 ▶ intr. com. v. "since it happened," "since it occurred," "since it came to pass"; the "Anterior Date Indicator" (ADI); T126 used as a "background marker" with the meaning "since" 2 ▶ prep. phr. "it happened at"; used in place name sequences

u-ti-ya *(utiy)* (T738:59:126) 1 ▶ intr. com. v. "since it happened," "since it occurred," "since it came to pass"; the "Anterior Date Indicator" (ADI); T126 used as a "background marker" with the meaning "since" 2 ▶ prep. phr. "it happened at"; used in place name sequences

u-ti-ya *(utiy)* (T846[520].59:125) 1 ▶ intr. com. v. "since it happened," "since it occurred," "since it came to pass"; the "Anterior Date Indicator" (ADI); T125 used as a "background marker" with the meaning "since" 2 ▶ prep. phr. "it happened at"; used in place name sequences

u-to-ma *(utom)* (T1:44:502) ▶ intr. incom. v. "it will happen," "it will occur," "it will come to pass"; the "Future Date Indicator" (FDI); incorporates the root *ut* "to happen/occur" and the subjunctive aspect marker *-om* "will"

u-to-ma *(utom)* (T3.44:563:142) ▶ intr. incom. v. "it will happen," "it will occur," "it will come to pass"; the "Future Date Indicator" (FDI); incorporates the root *ut* "to happen/occur" and the subjunctive aspect marker -*om* "will"

U . . . wa *(u . . . wa)* (T1 . . . 130) ▶ transitive completive verbal affix pattern; marks transitive completive verbs

U we'-ya *(u we'y)* (T1.nn:574:142.?:125) ▶ tr. incom. v. phr. "his/her/its eating of"

U . . . wi *(u . . . wi)* (T1 . . . 117) ▶ transitive completive verbal affix pattern; marks transitive completive verbs

u-xu-[lu] *(uxul)* (T1:756c) 1 ▶ n. "carving," "sculpture" 2 ▶ intr. v. "to carve," "to sculpt"

U ya-AJAW-wa TE' *(u yajaw te')* (T1:126.168:514:130) ▶ poss. n. "his/her/its Lord of the Tree"; possessed elite title

W

wa/WA *(wa)* (T130) 1 ▶ phonetic sign 2 ▶ pos. suf. *-w* 3 ▶ pos. v. "to erect" 4 ▶ n. "tortilla" 5 ▶ part. "and then" 6 ▶ prog. aspect marker on transitive verbs?

wa/WA *(wa)* (T335) 1 ▶ phonetic sign 2 ▶ pos. suf. *-w* 3 ▶ pos. v. "to erect" 4 ▶ n. "tortilla" 5 ▶ part. "and then" 6 ▶ progressive aspect marker on transitive verbs? ♦ Represents the teeth and eye of the "Snaggle Tooth Dragon"

wa/WA *(wa)* (T506) 1 ▶ phonetic sign 2 ▶ pos. suf. *-w* 3 ▶ pos. v. "to erect" 4 ▶ n. "tortilla" 5 ▶ n. "tamale" 6 ▶ part. "and then" ♦ Possibly represents a kernel of maize

wa/WA *(wa)* (Tnn) 1 ▶ phonetic sign 2 ▶ pos. suf. *-w* 3 ▶ pos. v. "to erect" 4 ▶ n. "tortilla" 5 ▶ part. "and then" ♦ Represents the profile of a human head turned toward the right

wa/WA *(wa)* (T130hv) 1 ▶ phonetic sign 2 ▶ pos. suf. *-w* 3 ▶ pos. v. "to erect" 4 ▶ n. "tortilla" 5 ▶ part. "and then" ♦ Represents the "Snaggle Tooth Dragon"

wa/WA *(wa)* (T130hv) 1 ▶ phonetic sign 2 ▶ pos. suf. *-w* 3 ▶ pos. v. "to erect" 4 ▶ n. "tortilla" 5 ▶ part. "and then" 6 ▶ progressive aspect marker on transitive verbs? ♦ Represents the teeth and eye of the "Snaggle Tooth Dragon"

WAK *(wak)* (TVI) 1 ▶ n. "six"; cardinal number 2 ▶ n. "something lifted," "something hoisted," "something erected," "something stood up"

WAK *(wak)* (T367) 1 ▶ n. "six"; cardinal number 2 ▶ n. "something lifted," "something hoisted," "something erected," "something stood up"

WAK *(wak)* (T1087v) 1 ▶ n. "six"; cardinal number 2 ▶ n. "something lifted," "something hoisted," "something erected," "something stood up" ♦ Represents an anthropomorphic head with axe infixed within the eye

WAK CHAAN-na AJAW/WAK KAAN-na AJAW *(Wak Chaan Ajaw/Wak Kaan Ajaw)* (TVI.170:561:130) 1 ▶ n. "Six Sky Lord" 2 ▶ n. "lifted/hoisted/erected/stood-up sky lord"; elite title

WAK-ki CHAAN/WAK-ki KAAN *(wak chaan/wak kaan)* (T367:561:102) 1 ▶ n. "six sky" 2 ▶ n. "lifted/hoisted/erected/stood-up sky"; elite title

wa-wa-aj-ni *(wawaan)* (T130hv.130:743:116) ▶ n. "a stood-up/lifted/erected/ raised-up thing"; used in name clauses of stelae

wa-wa-aj-ni *(wawaan)* (T335:743.335.1019) ▶ n. "a stood-up/lifted/ erected/raised-up thing"; used in name clauses of stelae

wa-WA-ji *(waj)* (T506:130.136) 1 ▶ n. "tortilla" 2 ▶ n. "tamale"

wa-WAY-{a}-[b'i] *(wayab')* (T130:539[585]) 1 ▶ n. "dreamer" 2 ▶ n. "spirit," "co-essence," *nawal*

WAXAK *(waxak)* (TVIII) ▶ n. "eight"; cardinal number

WAXAK *(waxak)* (T1006) ▶ n. "eight"; cardinal number ♦ Represents the head of the youthful Corn God

WAXAKLAJUN U B'A *(waxaklajun u b'a)* (TXVIII.13.757) 1 ▶ n. "Eighteen [Snake/Centipede] Heads"; proper name of the scaled Vision Serpent/ Centipede thought to derive from Teotihuacan imagery 2 ▶ n. "war helmet" 3 ▶ n. proper name of the 13th ruler of Copán in the Yax K'uk' Mo' lineage; possibly refers to the number of war serpent/centipede heads on the Temple of the Feathered Serpent at Teotihuacan in central Mexico

WAXAK NA CHAAK *(Waxak Na Chaak)* (TVIII.48:1011) ▶ n. proper name of God I (GI) of the Palenque Triad; "Eight First Chaak"?

WAY *(way)* (T539v) 1 ▶ n. "hole" 2 ▶ n. "entrance," "portal" 3 ▶ n. "water" 4 ▶ n. "spirit," "co-essence," *nawal* 5 ▶ n. "room," "quarter" 6 ▶ intr. v. "to sleep" ♦ The **AJAW** sign half-covered with jaguar pelt

WAY *(way)* (T769a) 1 ▶ n. "hole" 2 ▶ n. "entrance," "portal" 3 ▶ n. "water" 4 ▶ n. "spirit," "co-essence," *nawal* 5 ▶ n. "room," "quarter" 6 ▶ intr. v. "to sleep" ♦ Represents a "hole" or supernatural portal and the jaws of the "Snaggle Tooth Dragon"

wa-ya-k'a-wa *(wa yak'aw)* (T130.126:669:130) ▶ tr. v. "to give"; includes the possible progressive aspect marker *wa*

wa-ya-la-wa *(wa yalaw)* (T130.126:534:130) ▶ tr. v. "to say"; includes the possible progressive aspect marker *wa*

WAY-b'i-li *(wayb'il)* (T539[585]:82) 1 ▶ n. "sleeping room" 2 ▶ n. "lineage shrine"

WAYEB' *(Wayeb')* (T157:548) ▶ n. month sign; last "month" of the Maya Ja'ab' calendar; the final five-day unlucky period

WAY-ya *(way)* (T539:126) 1 ▶ n. "hole" 2 ▶ n. "entrance," "portal" 3 ▶ n. "water" 4 ▶ n. "co-essence," "spirit," *nawal* 5 ▶ n. "room," "quarter" 6 ▶ intr. v. "to sleep"

we'/WE' *(we')* (Tnn:574:142.?) 1 ▶ phonetic sign? 2 ▶ intr. v. "to eat"

we'/WE' *(we')* (T1008v[506]) 1 ▶ phonetic sign? 2 ▶ intr. v. "to eat"

wi/WI *(wi)* (T86) 1 ▶ phonetic sign 2 ▶ n. "root" 3 ▶ n. "one"; cardinal number

wi/WI *(wi)* (T86v) 1 ▶ phonetic sign 2 ▶ n. "root" 3 ▶ n. "one"; cardinal number

wi/WI *(wi)* (T117) 1 ▶ phonetic sign 2 ▶ n. "root" 3 ▶ n. "one"; cardinal number

wi/WI *(wi)* (T117) 1 ▶ phonetic sign 2 ▶ n. "root" 3 ▶ n. "one"; cardinal number

wi/WI *(wi)* (T117) 1 ▶ phonetic sign 2 ▶ n. "root" 3 ▶ n. "one"; cardinal number

WI CH'OK TE' NA *(wi ch'ok te' na)* (T117.600:87:4) ▶ n. "Root-Sprout Tree House"; proper name of a building; the "Lineage Founder" glyph

WINAL *(winal)* (T521) ▶ n. month of twenty days in the LC

WINAL *(winal)* (T741v) ▶ n. month of twenty days in the LC

WINIK *(winik)* (T521) 1 ▶ n. "man" 2 ▶ n. "person," "being"

wi-ti-ki AJAW *(Witik Ajaw)* (T117.513v:59 1000g) ▶ n. "Witik Lord"; elite title; *witik* of unknown meaning

WITZ *(witz)* (T529) 1 ▶ n. "hill" 2 ▶ n. "mountain" ♦ Represents a cleft mountain with infixed rain clouds (the so-called bunched grapes) and rainbow

wi-tzi *(witz)* (T117:507) 1 ▶ n. "hill" 2 ▶ n. "mountain"

wi-tzi mo-o *(Witz Mo')* (T117:507.582v[737]:279) ▶ n. "Mountain Macaw"; elite title

wi-tzi SAK-NIK-ki NAL *(Witz Sak Nik Nal)* (T117:507.79:102) ▶ n. "White Flowery Mountain Place"; proper name of the Kawak Monster on the Tablet of the Foliated Cross at Palenque

wi-WINIK-ki *(winik)* (T521:103.117) 1 ▶ n. "man" 2 ▶ n. "person," "being"

wi-WINIK-ki *(winik)* (T117.741v:102) 1 ▶ n. "man" 2 ▶ n. "person," "being"

. . . wi-ya *(. . . wiy?)* (T126.117) ▶ verbal suffix pattern used to derive an intransitive out of a transitive root

wo *(wo)* (T67) ▶ phonetic sign

wo *(wo)* (T67v) ▶ phonetic sign

wo *(wo)* (T67v) ▶ phonetic sign

WO *(Wo)* (T202:552v:142) ▶ n. month sign; second month of the Maya Ja'ab' calendar; sometimes spelled phonetically **EK'-ka-ta** for *Ik'kat*

wo-jo-li *(wojol)* (T67:607.24) ▶ n. "glyph," "character," "letter"

wo-la *(wol)* (T67:534) 1 ▶ n. "something round" 2 ▶ n. "heart" 3 ▶ tr. v. "to make round" 4 ▶ tr. v. "to wrap up"

WUK *(wuk)* (TVII) ▶ n. "seven"; cardinal number

WUK *(wuk)* (TVIIhv) ▶ n. "seven"; cardinal number ◆ Represents a zoomorphic head with a curl in its eye

X

xa/XA *(xa)* (T114) 1 ▶ phonetic sign 2 ▶ adv. pref. "already" 3 ▶ adv. pref. "again"; characterizes a verb as "happening again," "happening already"

xa/XA *(xa)* (T114) 1 ▶ phonetic sign 2 ▶ adv. pref. "already" 3 ▶ adv. pref. "again"; characterizes a verb as "happening again," "happening already"

xa-ma-na *(xaman)* (T114.566:23) ▶ n. "north"; cardinal direction

XAN-na *(xan)* (T202ms[585]:23) 1 ▶ intr. v. "to go" 2 ▶ intr. v. "to walk" 3 ▶ intr. v. "to travel"

xa-XAN-na *(xan)* (T114.202ms[585]:23) 1 ▶ intr. v. "to go" 2 ▶ intr. v. "to walk" 3 ▶ intr. v. "to travel"

xi *(xi)* (T736v) ▶ phonetic sign ◆ Represents a human skull

xi *(xi)* (T736v) ▶ phonetic sign ◆ Represents a human skull

xi *(xi)* (T736v) ▶ phonetic sign ◆ Represents a human skull

xi *(xi)* (T736v) ▶ phonetic sign ◆ Represents a human skull

XIB' *(xib')* (T1008) ▶ n. "man" ♦ Represents the head of a young man

xo *(xo)* (T536) ▶ phonetic sign

xo-ki *(xok)* (T536:102) 1 ▶ n. "shark" 2 ▶ n. "count"

xu *(xu)* (T756b) ▶ phonetic sign ♦ Represents the head of a leaf-nosed bat. See also **tz'i** and **SOTZ'**.

xu-[ku] *(xuk)* (T756d) 1 ▶ n. proper name of dance staff used at Yaxchilán; dance object 2 ▶ n. "bird"; possibly the mot-mot bird ♦ Represents the head of a leaf-nosed bat. Main sign of the Copán EG.

xu-[ku]-pi *(xukpi)* (T756d.177) 1 ▶ n. proper name of dance staff used at Yaxchilán; dance object 2 ▶ n. "bird"; possibly the mot-mot bird ♦ Main sign of the Copán EG with T177 **pi**

XUL *(Xul)* (T758v:116) ▶ n. month sign; sixth month of the Maya Ja'ab' calendar

xu-[lu] *(-xul)* (T756c) ▶ phonetic signs ♦ See **AJ u-xu-[lu]** and **u-xu-[lu]** for examples of usage; meaning outside of these contexts unknown

Y

ya *(ya)* (T125) 1 ▶ phonetic sign 2 ▶ background marker indicating the completive aspect 3 ▶ 3rd pers. prev. pron. used with words beginning in *a*: "he/she/it" 4 ▶ 3rd pers. prev. poss. pron. used with words beginning in *a*: "his/her/its"

ya *(ya)* (T126) 1 ▶ phonetic sign 2 ▶ background marker indicating the completive aspect 3 ▶ 3rd pers. prev. pron. used with words beginning in *a*: "he/she/it" 4 ▶ 3rd pers. prev. poss. pron. used with words beginning in *a*: "his/her/its"

ya *(ya)* (T126) 1 ▶ phonetic sign 2 ▶ background marker indicating the completive aspect 3 ▶ 3rd pers. prev. pron. used with words beginning in *a*: "he/she/it" 4 ▶ 3rd pers. prev. poss. pron. used with words beginning in *a*: "his/her/its"

ya *(ya)* (T126hv) 1 ▶ phonetic sign 2 ▶ background marker indicating the completive aspect 3 ▶ 3rd pers. prev. pron. used with words beginning in *a*: "he/she/it" 4 ▶ 3rd pers. prev. poss. pron. used with words beginning in *a*: "his/her/its" ◆ Represents a death's head with mouth scrolls

ya *(ya)* (T126hv) 1 ▶ phonetic sign 2 ▶ background marker indicating the completive aspect 3 ▶ 3rd pers. prev. pron. used with words beginning in *a*: "he/she/it" 4 ▶ 3rd pers. prev. poss. pron. used with words beginning in *a*: "his/her/its" ◆ Represents a death's head with mouth scrolls

ya-AJAW K'AK' *(Yajaw K'ak')* (T126:168:563a:122) ▶ poss. prep. phr. "Lord of the Fire," "Fire Lord"; elite title

ya-AJAW-wa *(yajaw)* (T126.533:130) ▶ poss. n. "his/her/its lord"; relationship glyph generally meaning "underlord," "subordinate"; elite title

ya-AJAW-wa TE' *(yajaw te')* (T126.168:513v.130) 1 ▶ poss. prep. phr. "Lord of the Tree," "Tree Lord" 2 ▶ poss. n. "his/her/its Tree Lord"; elite title

ya-AJAW-wa TE' *(yajaw te')* (T126.747a:130.87) 1 ▶ poss. prep. phr. "Lord of the Tree," "Tree Lord"; elite title 2 ▶ poss. n. "his/her/its Tree Lord"; elite title

ya-AL *(yal)* (T126.578af:670:142) ▶ poss. n. "child [of mother]"; literally "her harvest"; relationship glyph ♦ See also **ya CH'AM-ma/ya-CH'AM**.

ya-AL *(yal)* (T126.533:670) ▶ poss. n. "child [of mother]"; literally "her harvest"; relationship glyph ♦ See also **ya-CH'AM-ma/ya-CH'AM**.

ya-AL *(yal)* (T126.584:670) ▶ poss. n. "child [of mother]"; literally "her harvest"; relationship glyph ♦ See also **ya-CH'AM-ma/ya-CH'AM**.

ya-b'i-li *(yab'il)* (T126.743v[585]:24) ▶ poss. n. "his/her grandson"; relationship glyph

ya-CH'AM *(ya-ch'am)* (T126.533:670) ▶ poss. n. "child [of mother]"; literally "her harvest"; relationship glyph ♦ See also **ya-AL**.

ya-CH'AM *(ya-ch'am)* (T126.584:670) ▶ poss. n. "child [of mother]"; literally "her harvest"; relationship glyph ♦ See also **ya-AL**.

ya-CH'AM-ma *(ya-ch'am)* (T126.578af:670:142) ▶ poss. n. "child [of mother]"; literally "her harvest"; relationship glyph ♦ See also **ya-AL**.

ya-ja-li *(yajil)* (T125:60.1041:24) ▶ poss. n. "his/her/its termination"; "death"

ya-ja-wa *(yajaw)* (T126.683:130) ▶ poss. n. "lord of," "his/her/its lord"; relationship glyph

ya-k'a-wa *(yak'aw)* (T126.614b:130) 1 ▶ poss. n. "his/her/its giving" 2 ▶ poss. n. "his/her/its offering"

ya-k'a-wa *(yak'aw)* (T126.669b:130) 1 ▶ poss. n. "his/her/its giving" 2 ▶ poss. n. "his/her/its offering"

ya-k'u *(yak')* (T125:604v) 1 ▶ poss. n. "his/her/its giving" 2 ▶ poss. n. "his/her/its offering"

ya-la *(yal)* (T126.534) ▶ poss. n. "child [of mother]"; literally "her harvest"; relationship glyph ♦ See also **ya-CH'AM-ma/ya-CH'AM**.

ya-la-ja *(yalaj)* (T126.534:181) ▶ poss. n. "his/her/its throwing," "his/her/its hurling"

ya-la-ji *(yalij)* (T126.178:18v) ▶ poss. n. "his/her/its saying," "his/her/its utterance"

ya-la-ji-ya *(yalajiy)* (T126.534:246) ▶ poss. n. "his/her/its saying," "his/her/its utterance"

. . . ya-ni *(. . . yan)* (. . . T126.116) ▶ positional completive verbal affix pattern

ya-ta-ji *(yataj)* (T126.776:88) 1 ▶ poss. pl. n. "his/her/its companions" 2 ▶ tr. v. "to bathe," "to water"

ya-ta-na *(yatan)* (T126.552:23) ▶ poss. n. "the wife of," "his wife"; relationship glyph

ya-ti-ji *(yatij)* (T125.59:88v) ▶ tr. v. "to bathe," "to water"

ya-ti-ji *(yatij)* (T126.59:758v) ▶ tr. v. "to bathe," "to water"

YAX *(yax)* (T16) 1 ▶ adj. "green" 2 ▶ adj. "blue" 3 ▶ adj. "blue-green" 4 ▶ adj. "first"

YAX *(yax)* (T16) 1 ▶ adj. "green" 2 ▶ adj. "blue" 3 ▶ adj. "blue-green" 4 ▶ adj. "first"

YAX *(Yax)* (T16:528) ▶ n. month sign; tenth month of the Maya Ja'ab' calendar

YAX *(Yax)* (T16:528) ▶ n. month sign; tenth month of the Maya Ja'ab' calendar

ya-xa *(Yax)* (T126:114) 1 ▶ n. month sign; tenth month of the Maya Ja'ab' calendar 2 ▶ adj. "green" 3 ▶ adj. "blue" 4 ▶ adj. "blue-green" 5 ▶ adj. "first"

YAX CHIT *(yax chit)* (T16:580) ▶ adj. + n. "first father"?

YAX ch'a-CH'AM *(yax ch'am)* (T16:93v.617v:117) ▶ adj. + n. "first harvest"

YAX CH'AM *(yax ch'am)* (T16.617v:116?) ▶ adj. + n. "first harvest"

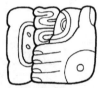

YAX CH'AM K'AWIL *(yax ch'am K'awil)* (T16.1030e:670) 1 ▶ v. phr. "first receiving [of] K'awil" 2 ▶ v. phr. "first harvesting [of] K'awil"

YAX K'AL TUN-ni *(yax k'al tun)* (T16:528.116:713a) ▶ v. phr. "closed the first *tun*," "closed the first stone"; general PE glyph for *tun*-endings

YAXK'IN *(Yaxk'in)* (T16:544.116) ▶ n. month sign; seventh month of the Maya Ja'ab' calendar

YAX k'o-jo *(yax k'oj)* (T16.220:607) ▶ adj. + n. "first image"

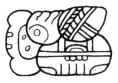

YAX PAS *(yax pas/Yax Pas)* (T16.222:561) 1 ▶ adj. + n. "first dawn" 2 ▶ n. name of sixteenth ruler of Copán in the Yax K'uk' Mo' lineage

YAX pa-{s} *(yax pas/Yax Pas)* (T16:602) 1 ▶ adj. + n. "first dawn" 2 ▶ n. name of sixteenth ruler of Copán in the Yax K'uk' Mo' lineage

ya-xu-na (?) *(yaxun?)* (T126:756b) ▶ poss. n. "his/her mother"

ye/YE *(ye/yej)* (T512) 1 ▶ phonetic sign 2 ▶ 3ʳᵈ pers. prev. pron. used with words beginning in *e*: "he/she/it" 3 ▶ 3ʳᵈ pers. prev. poss. pron. used with words beginning in *e*: "his/her/its" 4 ▶ adj. "revealed"

ye/YE *(ye/yej)* (T33:512) 1 ▶ phonetic sign 2 ▶ 3ʳᵈ pers. prev. pron. used with words beginning in *e*: "he/she/it" 3 ▶ 3ʳᵈ pers. prev. poss. pron. used with words beginning in *e*: "his/her/its" 4 ▶ adj. "revealed"

ye/YE *(ye/yej)* (T710) 1 ▶ phonetic sign 2 ▶ 3ʳᵈ pers. prev. pron. used with words beginning in *e*: "he/she/it" 3 ▶ 3ʳᵈ pers. prev. poss. pron. used with words beginning in *e*: "his/her/its" 4 ▶ adj. "revealed" ◆ Represents the back of a human hand turned downward

ye/YE *(ye/yej)* (T710v) 1 ▶ phonetic sign 2 ▶ 3ʳᵈ pers. prev. pron. used with words beginning in *e*: "he/she/it" 3 ▶ 3ʳᵈ pers. prev. poss. pron. used with words beginning in *e*: "his/her/its" 4 ▶ adj. "revealed" ♦ Represents the front of a human hand with curled fingers

ye/YE *(ye/yej)* (T1073) 1 ▶ phonetic sign 2 ▶ 3ʳᵈ pers. prev. pron. used with words beginning in *e*: "he/she/it" 3 ▶ 3ʳᵈ pers. prev. poss. pron. used with words beginning in *e*: "his/her/its" 4 ▶ adj. "revealed" ♦ Represents the head of an elderly man who wears an earflare and a distinctive forehead prefix incorporating crossed bands

ye/YE *(ye/yej)* (T32:nn:115.1073) 1 ▶ phonetic sign 2 ▶ 3ʳᵈ pers. prev. pron. used with words beginning in *e*: "he/she/it" 3 ▶ 3ʳᵈ pers. prev. poss. pron. used with words beginning in *e*: "his/her/its" 4 ▶ adj. "revealed" ♦ Represents a human head with earflare and a distinctive prefix that includes a hand or animal paw

ye-b'a-li *(yeb'al)* (T710.501:24?) ▶ poss. n. "his/her/its stairway," "the stairway of"

ye-ma-la *(yemal)* (T710v.74:534hv) ▶ adv. "below"

ye-ma-la *(yemal)* (T1073:142:178) ▶ adv. "below"

ye-te' *(yete')* (T512:87) 1 ▶ prep. "with" 2 ▶ prep. phr. "in the company of"; relationship glyph

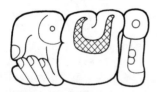

ye-te' *(yete')* (T710.587.87) 1 ▶ prep. "with" 2 ▶ prep. phr. "in the company of"; relationship glyph

ye-te' *(yete')* (T710v.78:514v) 1 ▶ prep. "with" 2 ▶ prep. phr. "in the company of"; relationship glyph

ye-te'-je *(yete'j)* (T512.78:514:69) 1 ▶ prep. "with" 2 ▶ prep. phr. "in the company of"; relationship glyph

ye-te'-je *(yete'j)* (T710v.78:514v:69) 1 ▶ prep. "with" 2 ▶ prep. phr. "in the company of"; relationship glyph

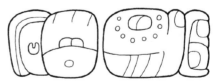

ye-te' k'a-b'a-li *(yete' k'ab'a-il)* (T512.580[646] 669[501].24) ▶ poss. n. "the namesake of"

yi *(yi)* (T17 and T18) 1 ▶ phonetic sign 2 ▶ 3rd pers. prev. pron. used with words beginning in *i*: "he/she/it" 3 ▶ 3rd pers. prev. poss. pron. used with words beginning in *i*: "his/her/its"

yi *(yi)* (T575) 1 ▶ phonetic sign 2 ▶ 3rd pers. prev. pron. used with words beginning in *i*: "he/she/it" 3 ▶ 3rd pers. prev. poss. pron. used with words beginning in *i*: "his/her/its"

yi *(yi)* (T17hv) 1 ▶ phonetic sign 2 ▶ 3rd pers. prev. pron. used with words beginning in *i*: "he/she/it" 3 ▶ 3rd pers. prev. poss. pron. used with words beginning in *i*: "his/her/its" ♦ Represents the head of a young man with infixed **yi**

yi-chi *(yich)* (T17.671) ▶ poss. n. "the surface of [for writing]," "its surface"

yi-chi-NAL *(yichnal)* (T17.671:86) 1 ▶ prep. phr. "in the company of" 2 ▶ prep. phr. "before them"; noun and third-person possessive pronoun *yi-*

yi-[chi]-NAL *(yichnal)* (T86:116?.606[671].116?) 1 ▶ prep. phr. "in the company of" 2 ▶ prep. phr. "before them"; noun and third-person possessive pronoun *yi-*

yi-ch'a-ki *(yich'ak)* (T17.603:100) ▶ poss. n. "his jaguar claw"; noun and third-person possessive pronoun *yi-* ♦ See also **ICH'AK-ki**.

yi-IL-ji *(yilij)* (T17.618v:88v) ▶ pron. + intr. com. v. "he/she saw/witnessed"; verb and third-person prevocalic possessive pronoun *yi-*

yi-IL-ji *(yilij)* (T17:618v:136) ▶ pron. + intr. com. v. "he/she/it saw/witnessed"; verb and third-person prevocalic possessive pronoun *yi-*

yi-IL-la-ja *(yilaj)* (T17.618v:178.181) ▶ pass. v. phr. "it was seen/witnessed by he/she/it"; verb and third-person prevocalic possessive pronoun *yi-*

yi-ka-tzo *(yikatz)* (T124:563b?:130) ▶ poss. n. "his/her/its tribute"; noun and third-person possessive pronoun *yi-*

yi-la-ji *(yilaj)* (T17.534:88) ▶ pass. v. phr. "was seen/witnessed by he/she/it"; verb and third-person possessive pronoun *yi-*

yi-li-aj-ji-ya *(yilajiy)* (T17:82:744v:246) ▶ pron. + intr. com. v. "he/she/it saw/witnessed"; verb and third-person possessive pronoun *yi-*

yi-ta *(yitaj)* (T17:565a) 1 ▶ prep. "with"; relationship glyph 2 ▶ prep. phr. "in the company of," "the companion of"; relationship glyph; noun and third-person possessive pronoun *yi-*

yi-ta-ji *(yitaj)* (T17.565:88) 1 ▶ prep. "with"; relationship glyph 2 ▶ prep. phr. "in the company of," "the companion of"; relationship glyph; noun and third-person possessive pronoun *yi-*

yi-[ta]-ji *(yitaj)* (T565:88) 1 ▶ prep. "with"; relationship glyph 2 ▶ prep. phr. "in the company of," "the companion of"; relationship glyph; noun and third-person possessive pronoun *yi-*

yi-tz'i-na *(yitz'in)* (T17.563:23) ▶ poss. n. "his/her younger brother"; relationship glyph; noun and third-person possessive pronoun *yi-*

yo/YOP *(yo/yop)* (T115) 1 ▶ phonetic sign 2 ▶ 3ʳᵈ pers. prev. pron. used with words beginning in *o*: "he/she/it" 3 ▶ 3ʳᵈ pers. prev. poss. pron. used with words beginning in *o*: "his/her/its" 4 ▶ n. "leaf" ♦ Represents a leaf

yo *(yo)* (T673) 1 ▶ phonetic sign 2 ▶ 3ʳᵈ pers. prev. pron. used with words beginning in *o*: "he/she/it" 3 ▶ 3ʳᵈ pers. prev. poss. pron. used with words beginning in *o*: "his/her/its" ♦ Represents a human hand with infixed crossed bands

yo-a-AT-ta *(yo-at)* (T115.229:552:103) ▶ adj. + n. "scarred penis" ♦ See also **YOP-a-AT-ta**.

yo-AT *(yo-at)* (T115.552v) ▶ adj. + n. "scarred penis" ♦ See also **YOP-AT**.

yo-AT-ta *(yo-at)* (T115.552:103) ▶ adj. + n. "scarred penis" ♦ See also **YOP-AT-ta**.

yo-AT-ti (?) *(yo-at)* (T115.761:59) ▶ adj. + n. "scarred penis" ♦ See also **YOP-AT-ti**.

yo-ko *(yok)* (T115:110) ▶ poss. n. "his/her/its foot"; noun and third-person possessive pronoun *yo-*

yo-OK-ki *(yok)* (T115.765v:103) ▶ poss. n. "his/her/its foot"; noun and third-person possessive pronoun *yo-*

yo-OK [K'IN]-ni *(yok k'in)* (T115.765[544]:116) ▶ n. elite title; title of unknown meaning

yo-OL-la *(yol)* (T115.574:178) ▶ poss. n. "his/her/its heart"; noun and third-person prevocalic possessive pronoun *yo-*

yo-OL-la TAN-na *(yol tan)* (T115v:506:178.606:23) ▶ poss. n. "his/her/its heart-center"; noun and third-person prevocalic possessive pronoun *yo-*

yo-OTOT *(yotot)* (T614:115.?:518v) ▶ poss. n. "his/her/its house"; noun and third-person prevocalic possessive pronoun *yo-*

yo-OTOT-ti *(yotot)* (T115.501:115v:59) ▶ poss. n. "his/her/its house"; noun and third-person prevocalic possessive pronoun *yo-*

yo-OTOT-ti *(yotot)* (T115.614:518v:59) ▶ poss. n. "his/her/its house"; noun and third-person prevocalic possessive pronoun *yo-*

yo-OTOT-ti *(yotot)* (T115.501:575v:59) ▶ poss. n. "his/her/its house"; noun and third-person prevocalic possessive pronoun *yo-*

YOP-a-AT-ta *(yop-at)* (T115.229:552:103) ▶ n. deity name or elite title ♦ See also **yo-a-AT-ta**.

YOP-AT *(yop-at)* (T115.552v) 1 ▶ n. deity name or elite title 2 ▶ n. name of the "founder" of the ruling lineage of Yaxchilán ♦ See also **yo-AT**.

YOP-AT-ta *(yop-at)* (T115.552:103) ▶ n. deity name or elite title ♦ See also **yo-AT-ta**.

YOP-AT-ti (?) *(yo-at)* (T115.761:59) ▶ n. deity name or elite title ♦ See also **yo-AT-ti**.

yo-to-ta-ti *(yotot-ti)* (T115.44:1016:59) ▶ prep. + poss. n. "in his/her/its house"; noun preceded by the third-person possessive pronoun *yo-* and followed by the preposition *ti* "in," "at"

yo-to-ti *(yotot)* (T115.44:563b:59) ▶ poss. n. "his/her/its house"; noun and third-person possessive pronoun *yo-*

yo-to-ti *(yotot)* (T115v.44:501:59) ▶ poss. n. "his/her/its house"; noun and third-person possessive pronoun *yo-*

yo-to-ti *(yotot)* (T673b:44.59) ▶ poss. n. "his/her/its house"; noun and third-person possessive pronoun *yo-*

yo-[xa]-AT-ti (?) *(yoxat)* (T115.761:59) ▶ poss. n. + adj. "his/its scarred penis"; noun, adjective, and third-person possessive pronoun *yo-*

yu *(yu)* (T61 and T62) 1 ▶ phonetic sign 2 ▶ 3ʳᵈ pers. prev. pron. used with words beginning in *u*: "he/she/it" 3 ▶ 3ʳᵈ pers. prev. poss. pron. used with words beginning in *u*: "his/her/its"

yu-b'u-te' *(yub'te')* (T61.21 86:518c.140) ▶ n. "tribute mantle," "tribute cloth"

yu-ch'a-b'a *(yuch'ab')* (T61.756af:501) ▶ poss. n. "his/her/its drinking vessel," "his/her/its drinking cup"; noun and third-person possessive pronoun *yu-*

yu-ch'a-b'i *(yuch'ab')* (T62.77:585) ▶ poss. n. "his/her/its drinking vessel," "his/her/its drinking cup"; noun and third-person possessive pronoun *yu-*

yu-NE-{n} *(yunen)* (T61v:nn) ▶ poss. n. "his child"; relationship glyph; "child of father" glyph; noun and third-person possessive pronoun *yu-*

yu-NE-{n} *(yunen)* (T62.856v) ▶ poss. n. "his child"; relationship glyph; "child of father" glyph; noun and third-person possessive pronoun *yu-*

yu-ta-{l} *(yutal)* (T61:565a) 1 ▶ poss. adj. "his/her/its fruited" 2 ▶ poss. n. "his/her/its seeds/beans"; **li** suf. optional; part of the "contents" prepositional phrase from the PSS, *ta yutal* "for his/her/its fruited [kakaw]," "for his/her/its seeds/beans [of kakaw]"; noun and third-person possessive pronoun *yu-*

yu-ta-la *(yutal)* (T61:565a.178v) 1 ▶ poss. adj. "his/her/its fruited" 2 ▶ poss. n. "his/her/its seeds/beans"; **li** suf. optional; part of the "contents" prepositional phrase from the PSS, *ta yutal* "for his/her/its fruited [kakaw]," "for his/her/its seeds/beans [of kakaw]"; noun and third-person possessive pronoun *yu-*

yu-tzi-li *(yutzil)* (T61.507c:24) ▶ poss. n. "his/her/its goodness"; noun and third-person possessive pronoun *yu-*

EMBLEM GLYPHS

Altar de Sacrificios (T168:715[1008]:23.59
or T168:239:23.59)

Altun Ha' (T33v.168:578.116)

B'ital (T32:585.168:676:130)

Bonampak (T168:197.743v.130)

Bonampak (T228.168:197.512v)

Calakmul (T32:25.168:764)

Cancuen (T168:626:130)

Caracol (T168:44:281.?)

Caracol (T32:281:23.74:518:89)

Caracol (T32:89.281.23:74v.518v)

Chinikiha (T16.168:41)

Comalcalco (T168:nn:561:130)

Copán (T38.168:756)

Copán (T34:568a.168:756dv:177)

Dos Pilas (T36.168:569:130v)

Dos Pilas (T36.168:716v)

Dos Pilas (T36.168:778v)

El Chorro (T168:42ms.116)

El Peru (T38.165:1008[544]
335.168:738)

Itzan (T38.686v[501]:87)

Ixkun (Tnn.168:653.177)

Ixtutz (T38v.168:526:140)

Lacanha (T168:756:25.4)

Lakamtun (T767.528:229.168:518)

Los Higos (T87.168:501)

Maasal (T74.168:518c:130)

Machaquilá (T32:552.168:174:513:130)

Motul de San José (T38v.168:503)

Nakum (T32.168:697)

Naranjo (T36.168:246v:552)

Nimlipunit (T41.168:738v:130)

Palenque (T38.168:570)

Palenque (T38.168:1045)

Palenque (T39.168:793:178)

Piedras Negras (yo-ki-b'i) *(Yokib')*
(T101v.168:585c)

Piedras Negras *(Yokib')* (T101v.168:585hv)

Piedras Negras (yo-yo-ki-b'i) *(Yokib')*
(T115.169:673.60:102.585c)

Pipa' (T32:177.168:743)

Pomoná, Tabasco (T38.168:602:25.21:534)

Pomoy (T168:582[622].115)

Pusilhá (T36.168:526hv:130)

Quirigua (T40.168:560:130)

Río Azul (T60:1008v[582v])

Sacul (T38.168:761:130)

Sak Tz'i (T58.168:563a)

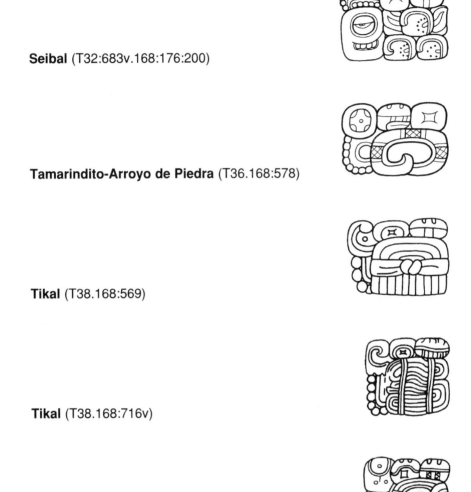

Seibal (T32:683v.168:176:200)

Tamarindito-Arroyo de Piedra (T36.168:578)

Tikal (T38.168:569)

Tikal (T38.168:716v)

Tikal (T40.168:778v)

Tikal (T36.539hv)

Toniná (T38[544].168:622v.279)

Toniná (T36.168:750[622].130)

Uaxactun (T36.168:562)

Ucanal (T281:23.168:130?:529)

Xcalumk'in (T38.168:561v:130)

Yaxchilán (T36.168:511:130)

Yaxchilán (T36.168:562:23)

Yaxhá (T16.168:743)

Yootz (T101.168:569v:124)

Lords of the Night

G1 (TIX:41:670)

G2 (T46.129:575?)

G3 (T32[25].126:60ms[624a]:23)

G4 (TVII.709hv)

G5 (TV.331:617)

G6 (TIX.176v?:578inv:142)

G7 (T4.1086)

G8 (T126:60ms[155v]:23)

G9 (T86.1014?[545])

INDICES

LANGUAGE INDICES

MAYAN INDEX

A

a vowel *a* (**a/AJ**) 25, 26
a 2ⁿᵈ pers. pron. you, yours (**a/AJ**) 25
ab' n. year; see *ja'ab'* (**AB'**) 26
ab' n. personal name (**AB'**)...26
ach n. penis (Ch'olan) (**ACH-cha**) 27
aj phonetic sign (**a/AJ**) 25, 26
aj masc. agentive pron. he (**a/AJ**) 25, 26
aj masc. agentive pref. he of (**a/AJ**) 25, 26
Ajaw n. day sign; twentieth day of the Maya Tzolk'in calendar (**AJAW**) 27
ajaw title, lord (**AJAW, AJAW-wa, a-ja-wa**) 27, 28, 29
ajawlel n. rulership, kingship (**AJAW-le-le**) 29
ajaw te' title, tree lord (**AJAW-wa TE'**) 29
aj k'ujun title, he of the sacred books, librarian (**AJ k'u-{JUN}-na**,
    AJ k'u-JUN-na) 30
aj naab' title, he of the water (**AJ na-b'i**) 30
aj payal title, he the leader (**AJ pa-ya-la**)...31
aj pitz title, he the ballplayer (youthful), ballplayer (**AJ pi-tzi**) 31
aj pitzlawal title, he of the ball game (youthful), ballplayer
    (**AJ pi-tzi-la-wa-{l}, AJ pi-tzi-la-wa-la**) 31
aj sul title, he the administrator, administrator (**AJ su-lu**) 32
aj tz'ib' title, he of the writing, scribe (**AJ tz'i-b'a**) 32
aj uxul title, he of the burnishing/scratching, he of the sculpture,
    sculptor (**AJ u-xu-[lu]**) 32
aj-X-b'ak title, he of X-number of captives; Count of Captives title
    (**AJ-X-B'AK**) 34
ak n. turtle (**a-ku**) 34
Akb'al n. day sign, third day of the Maya Tzolk'in calendar; darkness
    (**AKB'AL**) 34
ak' phonetic sign (**ak'/AK', ak'/AK'OT**) 34, 35
ak' n. tongue (**ak'/AK'**)...34
ak'ab' n. darkness (**AK'AB'**) 35
ak'ot n. dance (**a-AK'OT-ta, ak'/AK'OT, AK'OT-ta**) 26, 35
ak'ot tr. v. dance (**ak'/AK'OT, AK'OT-ta**)...35
ak'otaj pass. v. was danced (**AK'OT-ta-ja**) 35
aliy intr. v. say (**a-li-ya**) 36
aliy intr. v. it is said (**a-li-ya**) 36
am phonetic sign (**am**) 36
at phonetic sign (**at**) 36

at n. penis (Yucatec) (**AT, AT-ti**) 36, 37
awa ichnal? decl. phr. before you (**AJ-wa-chi-NAL**) 33
a winiken decl. phr. I am your servant (**AJ-wi-na-{i} ke-na**) 33
awol poss. n. your heart (**AJ-wo-la**) 33
aya v. phr. came into being (**a-ja-ya, a-ya, a-ya-ya**) 29, 37
ayin n. crocodile (**AYIN**) 37
ayin n. lizard (**AYIN**) 37

B'

b'a phonetic sign (**b'a, b'a/B'A**) 39
b'a n. being (**b'a/B'A**) 39
b'a adj. first (**b'a/B'A**) 39
b'a n. head (**b'a/B'A**) 39
b'a n. image (**b'a/B'A**) 39
b'a refl. suf. self (**b'a/B'A**) 39
b'a refl. suf. thing (**b'a/B'A**) 39
b'a ajaw title, first lord (**B'A AJAW**) 40
b'a ch'ok title, first sprout (**B'A ch'o-ko**) 40
b'a ch'ok title, first young person (**B'A ch'o-ko**) 40
b'a ch'ok title, first youth (**B'A ch'o-ko**) 40
b'a ch'ok title, first lineage member (**B'A ch'o-ko**) 40
b'aj n. image (**b'a-ja**) 40
b'ajin adv. indeed (**b'a-ji-ni**) 40
b'ak n. bone (**B'AK, b'a-ki**) 41
b'ak n. captive (**B'AK, b'a-ki**) 41
b'akab' title, standing one; first in the world (**b'a-ka-b'a**) 41
b'aktun See *pi, pi-i, pij, piy.*
b'alam n. jaguar (**B'ALAM**) 42
b'an tr. v. scatter (**b'a-na**) 42
b'ate' title, warrior (**b'a-te'**) 42
b'atz' n. howler monkey (**b'a-tz'u**) 42
b'a uxul title, first sculptor (**B'A u-xu-[lu]**) 42
b'a yal title, first born (**B'A YAL**) 43
b'e phonetic sign (**b'e/B'E**) 43
b'e n. road (**b'e/B'E**) 43
B'en n. day sign; thirteenth day of the Maya Tzolk'in calendar (**B'EN**) 43
b'i phonetic sign (**b'i/B'I**) 43, 44
b'i n. road (**b'i/B'I**) 43, 44
b'ixan incom. irreg. v. goes (**B'IXAN-na**) 44
b'ixan incom. irreg. v. walks (**B'IXAN-na**) 44
b'ixan incom. irreg. v. travels (**B'IXAN-na**) 44
b'ixan com. irreg. v. went (**B'IXAN-na**) 44
b'ixaniy com. irreg. v. went (**B'IXAN-ni-ya**) 44
b'o phonetic sign (**b'o**) 44
b'olon n. number nine; cardinal number (**B'OLON**) 44, 45
b'olon adj. many (**B'OLON**) 44, 45
b'olon iplaj n. many strengths (**B'OLON i-pi-[la]-ja**) 45
b'u phonetic sign (**b'u**) 45
b'uk pl. n. clothes (**b'u-ku**) 45
b'ul n. bean, beans (**b'u-la**) 46
b'uluk n. number eleven; cardinal number (**B'ULUK**) 46
b'utz' n. smoke (**B'UTZ'**) 46

CH

cha/ka phonetic sign (**cha/ka**) 47, 48
cha/ka n. two; cardinal number (**CHA/KA**) 48

Chaak n. Chaak; deity name, the Maya Rain God
   (**CHAAK, CHAAK-ki, cha-ki**) 48, 49, 53, 54
Chaak Chaan/Chaak Kaan n. deity name, Rain God Sky
   (**cha-ki CHAAN-na/cha-ki KAAN-na**) 54
chaan/kaan n. captor (**CHAAN/KAAN, CHAAN-na/KAAN-na**)..............................49, 50
chaan/kaan n. sky (**CHAAN/KAAN, CHAAN-na/KAAN-na**) 49, 50
chaanal/kaanal adj. heavenly (**CHAAN-na-NAL/KAAN-na-NAL**) 51
chaanal k'u/kaanal k'u adj. + pl. n. heavenly gods
   (**[CHAAN]-NAL K'U/[KAAN]-NAL K'U**) 51
chaan ch'en/kaan ch'en n. sky cave (**CHAAN CH'EN-na/KAAN**
   CH'EN-na, CHAAN-na CH'EN-na/KAAN-na CH'EN-na) 50
chaan ch'ul/kaan k'ul adj. + pl. n. heavenly gods (**CHAAN-na**
   CH'UL/KAAN-na K'UL) 51
Chaan K'awil/Kaan K'awil n. Sky K'awil; deity name
   (**CHAAN-na K'AWIL-la/KAAN-na K'AWIL-la**) 51
chak adj. red (**CHAK**) 52, 53
chak adj. great (**CHAK**)...52, 53
chak ch'ul ajaw/chak k'ul ajaw title, great holy lord
   (**CHAK CH'UL AJAW/CHAK K'UL AJAW**) 53
chak ch'ul ajaw/chak k'ul ajaw title, red holy lord
   (**CHAK CH'UL AJAW/CHAK K'UL AJAW**) 53
chak ek' adj. + n. great star, Venus (**CHAK EK'**) 53
Chak Xib' Chaak n. Chak Xib' Chaak; deity name (**CHAK XIB' cha-ki**) 54
Chak'at n. month sign; third month of the Maya Ja'ab' calendar;
   the month of Sip (**CHAK K'AT, CHAK-ka-ta, SIP**) 54, 218
chak'at n. dance object; name of the "basket staff" used in dances
   at Yaxchilán (**CHAK K'AT**) 54
chalajun/kalajun n. twelve; cardinal number (**CHALAJUN/KALAJUN**) 55
cham intr. v. die, death (**CHAM, CHAM-mi**) 55, 56
chamil intr. v. die, death (**CHAM-li**) 56
chamiy intr. incom. v. dies, death (**CHAM-mi-ya**) 56
chan/kan n. four; cardinal number (**CHAN/KAN**) 56, 57
chan/kan n. captor (**cha-CHAN/ka-KAN, CHAN/KAN, cha-nu/ka-nu**)..............52, 57, 58
chan/kan n. snake, serpent (**cha-CHAN/ka-KAN, CHAN/KAN**) 52, 57
chapat n. centipede (**CHAPAT**) 58
chatan prep. phr. in the center? (**cha-TAN-na**) 58
chat k'ab'a n. phr. *chat* name (**cha-te' K'AB'A**) 58
chay/kay n. fish (**CHAY/KAY, cha-ya**) 59
che phonetic sign (**che**) 59
cheb' n. quill pen (**che-b'u**) 60
che'en quot. part. says (so he/she/they/it) (**che-e-na, che-je-na**) 60
che'en tu b'ak v. phr. says on his/her/its bone (so it) (**che-e-na TU b'a-ki**) 60
chi phonetic sign (**chi/CHI**) 61
chi n. mouth (**chi/CHI**) 61
Chicchan n. day sign, fifth day of the Maya Tzolk'in calendar (**CHIKCHAN**) 61, 62
chij n. deer (white-tailed) (**CHIJ**) 61
chik'in n. west; cardinal direction (**chi-K'IN-ni**) 62
chik'inil prep. phr. in the west (**chi-[K'IN]-li**) 62
chi'lam n. interpreter (**chi-ji-la-ma**) 61
chi'lam n. speaker (**chi-ji-la-ma**) 61
chit n. father (**CHIT, CHIT-ti**) 62, 63
chitam n. peccary (**CHITAM**) 62
cho phonetic sign (**cho**) 63
chok tr. v. scatter (**CHOK**) 63
chok tr. v. throw (**CHOK**) 63
chokaw ch'aj tr. v. phr. scatter drops of liquid
   (**CHOK-ko-wa CH'A-ji, CHOK-wa CH'A-ji**) 64

chokaw ch'aj tr. v. phr. throw drops of liquid
    (**CHOK-ko-wa CH'A-ji, CHOK-wa CH'A-ji**) 64
chokij tr. v. phr. scatter drops (**CHOK-ji**) 63
chokij tr. v. phr. throw drops (**CHOK-ji**) 63
chu phonetic sign (**chu**) 64, 65
chuk tr. v. seize (**chu-ka, chu-[ku]**) 65
chuk tr. v. capture (**chu-ka, chu-[ku]**) 65
chukaj pass. v. captured (was) (**chu-ka-ja, chu-[ku]-ja**) 65, 66
chukjiy intr. com. v. captured (was) (**chu-[ku]-ji-ya**) 66
chum pos. v. accession (**CHUM, CHUM (?), CHUM-[mu]**) 66, 67
chum pos. v. seated (**CHUM, CHUM (?), CHUM-[mu]**) 66, 67
chumlajiy pos. com. v. accession (**CHUM-la-ji-ya, CHUM-[mu]-la-ji-ya**) 67
chumlajiy pos. com. v. seated (**CHUM-la-ji-ya, CHUM-[mu]-la-ji-ya**) 67
chum tun v. phr. seating of the stone, seating of the *tun*
    (**CHUM-[mu] TUN-ni, [CHUM] TUN-ni**) 68
chumwaniy pos. com. v. accession (**CHUM-[mu]-wa-ni-ya**) 68
chumwaniy pos. com. v. seated (**CHUM-[mu]-wa-ni-ya**) 68
chumwan ti ajawlel ti-construction v. phr. accession
    (**CHUM-wa-ni TI AJAW-le-{l}**) 68
chumwan ti ajawlel ti-construction v. phr. seated in lordship
    (**CHUM-wa-ni TI AJAW-le-{l}**) 68
Chuwen n. day sign, eleventh day of the Maya Tzolk'in calendar (**CHUWEN**) 69
chuwen n. artist, elite title (**CHUWEN**) 69

CH'

ch'a phonetic sign (**ch'a/CH'A, ch'a**) 71
ch'a n. drops, droplet (**ch'a/CH'A**) 71
ch'a n. drop of water, urine, or other liquid (**ch'a/CH'A**) 71
ch'ab' intr. v. do penance (**CH'AB', ch'a-b'a**) 72
ch'ab' intr. v. sacrifice (**CH'AB', ch'a-b'a**) 72
ch'ab' intr. v. pierce (**CH'AB', ch'a-b'a**) 72
ch'ab' intr. v. pierce with a lance (**CH'AB', ch'a-b'a**) 72
ch'aj n. drops, droplet (**ch'a-ji**) 73
ch'aj n. drop of water, urine, or other liquid (**ch'a-ji**) 73
ch'ajalte' n. type of drink (**ch'a-ja-{l}-te'**) 72
ch'ajom title, dripper (**ch'a-JOM, ch'a-jo-ma**) 73
ch'ajom title, scatterer (**ch'a-JOM, ch'a-jo-ma**) 73
ch'ak tr. v. chop (**CH'AK, CH'AK-ka**) 74
ch'ak tr. v. chop with a blow (**CH'AK, CH'AK-ka**) 74
ch'ak tr. v. decapitate (**CH'AK, CH'AK-ka**) 74
ch'akab' intr. v. self-axe (**CH'AK-ka-b'a**) 74, 75
ch'akab' intr. v. self-decapitate (**CH'AK-ka-b'a**) 74, 75
ch'akaj pass. v. axed (was) (**ch'a-ka-ja**) 74
ch'akaj pass. v. chopped (was) (**ch'a-ka-ja**) 74
ch'akaj pass. v. decapitated (was) (**ch'a-ka-ja**) 74
ch'am tr. v. receive (**CH'AM, CH'AM-ma**) 75, 76
ch'am tr. v. harvest (**CH'AM, CH'AM-ma**) 75, 76
ch'am n. harvest (**CH'AM, CH'AM-ma**) 75, 76
ch'am K'awil tr. v. receive K'awil (**CH'AM K'AWIL-la, CH'AM-ma K'AWIL-la**) 75, 76
ch'am K'awil tr. v. harvest K'awil (**CH'AM K'AWIL-la, CH'AM-ma K'AWIL-la**) 75, 76
ch'at n. dwarf (**ch'a-ti**) 76
ch'at n. hunchback (**ch'a-ti**) 76
Ch'en n. month sign, ninth month of the Maya Ja'ab' calendar
    (**CH'EN**) 77
ch'en n. cave (**CH'EN, CH'EN-na**) 77, 78
ch'o phonetic sign (**ch'o**) 78, 79
ch'ok n. youth (**ch'o-ko, ch'o-[ko]**) 79

ch'ok n. youngster (**ch'o-ko**, **ch'o-[ko]**) 79
ch'ok n. young one (**ch'o-ko**, **ch'o-[ko]**) 79
ch'ok adj. young (**ch'o-ko**, **ch'o-[ko]**) 79
ch'ok adj. unripe (**ch'o-ko**, **ch'o-[ko]**) 79
ch'ok k'ab'a adj. + n. youthful name (**ch'o-[ko] K'AB'A**) 80
ch'ok te' na n. sprout tree house (**CH'OK TE' NA**) 80
ch'ul/k'ul, ch'ujul/k'ujul adj. sacred, holy, divine
    (**CH'UL/K'UL (CH'UJUL/K'UJUL), CH'UL-lu/K'UL-lu**
    (**CH'UJUL-lu/K'UJUL-lu**)) 80, 81, 82, 84
ch'ul ajaw/k'ul ajaw, ch'ujul ajaw/k'ujul ajaw adj. + n. sacred/holy/divine
    lord (**CH'UL AJAW-wa/K'UL AJAW-wa**
    (**CH'UJUL AJAW-wa/K'UJUL AJAW-wa**)) 83
ch'ul chaan ch'ul kab'/k'ul kaan k'ul kab', ch'ujul chaan
    ch'ujul kab'/k'ujul kaan k'ujul kab' tit. phr.
    heavenly god, earthly god (**CH'UL CHAAN CH'UL**
    KAB'/K'UL KAAN K'UL KAB' (CH'UJUL CHAAN
    CH'UJUL KAB'/K'UJUL KAAN K'UJUL KAB')) 83
ch'ul chatan winik/k'ul chatan winik, ch'ujul chatan winik/k'ujul chatan winik
    tit. phr. sacred Chatan person (**CH'UL cha-TAN WINIK/K'UL cha-TAN**
    WINIK (CH'UJUL cha-TAN WINIK/K'UJUL cha-TAN WINIK), CH'UL
    cha-TAN-na wi-WINIK-ki/K'UL cha-TAN-na wi-WINIK-ki (CH'UJUL
    cha-TAN-na wi-WINIK-ki/K'UJUL cha-TAN-na wi-WINIK-ki))................83, 84
ch'ul ixik/k'ul ixik, ch'ujul ixik/k'ujul ixik adj. + n. sacred/holy/divine woman
    (**CH'UL IXIK-ki/K'UL IXIK-ki (CH'UJUL IXIK-ki/K'UJUL IXIK-ki**)) 84
ch'ul k'ab'a/k'ul k'ab'a adj. + n. sacred/holy/divine name
    (**CH'UL K'AB'A/K'UL K'AB'A**) 84
ch'ul tok'/k'ul tok', ch'ujul tok'/k'ujul tok' adj. + n. sacred/holy/divine flint
    (**CH'UL-lu to-k'a/K'UL-lu to-k'a (CH'UJUL-lu to-k'a/K'UJUL-lu to-k'a**))............85
Ch'ul Tok Tan Ajaw/K'ul Tok Tan Ajaw, Ch'ujul Tok Tan Ajaw/K'ujul Tok Tan
    Ajaw title, Sacred/Holy/Divine Cloud Center Lord
    (**CH'UL to-{k} TAN AJAW/K'UL to-{k} TAN AJAW**
    (**CH'UJUL to-{k} TAN AJAW/K'UJUL to-{k} TAN AJAW**)) 85
ch'ul winik/k'ul winik, ch'ujul winik/k'ujul winik adj. + n. sacred/holy/divine
    man (**CH'UL WINIK-ki/K'UL WINIK-ki**
    (**CH'UJUL WINIK-ki/K'UJUL WINIK-ki**)) 85
ch'ul winik/k'ul winik, ch'ujul winik/k'ujul winik adj. + n. sacred/holy/divine
    person (**CH'UL WINIK-ki/K'UL WINIK-ki**
    (**CH'UJUL WINIK-ki/K'UJUL WINIK-ki**)) 85

E

e vowel *e* (**e**) 87
Eb' n. day sign, twelfth day of the Maya Tzolk'in calendar (**EB'**)................88
eb' n. stairway, staircase (**e-b'u**, **EB'-[b'u]**)................88
ek' n. star (**EK'**) 89
ek' adj. black (**EK'**)................88, 89
Ek' n. Venus? (**EK'**) 89
ek' jun adj. + n. black headband (**EK' JUN**) 89
ek' waynal adj. + n. black hole (**EK' WAY-NAL**)................90
Ek' Waynal n. Black Hole Place (**EK' WAY-NAL**) 90
em intr. v. descend (**EM**) 90
Etz'nab' n. day sign, eighteenth day of the Maya Tzolk'in calendar (**ETZ'NAB'**) 90

I

i vowel *i* (**i/I**)................91, 92
i part. then, and then; Posterior Date Indicator (PDI) (**i/I**) 91
ib'ak' n. armadillo (**i-b'a-k'a**) 92

ich'ak n. jaguar claw (**ICH'AK, ICH'AK-ki**) 92, 93
ich'ak n. jaguar paw (**ICH'AK, ICH'AK-ki**) 92, 93
ich'ak tun n. jaguar claw stone (**ICH'AK TUN-ni**) 93
ich'ak tun n. jaguar paw stone (**ICH'AK TUN-ni**) 93
ikatz n. burden (**i-ka-tzi**) 93, 94
ikatz n. load (**i-ka-tzi**) 93, 94
ikatz n. tribute (**i-ka-tzi**) 93, 94
ikitz n. burden (**i-ki-tzi**) 94
ikitz n. load (**i-ki-tzi**) 94
ikitz n. tribute (**i-ki-tzi**) 94
Ik' n. day sign, second day of the Maya Tzolk'in calendar (**IK'**) 94
Ik' K'u n. Wind God, proper name of the Classic Maya Wind God (**IK' K'U**) 95
il tr. v. see (**IL**) 96
-il part. suf. (**-il**) 95, 96
ilaj pass. v. seen (was) (**IL-ja**) 97
ilij part. + tr. v. and then he/she saw it (**I-IL-ji**) 93
ilij part. + tr. v. and then he/she witnessed it (**I-IL-ji**) 93
Imix n. day sign, first day of the Maya Tzolk'in calendar (**IMIX**) 97
in 1st pers. pron. I (**IN**) 98
in 1st pers. poss. pron. my (**IN**) 98
in b'uk poss. n. my clothes (**IN-b'u-ku**) 98
in ch'en poss. n. my cave (**IN CH'EN**) 98
in kab' poss. n. my earth, my land (**IN KAB'**) 98
in pat poss. n. my tribute (**IN pa-ta**) 99
in tup poss. n. my earspool (**IN tu-pa**) 99
itz' n. essence (**ITZ'**) 99
itz' n. sweat (**ITZ'**) 99
itz' n. resin (**ITZ'**) 99
itz' n. flower nectar (**ITZ'**) 99
Itz'amná n. Itz'amná, proper name of the principal god of the
    Maya pantheon (**itz'-am-{na}**) 99
Itz'am Yej n. deity name; name of the Principal Bird Deity (**ITZ'AM ye-ji**) 100
itz'at n. artist (**ITZ'AT, i-tz'a-ta, ITZ'AT-ta**) 100, 101
itz'at n. learned one (**ITZ'AT, i-tz'a-ta, ITZ'AT-ta**) 100, 101
itz'at n. sage (**ITZ'AT, i-tz'a-ta, ITZ'AT-ta**) 100, 101
itz'at n. wise man (**ITZ'AT, i-tz'a-ta, ITZ'AT-ta**) 100, 101
itz'in n. younger brother (**i-tz'i-{n}**) 101
itz'in winik adj. + n. younger brother person (**i-tz'i-{n} WINIK, i-tz'i-{n}**
    wi-WINIK-ki) 101
i-ut part. + intr. v. then it happened; Posterior Date Indicator (PDI) (**i-u-ti**) 102
Ix n. day sign, fourteenth day of the Maya Tzolk'in calendar (**IX**) 102
ix n. woman (**IX/IXIK**) 103
ix fem. agentive pref. (**IX/IXIK**) 103
ix n. jaguar (**IX**) 102
ixik n. woman (**IXIK-ki, IX/IXIK**) 103
ixik fem. agentive pref. (**IXIK-ki, IX/IXIK**) 103
ix tz'am n. jaguar throne (**IX TZ'AM(?)**) 103
Ix Tz'am? Ku-aj n. Jaguar Throne Stone Place (**IX TZ'AM(?) ku-aj**) 103
i-yuwal progressive aspect marker (**i-yu-wa-la**) 104

J

ja phonetic sign (**ja**) 105
jal tr. v. say (**JAL, ja'-li**) 106, 111
jal tr. v. manifest (**JAL, ja'-li**) 106, 111
jal intr. v. rest (**JAL, ja'-li**) 106, 111
jal intr. v. terminate (**JAL, ja'-li**) 106, 111

jal-jiy tr. v. say (**JAL-ji-ya**)...106
jal-jiy tr. v. manifest (**JAL-ji-ya**) 106
jal-jiy intr. v. rest (**JAL-ji-ya**) 106
jal-jiy intr. v. terminate (**JAL-ji-ya**) 106
janaab' n. flower (**JANAAB'**, **ja-na-b'i**) 106, 107
janaab' pakal n. flower-shield (**[JANAAB'] PAKAL, [JANAAB'] PAKAL-la**) 107
Janaab' Pakal n. name of several Palenque Late Classic kings, including
    Janaab' Pakal the Great (**[JANAAB'] PAKAL, [JANAAB'] PAKAL-la**) 107
jasaw n. banner (**ja-sa-wa**) 108
jasaw n. flap-staff (**ja-sa-wa**) 108
jatz'ay tr. v. strike (**ja-tz'a-yi**) 108
jatz'ay tr. v. split (**ja-tz'a-yi**) 108
jatz'ay tr. v. wound (**ja-tz'a-yi**) 108
jawte' n. ceramic tripod plate (**ja-wa-te'**) 108, 109
jay n. thin-walled vessel, ceramic bowl (**ja-yi**) 109
ja' phonetic sign (**ja'**) 109
ja' n. water (**JA'**) 109, 110
ja'ab' n. year; see *ab'* (**JA'AB'**) 110
ja'-i dem. pron. this, that, that one; focus marker (**ja'-i**) 111
ja'ob' dem. pl. pron. they, these, they are, these are (**ja'-o-b'a**) 111
je phonetic sign (**je**) 111, 112
jem n. valley (**JEM**) 112
jem na n. valley house (**JEM NA**) 112
jemnal n. valley place (**JEM-NAL**) 112
ji phonetic sign (**ji**) 112, 113, 114
jich n. surface [for writing] (**ji-chi**) 114
jil intr. v. rest (**ji-li**) 115
jil intr. v. end (**ji-li**) 115
jix n. jaguar (**ji-IX, ji-JIX, JIX**) 114, 115
-jiy intr. com. verbal suf. pattern (**-ji-ya**) 115
jo phonetic sign (**jo**) 116
jo n. number five, cardinal number (**JO**) 116, 117
jol n. head (**JOL, JOL-lo**) 118
jom tr. v. destroy (**JOM**) 118, 119
jom tr. v. end (**JOM**) 118, 119
jom tr. v. throw down (**JOM**) 118, 119
joy tr. v. accede (**jo-JOY, JOY**) 117, 119
joy tr. v. emerge, come out (**jo-JOY, JOY**) 117, 119
joyaj pass. v. accede (did) (**jo-JOY-ja, JOY-ja**) 117, 119
joyaj pass. v. emergent (was), come out (was) (**jo-JOY-ja, JOY-ja**) 117, 119
joyajiy intr. com. v.?, acceded (**JOY-[ja]-ji-ya**) 120
joyajiy tr. v. emerge, come out (**JOY-[ja]-ji-ya**) 120
joyaj ti ajawlel pass. v. phr. acceded in lordship (**jo-JOY-ja TI AJAW-le-{l}**) 117
joyaj ti ajawlel pass. v. phr. acceded as ruler (**jo-JOY-ja TI AJAW-le-{l}**) 117
ju phonetic sign (**ju**) 120
jub' n. shell (**JUB', JUB'-b'a**) 121
jub' n. shell trumpet (**JUB', JUB'-b'a**) 121
jub' intr. v. take down; war (**JUB' (?)**) 121
jub' intr. v. bring down; war (**JUB' (?)**) 121
jub'-Emblem Glyph intr. v. bring down [a site/location/polity]; war
    (**JUB'-EMBLEM GLYPH**) 121
jub'uy intr. v. taken down, war (**ju-b'u-yi, JUB'(?)-yi, JUB'(?)-yi-ya**) 122
jub'uy intr. v. brought down, war (**ju-b'u-yi, JUB'(?)-yi, JUB'(?)-yi-ya**) 122
jul intr. v. arrive (**JUL, ju-li**) 123, 124
jul tr. v. pierce (**JUL, ju-li, JUL-li**) 123, 124
jul tr. v. shoot (**JUL, ju-li, JUL-li**) 123, 124
jul tr. v. spear (**JUL, ju-li, JUL-li**) 123, 124

jul tr. v. throw (**JUL, ju-li, JUL-li**) 123, 124
jul n. engraving (**JUL**) 123
julaj pass. v. arrived (was) (**JUL-li-ja**)..124
julaj pass. v. thrown (was) (**JUL-li-ja**)..124
julaj pass. v. shot (was) (**JUL-li-ja**) 124
julaj pass. v. speared (was) (**JUL-li-ja**) 124
juliy intr. com. v. arrived (**ju-li-ya**) 125
julob' intr. pl. v. arrived (they) (**ju-li-OB'**) 124
julob' intr. pl. v. threw (they) (**ju-li-OB'**) 124
julob' intr. pl. v. shot (they) (**ju-li-OB'**) 124
jun n. number one; cardinal number (**JUN**) 125
jun n. paper (**JUN, ju-na**)..125, 126
jun n. book (**JUN, ju-na**) 125, 126
jun n. paper headband (**JUN, ju-na**) 125, 126
junal n. headband (**ju-na-la**) 126
Jun Nal Ye n. deity name, proper name of the Maize God (**JUN NAL YE**)................127
jun tan adj. beloved (**JUN TAN-na**)..127
jun tan adj. cherished (**JUN TAN-na**) 127

K

ka phonetic sign (**ka**) 129
kaan See *chaan.*
kab' n. earth (**KAB'**) 129, 130
kab'al k'u adj. + n. earthly gods (**KAB'-la K'U**)..131
Kab'an n. day sign, seventeenth day of the Maya Tzolk'in calendar (**KAB'AN**)............130
kab'ij relat. under the auspices, under the authority (**KAB'-ji**) 130
kab'ij tr. v. did it (**KAB'-ji**)..130
kab'iy relat. under the auspices, under the authority (**KAB'-ya**) 131
kab'iy tr. v. did it (**KAB'-ya**)..131
kab'jiy relat. under the auspices, under the authority (**KAB'-ji-ya**) 131
kab'jiy tr. v. did it (**KAB'-ji-ya**)..131
kakaw n. cacao, chocolate (**ka-{ka}-wa, ka-ka-wa**)..132
kalomte' title of unknown meaning (**KALOMTE', ka-KALOMTE'-te',**
    ka-lo-ma-te', KALOMTE'-te')..132, 133
kan See *chan.*
Kawak n. day sign, nineteenth day of the Maya Tzolk'in calendar (**KAWAK**)................133
ke phonetic sign (**ke**) 134
Kej n. month sign, twelfth month of the Maya Ja'ab' calendar (**KEJ**) 134
kelem n. youth (**ke-KELEM, ke-le-ma**) 134
kelem adj. strong (**ke-KELEM, ke-le-ma**) 134
ki phonetic sign (**ki**) 134, 135
Kib' n. day sign, sixteenth day of the Maya Tzolk'in calendar (**KIB'**) 135
Kimi n. day sign, sixth day of the Maya Tzolk'in calendar (**KIMI**) 135
kix? n. stingray spine (**KIX (?)**) 135, 136
ko phonetic sign (**ko**) 136
kojaw n. helmet (**KOJAW, KOJAW-wa, ko-ja-wa**)..136, 137
kojaw n. headdress (**KOJAW, KOJAW-wa, ko-ja-wa**) 136, 137
kojoy intr. v. go down (**ko-jo-yi**) 137
kokonob' n. guardians (**ko-ko-no-OB'**) 137
kotz' tr. v. roll up (**ko-tz'o**)..137
ku phonetic sign (**ku**) 137
kuch n. burden (**KUCH, ku-chu**) 138
kuch n. cargo (**KUCH, ku-chu**) 138
kuch n. load (**KUCH, ku-chu**) 138
kuch tr. v. carry (**KUCH, ku-chu**) 138
kuch ab'ak n. inkpot (**KUCH AB'AK**) 138
kuch-taj pass. v. carried (was) (**KUCH-ta-ja**)..138

kuch tun adj. + n. burden stone (**KUCH TUN**) 138
Kumk'u n. month sign, eighteenth month of the Maya Ja'ab' calendar (**KUMK'U**) 139
kutz' n. turkey, ocellated turkey (**ku-tz'u**) 139

K'

k'a/ch'a phonetic sign (**k'a/ch'a (K'A/CH'A?), k'a/ch'a**) 141, 142
k'a/ch'a pos. v. lying down (**k'a/ch'a (K'A/CH'A?)**) 141
k'a/ch'a pos. v. horizontal (**k'a/ch'a (K'A/CH'A?)**) 141
k'ab' n. hand (**K'AB', k'a-[b'a]**) 142
k'ab' n. arm (**k'a-[b'a]**) 142
k'ab'a n. name (**K'AB'A**) 142
k'a chaan pos. + n. lying down sky (**K'A CHAAN-na**) 142
k'ak' n. fire (**K'AK', k'a-K'AK', K'AK'-k'a**) 143
k'ak' b'utz' n. fire [and] smoke (**K'AK'-k'a B'UTZ'-tz'i**) 144
k'ak' naab' adj. + n. fire sea, primordial sea, fiery water place (**K'AK' NAAB'**) 144
k'al tr. v. bind (**K'AL**) 144
k'al tr. v. close (**K'AL**) 144
k'al tr. v. set (**K'AL**) 144
k'al tr. v. tie (**K'AL**) 144
k'al tr. v. wrap (**K'AL**) 144
k'al n. completion (**K'AL**) 144
k'al n. number twenty; cardinal number (**K'AL**) 144
k'al tr. incom. v. closing (**k'a-li**) 144
k'alaj pass. v. bound (was) (**K'AL-ja**) 145
k'alaj pass. v. closed (was) (**K'AL-ja**) 145
k'alaj pass. v. set (was) (**K'AL-ja**) 145
k'alaj pass. v. tied (was) (**K'AL-ja**) 145
k'alaj pass. v. wrapped (was) (**K'AL-ja**) 145
k'alaj mayij? pass. v. phr. bound the deer hoof (was) (**K'AL-ja MAY(?)-ji**) 145
k'alaj mayij? pass. v. phr. tied the deer hoof (was) (**K'AL-ja MAY(?)-ji**) 145
k'alaj mayij? pass. v. phr. wrapped the deer hoof (was) (**K'AL-ja MAY(?)-ji**) 145
k'al-jiy sak jun tr. v. phr. bound the white headband (**K'AL-ji-ya SAK JUN**) 145
k'al-jiy sak jun tr. v. phr. closed the white headband (**K'AL-ji-ya SAK JUN**) 145
k'al-jiy sak jun tr. v. phr. tied the white headband (**K'AL-ji-ya SAK JUN**) 145
k'al-jiy sak jun tr. v. phr. wrapped the white headband (**K'AL-ji-ya SAK JUN**) 145
k'al jun tr. v. phr. bound the headband (**K'AL JUN-na**) 145
k'al jun tr. v. phr. closed the headband (**K'AL JUN-na**) 145
k'al jun tr. v. phr. tied the headband (**K'AL JUN-na**) 145
k'al jun tr. v. phr. wrapped the headband (**K'AL JUN-na**) 145
k'al jun na n. accession house (**K'AL JUN NA**) 146
k'al sak jun v. phr. bound the white headband
    (**K'AL SAK JUN, K'AL SAK ju-na**) 146
k'al sak jun v. phr. closed the white headband
    (**K'AL SAK JUN, K'AL SAK ju-na**) 146
k'al sak jun v. phr. tied the white headband
    (**K'AL SAK JUN, K'AL SAK ju-na**) 146
k'al sak jun v. phr. wrapped the white headband
    (**K'AL SAK JUN, K'AL SAK ju-na**) 146
k'al tun intr. v. phr. stone-binding (**K'AL TUN-ni**) 146
k'al tun pass. v. phr. closed the stone (was) (**K'AL TUN-ni**) 146
k'al tun pass. v. phr. set the stone (was) (**K'AL TUN-ni**) 146
k'al tun intr. v. phr. tie the stone (**K'AL TUN-ni**) 146
k'al tun intr. v. phr. wrap the stone (**K'AL TUN-ni**) 146
K'an n. day sign, fourth day of the Maya Tzolk'in calendar (**K'AN**) 147
k'an adj. yellow (**K'AN, K'AN-na**) 147
k'an adj. precious (**K'AN, K'AN-na**) 147
K'anal Eb' adj. + n. Precious Stairway Place (**K'AN-NAL-la e-b'u**) 148

K'ank'in n. month sign, fourteenth month of the Maya Ja'ab' calendar
(**K'ANK'IN**) 147

k'an tun adj. + n. yellow stone (**K'AN TUN-ni**) 148

k'an tun adj. + n. precious stone (**K'AN TUN-ni**) 148

k'atun n. period of twenty years (years of 360 days) used in the LC
(**K'ATUN**) 148

K'awil n. deity name; proper name of the god K'awil
(**ka-K'AWIL, K'AWIL, K'AWIL-la, K'AWIL-li**) 143, 149

K'awilnalob' pl. n. deity name; K'awilnals (pl.) (**K'AWIL-NAL-OB'**) 149

K'awilob' pl. n. deity name; K'awils (pl.) (**K'AWIL-OB'**) 150

K'awinal winik n. K'awilnal person (**k'a-wi-NAL WINIK**) 150

k'ay/ch'ay intr. incom. v. terminates (**k'a-yi/ch'a-yi**) 150

k'ay/ch'ay intr. incom. v. flies (**k'a-yi/ch'a-yi**) 150

K'ayab' n. month sign, seventeenth month of the Maya Ja'ab' calendar
(**K'AYAB'**)..150

k'ay u sak nik ik'il/
ch'ay u sak nich ik'il intr. incom. v. phr. terminates his/her resplendent soul
(**k'a-yi U SAK NIK IK'-li/ch'a-yi U SAK NICH IK'-li**) 151

k'in n. day (**K'IN, K'IN (?), K'IN-ni**) 151, 152, 153

k'in n. sun (**K'IN, K'IN-ni**) 151, 152, 153

k'in n. period of one day in the Maya LC calendar and DNs (**K'IN, K'IN (?)**).........151, 152

k'ina adj. sun-eyed (**K'INA/K'INICH, K'INICH, K'INICH-ni**) 152

k'ina adj. sun-faced (**K'INA/K'INICH, K'INICH, K'INICH-ni**) 152

K'in Ajaw title, Sun Lord (**K'IN-ni AJAW**) 153

k'inich adj. sun-eyed (**K'INA/K'INICH, K'INICH, K'INICH-ni**)..............152

k'inich adj. sun-faced (**K'INA/K'INICH, K'INICH, K'INICH-ni**) 152

K'inich Tzam? Tun adj. + n. Sun-Faced Throne Stone; proper name of
an altar (**K'IN-ni-chi TZAM(?) TUN-ni**) 153

K'in Ja'nal n. Sun Water Place (**K'IN-ni JA'-NAL**) 154

k'o phonetic sign (**k'o**) 154

k'ob'a n. image (**k'o-b'a**) 154

k'ob'a n. mask (**k'o-b'a**) 154

k'ob'a n. statue (**k'o-b'a**) 154

k'oj n. image (**k'o-jo**) 154

k'oj n. mask (**k'o-jo**) 154

k'oj n. statue (**k'o-jo**) 154

k'u phonetic sign (**k'u, k'u/K'U**) 154, 155

k'u n. god, divinity (**k'u/K'U**) 154, 155

k'u adj. divine, sacred (**k'u/K'U**) 154, 155

k'uj n. god, divinity (**k'u-ju**) 155

k'uk' n. quetzal bird (**K'UK'**) 155

k'ul/k'ujul See *ch'ul/ch'ujul.*

k'uxaj pass. v. eaten (was) (**k'u-xa-ja**) 156

k'uxaj pass. v. ground (was) (**k'u-xa-ja**) 156

k'uxaj pass. v. hurt (was) (**k'u-xa-ja**) 156

k'uxajiy tr. com. v. ate (**k'u-xa-ji-ya**) 156

k'uxajiy tr. v. grind (**k'u-xa-ji-ya**) 156

k'uxajiy tr. v. hurt (**k'u-xa-ji-ya**) 156

K'uy Nik Ajaw title, Bird Flower Lord (**k'u-yu NIK-ki AJAW**) 156

L

la phonetic sign (**la**) 157

-laj pos. com. verbal suffix pattern (**-la-ja, [la]-ja, -la-ji**) 157, 158

-laj tr. v. end (**-la-ja**) 157

-laj tr. v. finish (**-la-ja**)..157

lajun n. number ten; cardinal number (**LAJUN**) 158

lak n. plate (**LAK, la-ka**) 159

lakam n. banner (**LAKAM, la-ka-ma**) 159
lakam adj. large, big (**LAKAM, la-ka-ma**) 159
lakam adj. great (**LAKAM, la-ka-ma**) 159
lakam ja' adj. + n. great water (**LAKAM JA'**) 160
lakam ja' adj. + n. wide water (**LAKAM JA'**) 160
lakam tun adj. + n. banner stone (**LAKAM TUN, LAKAM TUN-ni**) 160
lakam tun adj. + n. big stone (**LAKAM TUN, LAKAM TUN-ni**) 160
lakam tun adj. + n. great stone (**LAKAM TUN, LAKAM TUN-ni**) 160
lakam tun adj. + n. large (**LAKAM TUN, LAKAM TUN-ni**) 160
lak'in n. east; cardinal direction (**LAK-K'IN-ni**) 160
Lamat n. day sign, eighth day of the Maya Tzolk'in calendar (**LAMAT**) 161
-lat temp. suf. meaning "X-number of days later" (**la-ta**) 161
lat n. day (**la-ta**) 161
le phonetic sign (**le**) 161
li phonetic sign (**li**) 161, 162
lo phonetic sign (**lo**) 163
lok'iy intr. com. v. came out (**LOK'-yi**) 163
lok'iy intr. com. v. emerged (**LOK'-yi**) 163
lok'iy intr. com. v. escaped (**LOK'-yi**) 163
lok'-ta intr. v. came out from (**lo-k'u-ta**) 163
lok'-ta intr. v. emerged from (**lo-k'u-ta**) 163
lom n. lance (**lo-mu**) 163
lom n. staff (**lo-mu**) 163
lu phonetic sign (**lu**) 163, 164
luk' n. mud (**lu-k'u**) 164
luk' n. clay (**lu-k'u**) 164
lum n. earth (**lu-mi**) 164

M

ma phonetic sign (**ma/MA, ma**) 165, 166
ma negative marker (**ma/MA**) 165, 166
ma adv. not (**ma/MA**) 165, 166
ma ilaj pass. v. not seen (was) (**MA-[IL]-aj**) 166
Mak n. month sign, thirteenth month of the Maya Ja'ab' calendar
  (**MAK, ma-ka**) 167
mak tr. v. close (**ma-ka**) 167
mak tr. v. cover (**ma-ka**) 167
mak tr. v. betroth (**ma-ka**) 167
mak n. cover, lid (**ma-ka**) 167
mak n. capstone (**ma-ka**) 167
makaj pass. v. closed (was) (**ma-ka-ja**) 167
makaj pass. v. covered (was) (**ma-ka-ja**) 167
makaj pass. v. betrothed (was) (**ma-ka-ja**) 167
makax tr. v. close (**ma-ka-xa**) 167
makax tr. v. cover (**ma-ka-xa**) 167
makax tr. v. betroth (**ma-ka-xa**) 167
makom n. calabash tree (**ma-ko-ma**) 168
mam n. ancestor (**MAM**) 168
mam n. maternal grandfather (**MAM**) 168
Manik' n. day sign, seventh day of the Maya Tzolk'in calendar (**MANIK'**) 168
matawil divinity title, specific meaning unknown (**ma-ta-wi-la**) 168
max n. monkey, spider monkey (**ma-xi**) 168, 169
may? n. deer hoof (**MAY (?)**) 169
may? n. tobacco (**MAY (?)**) 169
may? n. fawn (**MAY (?)**) 169
Men n. day sign, fifteenth day of the Maya Tzolk'in calendar (**MEN**) 169
mi phonetic sign (**mi, mi/MI**) 169, 170

mi n. nothing, zero; negative marker (**mi, mi/MI**)................................169, 170
mi ol negative marker + n. no heart (**MI OL-la**)....................................170
mo phonetic sign (**mo/MO', mo**)...170, 171
mokoch n. Knot-Mouth; proper name of a lesser god (**mo-ko-chi**) 171
Mol n. month sign, eighth month of the Maya Ja'ab' calendar (**MOL**) 171
mol? n. jaguar claw (**MOL (?)**)...171
mol? n. jaguar paw (**MOL (?)**)..171
mol tun? n. jaguar claw stone (**MOL(?) TUN-ni**)..............................171
mol tun? n. jaguar paw stone (**MOL(?) TUN-ni**) 171
mo' n. macaw (**mo/MO', MO'**)...171, 172
Mo' Witz n. Macaw Mountain; proper name of location (**MO' WITZ**) 172
Mo' Witz Ajaw n. Macaw Mountain Lord
     (**mo-o WITZ AJAW, mo-o wi-tzi AJAW**) 172
mu phonetic sign (**mu**) 172, 173
muk tr. v. bury (**mu-ka**) 173
mukaj pass. v. buried (was) (**mu-ka-ja**) 173
mukuy n. dove (**mu-ku-yi**) 174
mukuy n. pigeon (**mu-ku-yi**)...174
Muluk n. day sign, ninth day of the Maya Tzolk'in calendar (**MULUK**)........174
mut n. bird (**mu-ti**) 174
mut n. omen (**mu-ti**) 174
mutul n. bird, species unknown; main sign of the Tikal EG (**MUTUL**) 174, 175
Mutul Ajaw-tak pl. n. Mutul Lords (**MUTUL AJAW-TAK**) 175
muwan n. bird; mythological bird; type of sparrow hawk?
     (**MUWAN-ni, mu-wa-ni, MUWAN-na**) 175, 176
Muwan n. month sign; fifteenth month of Maya Ja'ab' calendar
     (**MUWAN-ni, mu-wa-ni, MUWAN-na**) 175, 176
muyal n. cloud (**MUYAL**) 176

N

na phonetic sign (**na/NA/NAJ**) 177, 178
na adj. first; ordinal number (**na/NA/NAJ**)............................177, 178
na n. house (**na/NA/NAJ**)..177, 178
na n. lady (**na/NA/NAJ**)...178
na n. mother (**na/NA/NAJ**) 178
naab' n. plaza (**NAAB', na-b'i**)..178, 179
naab' n. sea (**NAAB', na-b'i**) 178, 179
naab' n. water (**NAAB', na-b'i**) 178, 179
naab' n. water lily? (**NAAB', na-b'i**) 178, 179
naab' tunich adj. + n. watery stone (**NAAB' TUN-chi**) 179
naj adj. first; ordinal number (**na/NA/NAJ**) 177, 178
naj n. house (**na/NA/NAJ**) 177, 178
naj n. lady (**na/NA/NAJ**) 178
naj n. mother (**na/NA/NAJ**) 178
-naj verbal ending?; part of the PSS dedication phrase (**na-ja**)........179
najiy tr. incom. v. fills up (**na-ja-yi**) 180
nak num. class. for counts with titles (**na-ku**) 180
nak tr. v. conquer (**na-ku**) 180
nak intr. v. ascend (**na-ku**) 180
nak intr. v. elevate (**na-ku**) 180
nak intr. v. rise (**na-ku**) 180
nak n. crown (**na-ku**) 180
nak n. diadem (**na-ku**) 180
nak n. face (**na-ku**)..180
nak n. mask (**na-ku**) 180
Na Kan n. deity name; part of the name of a Vision Serpent (**NA ka-KAN**) 180
nal n. maize, maize curl (**NAL**) 180, 181

nal n. part of the proper name of the Maize God (**NAL**).....................................180, 181
nal n. north; cardinal direction (**NAL (?), na-NAL (?)**).....................................181
-nal loc. determinative suffix meaning "place" (**NAL**) 180, 181
na ototaj n. house (**NA OTOT-ja**) 181
nawaj pass. v. adorned (was) (**na-wa-ja**) 182
ne phonetic sign (**ne/NE**) 182
ne n. tail (**ne/NE**) 182
ni phonetic sign (**ni**) 183
nich n. flower (**NICH/NIK**) 183
nich n. son, relat. glyph (**NICH/NIK**) 183
nichil n. flower (**NICH-li/NIK-li**).....................................184
nichil n. son, relat. glyph (**NICH-li/NIK-li**) 184
nichim n. flower (**ni-chi-{m}**).....................................183
nichim n. son, relat. glyph (**ni-chi-{m}**) 183
nik n. flower (**NICH/NIK**) 183
nik n. son, relat. glyph (**NICH/NIK**) 183
nikil n. flower (**NICH-li/NIK-li**) 184
nikil n. son, relat. glyph (**NICH-li/NIK-li**) 184
nikte' n. flower, possibly the mayflower (**NIKTE', NIKTE'-te'**) 184, 185
no phonetic sign (**no**).....................................185
noj adj. great? (**NOJ**) 185, 186
nojol n. north; cardinal direction (**NOJOL**) 186
nu phonetic sign (**nu**) 186, 187
nuk adj. great (**nu-ku**) 188
nuk adj. large (**nu-ku**) 188
nuk adj. wide (**nu-ku**).....................................188
nuun n.? meaning unknown (**NUUN**) 188

O

o vowel *o* (**o**) 189, 190, 191
och intr. v. enter (**OCH, OCH-chi**).....................................191, 192, 193
och/ok n. foot (**OCH/OK**) 192
ochaj pass. v. was entered (**OCH-ja/OK-ja**) 194
och b'i tr. v. phr. entered the road; death (**OCH B'I**) 192
och b'i-aj pass. v. phr. entered the road (was); death (**OCH B'I-ja**) 192
och b'ij-jiy tr. v. phr. road-entered; death (**OCH B'I-ji-ji-ya**) 193
och ja' v. phr. entered the water, water-entered; death (**OCH JA'**) 194
och ja'-aj pass. v. phr. entered the water (was); death (**OCH JA'-ja**) 194
och k'ak' tr. v. phr. entered the fire, fire-entered; dedication
 (**OCH-chi K'AK', OCH K'AK'**).....................................193, 194
och k'in n. west; cardinal direction (**OCH K'IN**).....................................195
och ta chaan/ok ta kaan tr. v. phr. entered into the sky, became the sky,
 sky-entered (**OCH TA CHAAN-na/OK TA KAAN-na**) 195
och te' tr. v. phr. entered the tree, tree-entered (**OCH TE'/OK TE'**) 195
Ok n. day sign, tenth day of the Maya Tzolk'in calendar (**OK**) 195
ok te' tr. v. phr. entered the tree, tree-entered (**OCH TE'/OK TE'**) 195
ol n. middle, center (**OL**) 196
ol n. heart (**OL**) 196
olas n. phr. whole (the) (**o-la-si**) 196
olas adj. + n. whole set (the) (**o-la-si**).....................................196
olas k'u n. phr. whole set of gods (the)?, all the gods? (**o-la-si K'U**) 196
olis n. phr. whole (the) (**o-OL-si**) 196, 197
olis adj. + n. whole set (the)? (**o-OL-si**) 196, 197
olis k'u n. phr. whole set of gods (the)?, all the gods? (**o-OL-si K'U**) 197
otot n. house (**OTOT**).....................................197
ototaj pass. v. housed (was) (**OTOT-ja**).....................................197
ox n. number three; cardinal number (**OX**) 197, 198

ox adj. many (**OX**) 197, 198
ox ajal v. phr. thrice said (**OX aj-ja-li**) 198
ox ajal v. phr. thrice manifested (**OX aj-ja-li**)..198
Ox B'olon Chaak n. deity name, proper name of deity; possibly GI of the
    Palenque Triad (**OX B'OLON CHAAK**) 198

P

pa phonetic sign (**pa/PAJ**) 199
paj n. wall (**pa/PAJ**) 199
paj tr. v. choose (**pa/PAJ**)..199
pakab' n. lintel (**pa-ka-b'a**) 200
pakal n. shield (**PAKAL, pa-ka-la**)...200
pakal n. name of several Palenque Classic Period kings
    (**PAKAL, pa-ka-la**) 200
paklaj pos. v. doubled over (was) (**pa-ka-la-ja**) 200
paklaj pos. v. faced down (was) (**pa-ka-la-ja**) 200
pakax v. phr. (someone) coming back (**pa-ka-xa**) 201
pak' tr. v. mold (**pa-k'a**) 201
pak' tr. v. form in clay (**pa-k'a**) 201
pak' tr. v. plant (**pa-k'a**) 201
pak' tr. v. hoist (**pa-k'a**) 201
pak'ajiy intr. com. v. molded (**pa-k'a-ji-ya**) 201
pak'ajiy intr. com. v. phr. formed in clay (**pa-k'a-ji-ya**) 201
pak'ajiy intr. com. v. planted (**pa-k'a-ji-ya**) 201
pak'ajiy intr. com. v. hoisted (**pa-k'a-ji-ya**)..201
pas/pasaj tr. v. open (**PAS/PASAJ, pa-sa**) 202
pas/pasaj n. dawn (**PAS/PASAJ, pa-sa**) 202
pasil n. opening (**pa-si-li**) 202
pasil n. doorway (**pa-si-li**) 202
pat tr. v. form (**PAT, pa-ti, PAT-ta**) 202, 203, 204
pat tr. v. make (**PAT, pa-ti, PAT-ta**) 202, 203, 204
pat n. back; body part (**PAT, pa-ti, PAT-ta**) 202, 203, 204
pat n. shoulders; body part (**PAT, pa-ti, PAT-ta**) 202, 203, 204
pat n. tribute (**PAT, pa-ti, PAT-ta**)..202, 203, 204
patan n. tribute (**pa-ta-{n}, pa-ta-na**) 203
pat b'uj tr. com. v. formed (**PAT-ta-b'u-ji**) 205
pat b'uj tr. com. v. made (**PAT-ta-b'u-ji**) 205
pat b'uy tr. com. v. formed (**PAT-b'u-ya**) 204
pat b'uy tr. com. v. made (**PAT-b'u-ya**)...204
patlaj pos. com. v. formed (was) (**PAT-[la]-ja**) 204
patlaj pos. com. v. made (was) (**PAT-[la]-ja**) 204
patwan com. v. formed (**PAT-ta-wa-ni, PAT-wa-ni**) 205
patwan com. v. made (**PAT-ta-wa-ni, PAT-wa-ni**) 205
Pax n. month sign, sixteenth month of the Maya Ja'ab' calendar (**PAX**) 205, 206
pet intr. v. rotate (**PET**) 206
pet intr. v. turn (**PET**) 206
pet n. jewel (**PET**) 206
pet n. island (**PET**) 206
petjiy intr. com. v. rotated (**PET-ji-ya**)...206
petjiy intr. com. v. turned (**PET-ji-ya**) 206
pi phonetic sign (**pi, pi/PI/PIJ**)..206, 207
pi n. period of 400 years of 360 days each, used in the Maya LC calendar;
    B'aktun (**pi/PI/PIJ, pi-ji**)...207, 208
pi n. bundle (**pi/PI/PIJ, pi-ji**) 207
pib' naj n. sweat bath, *temescal* (**pi-b'i NA-aj**) 207
pib'nal n. sweat bath, *temescal* (**pi-b'i-NA-li**) 207

pi-i n. period of 400 years of 360 days each, used in the Maya LC calendar;
B'aktun (**PI-ya**) 209
pij n. bundle (**pi/PI/PIJ**) 207
pij n. period of 400 years of 360 days each, used in the Maya LC calendar;
B'aktun (**pi/PI/PIJ, pi-ji**)...207, 208
pik num. class. units/groups of 8,000 (**PIK**) 208
pis num. class. "measure"; for counts of periods of time (**pi-si**)..................208
pitz adj. youthful (**pi-tzi**)..208
pitz n. ball game (**pi-tzi**) 208
pitz n. ball player (**pi-tzi**) 208
pitzal adj. youthful (**pi-tzi-la**) 209
pitzal intr. v. play ball (**pi-tzi-la**) 209
pitzalaj adj. youthful (was) (**pi-tzi-la-ja**) 209
pitzalaj pos. com. v. played ball (**pi-tzi-la-ja**)....................................209
pixom n. headdress (**pi-xo-ma**) 209
pixom tr. v. wrap (**pi-xo-ma**)..209
piy n. bundle (**PI-ya**) 209
piy n. period of 400 years (years of of 360 days each) used in the
Maya LC calendar; B'aktun (**PI-ya**) 209
po phonetic sign (**po**) 209
Pop n. month sign, first month of the Maya Ja'ab' calendar (**POP**) 210
pu phonetic sign (**pu/PU/PUJ**) 210
pu n. cattail reed (**pu/PU/PUJ**)...210
pu n. reed (**pu/PU/PUJ**) 210
pu n. bullrush (**pu/PU/PUJ**) 210
Pu n. proper name of Tollan in Mayan (**pu/PU/PUJ**) 210
puj n. bullrush (**pu/PU/PUJ**) 210
puj n. cattail reed (**pu/PU/PUJ**) 210
puj n. reed (**pu/PU/PUJ**) 210
puliy intr. com. v. burned (**pu-lu-yi**, **PUL-[yi]**) 210
puliy intr. com. v. sprinkled (**pu-lu-yi**, **PUL-[yi]**) 210

S

sa phonetic sign (**sa**, **sa/SA**) 211, 212
sa n. maize/corn gruel, *atole* (**sa/SA**) 211
sajal title, underlord; elite title of unknown specific meaning (**sa-ja-la**) 213
sajal title, one who fears (**sa-ja-la**) 213
sajmiy temp. phr. earlier today (**sa-aj-mi-ya**) 212
Sak n. month sign, eleventh month of the Maya Ja'ab' calendar (**SAK**) 213
sak adj. pure (**SAK**) 213
sak adj. resplendent (**SAK**) 213
sak adj. white (**SAK**) 213
sak chuwen adj. + n. pure, resplendent artist (**SAK CHUWEN**) 214
Sak Ik' Ek' n. deity name; proper name of god with "wind" manifestations;
"Resplendent Wind God Star"? (**SAK IK' EK'**) 214
sak lak tun n. incensario (**SAK la-ka-TUN, SAK la-ka-TUN-ni**) 214
sak nik adj. white flowery (**SAK NIK**) 215
Sak Nuk Naj n. White Great House; proper name of building
(**SAK nu-ku NAJ**) 215
Sak Te' Ajaw title, White Tree Lord (**SAK TE' AJAW-wa**) 215
samiy temp. phr. earlier today (**sa-mi-ya**) 216
sat tr. v. destroy (**sa-ta**) 216
sat tr. v. lose (**sa-ta**) 216
satay intr. com. v. destroyed (**sa-ta-yi**) 216
satay intr. com. v. lost (**sa-ta-yi**) 216
se phonetic sign (**se**) 216

Sek n. month sign, fifth month of the Maya Ja'ab' calendar (**SEK**) 216
si phonetic sign (**si**) 217
si intr. v. be born (**SI**) 217
sij-ya n. birth (**SI-ji-ya**) 217
sij-ya intr. com. v. born (**SI-ji-ya**) 217
Sip n. month sign, third month of the Maya Ja'ab' calendar (**SIP**) 218
sitz winik n. glutton (**si-tzi WINIK-ki**) 218
siyaj pass. v. born (was) (**SI-ya-ja**) 218
Sotz' n. month sign, fourth month of the Maya Ja'ab' calendar (**SOTZ'**) 218
su phonetic sign (**su**) 218
sukun n. older brother (**su-ku-{n}**) 219
sukun winik adj. + n. older brother person (**su-ku-{n} WINIK-ki**) 219
susaj pass. v. cut up (was) (**su-sa-ja**) 219
susaj pass. v. rasped (was) (**su-sa-ja**) 219
sutz' n. bat (**su-tz'i**) 219

T

ta phonetic sign (**ta/TA**) 221, 222
ta prep. at (**ta/TA**) 221, 222
ta prep. in (**ta/TA**) 221, 222
ta prep. to (**ta/TA**) 221, 222
ta prep. with (**ta/TA**) 221, 222
tab' tr. v. ascend (**TAB'**) 223
tab' tr. v. go up (**TAB'**) 223
tab' tr. v. rise up (**TAB'**) 223
tab' tr. v. present (**TAB'**) 223
tab'iy intr. com. v. ascended (**TAB'-[yi]**) 223, 224
tab'iy intr. com. v. presented (**TAB'-[yi]**) 223, 224
tab'iy intr. com. v. rose up (**TAB'-[yi]**) 223, 224
tab'iy intr. com. v. went up (**TAB'-[yi]**) 223, 224
taj n. torch, pine torch (**TAJ**) 224
taj n. obsidian (**ta-ji**) 224
taj tun n. torch stone (**TAJ TUN**) 225
-tak pl. suf. (**TAK, ta-ki, TAK-ki**) 225
takaj pass. v. come (have) (**ta-ki-ja**) 225
takaj pass. v. come (was) (**ta-ki-ja**) 225
tal intr. v. arrive (**TAL, ta-li**) 226
tal intr. v. come (**TAL, ta-li**) 226
tal num. class. for ordinal numbers (**TAL, ta-li**) 226
tan loc. prep. in (**TAN, TAN-na**) 226, 228
tan prep. phr. in the center of (**TAN, TAN-na**) 226, 228
tan prep. phr. in front of (**TAN, TAN-na**) 226, 229
tan prep. phr. in the middle of (**TAN, TAN-na**) 226, 229
tan ch'en double loc. phr. within the cave (**TAN CH'EN-na**) 227
tan ch'en double loc. phr. in front of the cave (**TAN CH'EN-na**) 227
tan ch'en Ox Witzaj double loc. phr. within the cave Three Hill Water
    (**TAN CH'EN OX WITZ-aj**) 227
tan ch'en Ox Witzaj double loc. phr. in front of the cave Three Hill Water
    (**TAN CH'EN OX WITZ-aj**) 227
tan lam adj. half diminished; "half period" (**[TAN] LAM**) 227
tan lamaj pass. v. half diminished (was); "half period" (**[TAN] LAM-ja**) 227
ta ochlel prep. phr. at the foot of (**TA OCH-le-{l}**) 228
ta ochlel prep. phr. at the enter-treeship (**TA OCH-le-{l}**) 228
ta yutal prep. phr. for his/her seeds/beans (of cacao) (**TA yu-ta-{l}**) 228
ta yutal prep. phr. for his/her fruited (cacao) (**TA yu-ta-{l}**) 228
tek' tr. v. phr. step on (**te'-k'a**) 230

tek'aj pass. v. phr. stepped on (was) (**te'-k'a-ja**) 230
te'/che' phonetic sign (**te'/TE' (che'/CHE')**) 228, 229, 230
te'/che' n. tree (**te'/TE' (che'/CHE')**) 228, 229, 230
te'/che' n. wood (**te'/TE' (che'/CHE')**) 228, 229, 230
te'el adj. tree-fresh (**te'-TE'-le**) 231
ti phonetic sign (**ti/TI**) 231
ti prep. at (**ti/TI**) 231
ti prep. from (**ti/TI**) 231
ti prep. in (**ti/TI**) 231
ti prep. on (**ti/TI**) 231
ti prep. to (**ti/TI**) 231
ti prep. with (**ti/TI**) 231
ti ajawlel prep. phr. in kingship (**TI AJAW le-{l}**) 231
ti ajawlel prep. phr. in lordship (**TI AJAW le-{l}**) 231
ti ajawlel prep. phr. in rulership (**TI AJAW le-{l}**) 231
tikal tr. v. phr. get drunk on (**ti-ka-la**) 232
tikil prep. phr. as the . . . (**ti-ki-li**) 232
til n. tapir (**TIL**) 232
ti xukpi prep. phr. with a bird, prep. + proper name of dance staff
    (**ti-xu-[ku]-pi**) 232
ti yak'il? prep. phr. in the tongue (**TI ya-AK'-il**) 232
to phonetic sign (**to**) 233
tojol n. payment (**to-jo-li**) 233
tojol n. tribute (**to-jo-li**) 233
tok n. cloud (**to-ko**) 233
tok tan n. cloud center (**to-ko-TAN-na**) 234
Tok Tan Ajaw title, Cloud Center Lord (**to-ko TAN AJAW**) 234
Tok Tan Winik title, Cloud Center Person (**to-ko TAN WINIK-ki**) 234
tok' n. flint (**TOK', to-k'a**) 234, 235
tok' pakal n. flint [and] shield (**to-k'a pa-ka-la, TOK' PAKAL**) 235
toxat n. bled penis (**to-[xa]-AT-ti, to-XAT**) 235, 236
tu prep. + 3rd pers. poss. pron. in his/her/its (**TU**) 236
tukun n. dove (**tu-ku-nu**) 236
tuk'ul prep. phr. in his/her/its divinity (**TU K'U-li**) 236
tul n. rabbit (**TUL**) 236
tun n. year of 360 days used in the Maya LC calendar and DNs
    (**TUN, TUN-ni**) 237, 238
tun n. stone (**TUN, TUN-ni**) 237, 238
tu naj prep. phr. in his/her/its house (**TU na-ja**) 238
tu naj prep. phr. in his/her/its structure (**TU na-ja**) 238
tup n. earflare (**tu-pa**) 238
tupaj pass. v. adorned (was) (**tu-pa-ja**) 239
tupaj pass. v. ear-flared (was) (**tu-pa-ja**) 239
tu wayb'il prep. phr. in his/her/its dreaming place (**TU WAY-[b'i]-li**) 239
tu wayb'il prep. phr. in his/her/its sleeping place (**TU WAY-[b'i]-li**) 239

TZ

tza phonetic sign (**tza**) 241
tzak intr. v. appear (**tza-[ka]**) 241, 242
tzak tr. v. conjure (**tza-[ka]**) 241, 242
tzak tr. v. grab (**tza-[ka]**) 241, 242
tzak tr. v. grasp (**tza-[ka]**) 241, 242
tzakaw tr. v. conjure (**tza-[ka]-wa**) 242
tzakaw tr. v. grab (**tza-[ka]-wa**) 242
tzakaw tr. v. grasp (**tza-[ka]-wa**) 242
tzakaw tr. v. make appear (**tza-[ka]-wa**) 242

tzakaw ch'ul/tzakaw k'ul tr. v. phr. conjure god/divinity/holiness
   (**tza-[ka]-wa CH'UL/tza-[ka]-wa K'UL**) 242
tzakaw ch'ul/tzakaw k'ul tr. v. phr. make appear god/divinity/holiness
   (**tza-[ka]-wa CH'UL/tza-[ka]-wa K'UL**) 242
tzakaw ch'ul/tzakaw k'ul tr. v. phr. manifest god/divinity/holiness
   (**tza-[ka]-wa CH'UL/tza-[ka]-wa K'UL**) 242
tzi phonetic sign (**tzi, tzi/TZI**) 242, 243
tzi adj. fresh (**tzi/TZI**) 243
tzi adj. new (**tzi/TZI**) 243
tzi adj. seasoned (**tzi/TZI**) 243
tzik ja'ab'?/tzik ab'? intr. v. phr. the count of years?; the Initial Series
   Introductory Glyph (**tzi-ka JA'AB' (?)/tzi-ka AB' (?)**) 243
tzo phonetic sign (**tzo**) 243, 244
tzu phonetic sign (**tzu/TZU, tzu**) 243, 244
tzul n. dog (**tzu-lu**) 244
tzutz tr. v. end (**TZUTZ**) 244, 245
tzutz tr. v. expire (**TZUTZ**) 244, 245
tzutz tr. v. terminate (**TZUTZ**) 244, 245
tzutz tr. v. join (**TZUTZ**) 244, 245
tzutzaj pass. v. ended (was) (**TZUTZ-ja, tzu-tzu-ja**) 245
tzutzaj pass. v. expired (was) (**TZUTZ-ja, tzu-tzu-ja**) 245
tzutzaj pass. v. terminated (was) (**TZUTZ-ja, tzu-tzu-ja**) 245
tzutziy intr. com. v. ended (**TZUTZ-yi**) 246
tzutziy intr. com. v. expired (**TZUTZ-yi**) 246
tzutziy intr. com. v. terminated (**TZUTZ-yi**) 246

TZ'

tz'a phonetic sign (**tz'a/TZ'A**) 247
tz'a tr. v. give (**tz'a/TZ'A**) 247
tz'ak tr. v. put in order (**TZ'AK**) 247
tz'ak tr. v. count (**TZ'AK**) 247
tz'ak tr. v. increase (**TZ'AK**) 247
tz'ak adj. whole (**TZ'AK**) 247
tz'akaj pass. v. counted (was) (**TZ'AK-aj**) 247
tz'akaj pass. v. increased (was) (**TZ'AK-aj**) 247
tz'akaj pass. v. put in order (was) (**TZ'AK-aj**) 247
tz'ak b'ul tr. v. count (**TZ'AK b'u-li**) 248
tz'ak b'ul tr. v. increase (**TZ'AK b'u-li**) 248
tz'ak b'ul tr. v. put in order (**TZ'AK b'u-li**) 248
tz'am? n. throne (**TZ'AM (?)**) 248
tz'ap pos. v. plant upright (**tz'a-[pa]**) 248
tz'ap pos. v. hoist (**tz'a-[pa]**) 248
tz'ap tr. v. pile up (**tz'a-[pa]**) 248
tz'ap tr. v. stack (**tz'a-[pa]**) 248
tz'apa pass. v. hoisted (was) (**tz'a-pa-ja, tz'a-[pa]-ja**) 248, 249
tz'apaj pass. v. planted upright (was) (**tz'a-pa-ja, tz'a-[pa]-ja**) 248, 249
tz'apaj pass. v. piled up (was) (**tz'a-pa-ja, tz'a-[pa]-ja**) 248, 249
tz'apaj pass. v. stacked (was) (**tz'a-pa-ja, tz'a-[pa]-ja**) 248, 249
tz'apajiy intr. com. v. planted upright (**tz'a-pa-ji-ya**) 249
tz'apajiy intr. com. v. hoisted (**tz'a-pa-ji-ya**) 249
tz'apajiy intr. com. v. piled up (**tz'a-pa-ji-ya**) 249
tz'apajiy intr. com. v. stacked (**tz'a-pa-ji-ya**) 249
tz'apwa pos. v. plant upright (**tz'a-[pa]-wa**) 249
tz'apwa pos. v. hoist (**tz'a-[pa]-wa**) 249
tz'apwa pos. v. pile up (**tz'a-[pa]-wa**) 249
tz'apwa pos. v. stack (**tz'a-[pa]-wa**) 249
tz'i phonetic sign (**tz'i**) 249, 250, 251

tz'i n. dog (**TZ'I**, **tz'i-i**)) 250, 252
tz'ib' n. painting (**tz'i-b'a**, **tz'i-b'i**) 251
tz'ib' n. writing (**tz'i-b'a**, **tz'i-b'i**) 251
tz'o phonetic sign (**tz'o**) 252
tz'u phonetic sign (**tz'u**) 252
tz'unun n. hummingbird (**tz'u-nu-{n}**) 252

U

u vowel *u* (**u/U**) 253, 254, 255
u 3rd pers. pron. he, she, it (**u/U**) 253, 254, 255
u 3rd pers. poss. pron. his, hers, its (**u/U**) 253, 254, 255
u b'a poss. n. his/her/its doing (**U B'A**) 255, 256
u b'a poss. n. the doing of (**U B'A**) 255, 256
u b'a poss. n. his/her/its image (**U B'A**) 255, 256
u b'a poss. n. the image of (**U B'A**) 255, 256
uch' n. drink (**UCH'**) 256
uch' intr. v. drink (**UCH'**) 256
ul n. maize/corn gruel, *atole* (**u-lu**) 256
unen relat. child [of father] (**u-ne-{n}**) 256
ut intr. v. come to pass (**u-ti**) 257
ut intr. v. happen (**u-ti**) 257
ut intr. v. occur (**u-ti**) 257
utiy intr. com. v. since it came to pass; Anterior Date Indicator (ADI)
     (**u-ti-ya**) 257, 258
utiy intr. com. v. since it happened; Anterior Date Indicator (ADI)
     (**u-ti-ya**) 257, 258
utiy intr. com. v. since it occurred; Anterior Date Indicator (ADI)
     (**u-ti-ya**) 257, 258
utiy prep. phr. it happened at (**u-ti-ya**) 257, 258
utjiy intr. com. v. since it came to pass; Anterior Date Indicator (ADI)
     (**u-ti-ji-ya**) 257
utjiy intr. com. v. since it happened; Anterior Date Indicator (ADI)
     (**u-ti-ji-ya**) 257
utjiy intr. com. v. since it occurred; Anterior Date Indicator (ADI)
     (**u-ti-ji-ya**) 257
utjiy prep. phr. it happened at (**u-ti-ji-ya**) 257
utom intr. incom. v. it will come to pass; Future Date Indicator (FDI)
     (**u-to-ma**) 258, 259
utom intr. incom. v. it will happen; Future Date Indicator (FDI) (**u-to-ma**) 258, 259
utom intr. incom. v. it will occur; Future Date Indicator (FDI) (**u-to-ma**) 258, 259
u . . . wa tr. com. verbal affix pattern (**U . . . wa**) 259
u we'y tr. incom. v. phr. his/her/its eating of (**U we'-ya**) 259
u . . . wi tr. com. verbal affix pattern (**U . . . wi**) 259
uxul n. carving (**u-xu-[lu]**) 260
uxul n. sculpture (**u-xu-[lu]**) 260
uxul intr. v. carve (**u-xu-[lu]**) 260
uxul intr. v. sculpt (**u-xu-[lu]**) 260
u yajaw te' poss. title, his Lord of the Tree (**U ya-AJAW-wa TE'**) 260

W

wa phonetic sign (**wa/WA**) 261, 262
wa pos. suf. -*w* (**wa/WA**) 261, 262
wa pos. v. erect (**wa/WA**) 261, 262
wa n. *tortilla* (**wa/WA**) 261, 262
wa n. *tamale* (**wa/WA**) 261
wa part. and then (**wa/WA**) 261, 262

wa prog. aspect marker on transitive verbs? (**wa/WA**) 261, 262
waj n. *tortilla* (**wa-WA-ji**) 264
waj n. *tamale* (**wa-WA-ji**) 264
wak n. number six; cardinal number (**WAK**) 262, 263
wak n. something erected (**WAK**) 262, 263
wak n. something hoisted (**WAK**) 262, 263
wak n. something lifted (**WAK**) 262, 263
wak n. something stood up (**WAK**)..262, 263
wak chaan/wak kaan n. erected sky (**WAK-ki CHAAN/WAK-ki KAAN**) 263
wak chaan/wak kaan n. hoisted sky (**WAK-ki CHAAN/WAK-ki KAAN**) 263
wak chaan/wak kaan n. lifted sky (**WAK-ki CHAAN/WAK-ki KAAN**) 263
wak chaan/wak kaan n. six sky (**WAK-ki CHAAN/WAK-ki KAAN**) 263
wak chaan/wak kaan n. stood-up sky (**WAK-ki CHAAN/WAK-ki KAAN**) 263
Wak Chaan Ajaw/Wak Kaan Ajaw title, Erected Sky Lord
    (**WAK CHAAN-na AJAW/WAK KAAN-na AJAW**) 263
Wak Chaan Ajaw/Wak Kaan Ajaw title, Hoisted Sky Lord
    (**WAK CHAAN-na AJAW/WAK KAAN-na AJAW**) 263
Wak Chaan Ajaw/
Wak Kaan Ajaw title, Lifted Sky Lord
    (**WAK CHAAN-na AJAW/WAK KAAN-na AJAW**) 263
Wak Chaan Ajaw/
Wak Kaan Ajaw title, Six Sky Lord
    (**WAK CHAAN-na AJAW/WAK KAAN-na AJAW**) 263
Wak Chaan Ajaw/Wak Kaan Ajaw title, Stood-Up Sky Lord
    (**WAK CHAAN-na AJAW/WAK KAAN-na AJAW**) 263
wawaan n. erected thing (**wa-wa-aj-ni**) 264
wawaan n. lifted thing (**wa-wa-aj-ni**) 264
wawaan n. raised-up thing (**wa-wa-aj-ni**) 264
wawaan n. stood-up thing (**wa-wa-aj-ni**) 264
waxak n. number eight; cardinal number (**WAXAK**) 265
Waxaklajun U B'a n. Eighteen [Snake/Centipede] Heads; proper name of
    the scaled Vision Serpent/centipede thought to derive from
    Teotihuacan imagery (**WAXAKLAJUN U B'A**) 265
Waxaklajun U B'a n. proper name of the 13th ruler of Copán in the
    Yax K'uk' Mo' lineage (**WAXAKLAJUN U B'A**)..................................265
waxaklajun u b'a n. war helmet (**WAXAKLAJUN U B'A**) 265
Waxak Na Chaak n. proper name of God I (GI) of the Palenque Triad;
    Eight First Chaak? (**WAXAK NA CHAAK**)..265
way n. entrance (**WAY, WAY-ya**) 266, 267
way n. hole (**WAY, WAY-ya**) 266, 267
way n. portal (**WAY, WAY-ya**) 266, 267
way n. water (**WAY, WAY-ya**)..266, 267
way n. co-essence, *nawal* (**WAY, WAY-ya**) 266, 267
way n. spirit, *nawal* (**WAY, WAY-ya**) 266, 267
way n. quarter (**WAY, WAY-ya**) 266, 267
way n. room (**WAY, WAY-ya**) 266, 267
way intr. v. sleep (**WAY, WAY-ya**) 266, 267
wayab' n. dreamer (**wa-WAY-{a}-[b'i]**) 264
wayab' n. co-essence, *nawal* (**wa-WAY-{a}-[b'i]**) 264
wayab' n. spirit, *nawal* (**wa-WAY-{a}-[b'i]**) 264
wa yak'aw tr. v. give (**wa-ya-k'a-wa**) 266
wa yalaw tr. v. say (**wa-ya-la-wa**) 266
wayb'il n. sleeping room (**WAY-b'i-li**) 267
wayb'il n. lineage shrine (**WAY-b'i-li**) 267
Wayeb' n. month sign, last "month" of the Maya Ja'ab' calendar;
    the final five-day unlucky period (**WAYEB'**) 267
we' phonetic sign? (**we'/WE'**) 267, 268
we' intr. v. eat (**we'/WE'**) 267, 268

wi phonetic sign (**wi/WI**) 268, 269
wi n. root (**wi/WI**) 268, 269
wi n. number one; cardinal number (**wi/WI**) 268, 269
Wi Ch'ok Te' Na n. Root-Sprout Tree House; the "Lineage Founder" glyph
    (**WI CH'OK TE' NA**) 269
winal n. month of twenty days in LC (**WINAL**) 269
winik n. being (**WINIK, wi-WINIK-ki**) 269, 271
winik n. man (**WINIK, wi-WINIK-ki**) 269, 271
winik n. person (**WINIK, wi-WINIK-ki**) 269, 271
Witik Ajaw title, Witik Lord (**wi-ti-ki AJAW**) 270
witz n. hill (**WITZ, wi-tzi**) 270
witz n. mountain (**WITZ, wi-tzi**) 270
Witz Mo' n. Mountain Macaw (**wi-tzi mo-o**) 270
Witz Sak Nik Nal n. White Flowery Mountain Place; proper name of the
    Kawak Monster on the Tablet of the Foliated Cross at Palenque
    (**wi-tzi SAK-NIK-ki NAL**) 271
. . . wiy verbal suffix pattern used to derive an intransitive out of a
    transitive root (**. . . wi-ya**) 271
wo phonetic sign (**wo**) 272
Wo title, month sign, second month of the Maya Ja'ab' calendar (**WO**) 272
wojol n. character (**wo-jo-li**) 272
wojol n. glyph (**wo-jo-li**) 272
wojol n. letter (**wo-jo-li**) 272
wol n. something round (**wo-la**) 273
wol n. heart (**wo-la**) 273
wol tr. v. make round (**wo-la**) 273
wol tr. v. wrap up (**wo-la**) 273
wuk n. number seven; cardinal number (**WUK**) 273

X

xa phonetic sign (**xa/XA**) 275
xa adv. pref. already (**xa/XA**) 275
xa adv. pref. again (**xa/XA**) 275
xaman n. north; cardinal direction (**xa-ma-na**) 275
xan intr. v. go (**XAN-na, xa-XAN-na**)...275, 276
xan intr. v. walk (**XAN-na, xa-XAN-na**) 275, 276
xan intr. v. travel (**XAN-na, xa-XAN-na**) 275, 276
xi phonetic sign (**xi**) 276
xib' n. man (**XIB'**) 277
xo phonetic sign (**xo**)..277
xok n. count (**xo-ki**) 277
xok n. shark (**xo-ki**) 277
xu phonetic sign (**xu**) 277
xuk n. dance object, proper name of dance staff used at Yaxchilán
    (**xu-[ku]**) 277
xuk n. bird; possibly the mot-mot bird (**xu-[ku]**) 277
xukpi n. dance object, proper name of dance staff used at Yaxchilán
    (**xu-[ku]-pi**) 278
xukpi n. bird; possibly the mot-mot bird (**xu-[ku]-pi**) 278
Xul n. month sign, sixth month of the Maya Ja'ab' calendar (**XUL**) 278
-xul phonetic signs (**xu-[lu]**) 278

Y

ya phonetic sign (**ya**)...279, 280
ya background marker indicating the completive aspect (**ya**) 279, 280
ya pron. he/she/it; 3rd pers. prevocalic pron. used with words beginning
    in *a* (**ya**) 279, 280

ya poss. pron. his/her/its; 3ʳᵈ pers. prevocalic poss. pron. used with words
    beginning in *a* (**ya**) 279, 280
yab'il poss. n. grandson (his/her) (**ya-b'i-li**) 282
ya-ch'am poss. n. child [of mother]; literally "her harvest"
    (**ya-CH'AM, ya-CH'AM-ma**)...282, 283
yajaw poss. n. lord (his/her/its); generally "underlord" (**ya-AJAW-wa, ya-ja-wa**) 280, 283
Yajaw K'ak' poss. prep. phr. Lord of the Fire, Fire Lord; title
    (**ya-AJAW K'AK'**) 280
Yajaw Te' poss. prep. phr. Lord of the Tree, Tree Lord; title
    (**ya-AJAW-wa TE'**) 281
Yajaw Te' poss. n. Tree Lord (his/her/its); title (**ya-AJAW-wa TE'**) 281
Yajaw Te', u poss. n. Lord of the Tree (his/her/its); title (**U ya-AJAW-wa TE'**) 260
yajil poss. n. termination (his/her/its) (**ya-ja-li**) 283
yak' poss. n. giving (his/her/its) (**ya-k'u**) 284
yak' poss. n. offering (his/her/its) (**ya-k'u**) 284
yak'aw poss. n. giving (his/her/its) (**ya-k'a-wa**) 283, 284
yak'aw poss. n. offering (his/her/its) (**ya-k'a-wa**)............................283, 284
yal poss. n. child [of mother]; literally "her harvest" (**ya-AL, ya-la**) 281, 282, 284
yalaj poss. n. hurling (his/her/its) (**ya-la-ja**) 284
yalaj poss. n. throwing (his/her/its) (**ya-la-ja**) 284
yalajiy poss. n. saying (his/her/its) (**ya-la-ji-ya**) 285
yalajiy poss. n. utterance (his/her/its) (**ya-la-ji-ya**) 285
yalij poss. n. saying (his/her/its) (**ya-la-ji**) 285
yalij poss. n. utterance (his/her/its) (**ya-la-ji**) 285
. . . yan pos. com. verbal affix pattern (**. . . ya-ni**) 285
yataj poss. pl. n. companions (his/her/its) (**ya-ta-ji**) 285
yataj tr. v. bathe, water (**ya-ta-ji**) 285
yatan poss. n. wife (his) (**ya-ta-na**) 286
yatan poss. n. wife of (**ya-ta-na**) 286
yatij tr. v. bathe, water (**ya-ti-ji**) 286
Yax n. month sign, tenth month of the Maya Ja'ab' calendar (**YAX, ya-xa**) 287
yax adj. green (**YAX, ya-xa**) 286, 287
yax adj. blue (**YAX, ya-xa**) 286, 287
yax adj. blue-green (**YAX, ya-xa**) 286, 287
yax adj. first (**YAX, ya-xa**) 286, 287
yax chit adj. + n. first father? (**YAX CHIT**) 287
yax ch'am adj. + n. first harvest (**YAX CH'AM, YAX ch'a-CH'AM**) 288
yax ch'am K'awil v. phr. first harvesting [of] K'awil (**YAX CH'AM K'AWIL**) 288
yax ch'am K'awil v. phr. first receiving [of] K'awil (**YAX CH'AM K'AWIL**) 288
yax k'al tun v. phr. closed the first stone (**YAX K'AL TUN-ni**) 288
yax k'al tun v. phr. closed the first *tun* (**YAX K'AL TUN-ni**) 288
Yaxk'in n. month sign, seventh month of the Maya Ja'ab' calendar (**YAXK'IN**) 289
yax k'oj adj. + n. first image (**YAX k'o-jo**) 289
yax pas adj. + n. first dawn (**YAX PAS, YAX pa-{s}**) 289
Yax Pas n. name of sixteenth ruler of Copán in the Yax K'uk' Mo' Lineage
    (**YAX PAS, YAX pa-{s}**) 289
yaxun? poss. n. mother (his/her) (**ya-xu-na (?)**) 290
ye phonetic sign (**ye/YE**) 290, 291
ye pron. he/she/it; 3ʳᵈ pers. prevocalic pron. used with words beginning
    in *e* (**ye/YE**) 290, 291
ye pron. his/her/its; 3ʳᵈ pers. prevocalic poss. pron. used with words
    beginning in *e* (**ye/YE**) 290, 291
ye adj. revealed (**ye/YE**) 290, 291
yeb'al poss. n. stairway (his/her/its) (**ye-b'a-li**) 291
yeb'al poss. n. stairway of (**ye-b'a-li**) 291
yej adj. revealed (**ye/YE**) 290, 291
yemal adv. below (**ye-ma-la**) 292
yete' prep. with (**ye-te'**)..292, 293

yete' prep. phr. company of (in the) (**ye-te'**) 292, 293
yete'j prep. with (**ye-te'-je**) 293
yete'j prep. phr. company of (in the) (**ye-te'-je**) 293
yete' k'ab'a-il poss. n. namesake of (**ye-te' k'a-b'a-li**) 293
yi phonetic sign (**yi**) 294
yi pron. he/she/it; 3ʳᵈ pers. prevocalic pron. used with words beginning
    in *i* (**yi**) 294
yi pron. his/her/its; 3ʳᵈ pers. prevocalic poss. pron. used with words
    beginning in *i* (**yi**)..294
yich poss. n. surface [for writing] (its) (**yi-chi**) 294
yichnal prep. phr. company of (in the) (**yi-chi-NAL, yi-[chi]-NAL**) 295
yichnal prep. phr. before them (**yi-chi-NAL, yi-[chi]-NAL**)...................................295
yich'ak poss. n. jaguar claw (his/her/its) (**yi-ch'a-ki**) 295
yikatz poss. n. tribute (his/her/its) (**yi-ka-tzo**) 296
yilaj pass. v. phr. seen by he/she/it (was) (**yi-IL-la-ja, yi-la-ji**) 296
yilaj pass. v. phr. witnessed by he/she/it (was) (**yi-IL-la-ja, yi-la-ji**) 296
yilajiy pron. + intr. com. v. saw (he/she/it) (**yi-li-aj-ji-ya**) 297
yilajiy pron. + intr. com. v. witnessed (he/she/it) (**yi-li-aj-ji-ya**) 297
yilij pron. + intr. com. v. saw (he/she/it) (**yi-IL-ji**) 295, 296
yilij pron. + intr. com. v. witnessed (he/she/it) (**yi-IL-ji**) 295, 296
yitaj prep. with (**yi-ta, yi-ta-ji, yi-[ta]-ji**) 297
yitaj prep. phr. company of (in the), companion of (**yi-ta, yi-ta-ji, yi-[ta]-ji**) 297
yitz'in poss. n. younger brother (his/her) (**yi-tz'i-na**) 298
yo phonetic sign (**yo/YOP, yo**)..298
yo pron. he/she/it; 3ʳᵈ pers. prevocalic pron. used with words beginning
    in *o* (**yo/YOP, yo**) 298
yo pron. his/her/its; 3ʳᵈ pers. prevocalic poss. pron. used with words
    beginning in *o* (**yo/YOP, yo**) 298
yo-at adj. + n. scarred penis (his/its) (**yo-a-AT-ta, yo-AT, yo-AT-ta, yo-AT-ti**)......298, 299
yok poss. n. foot (his/her/its) (**yo-ko, yo-OK-ki**)..................................299, 300
yok k'in title of unknown meaning (**yo-OK [K'IN]-ni**) 300
yol poss. n. heart (his/her/its) (**yo-OL-la**) 300
yol tan poss. n. heart-center (his/her/its) (**yo-OL-la TAN-na**)...............................300
yop n. leaf (**yo/YOP**) 298
yop-at n. deity name or elite title
    (**YOP-a-AT-ta, YOP-AT, YOP-AT-ta, YOP-AT-ti (?)**) 302
yop-at n. name of the "founder" of the royal lineage of Yaxchilán (**YOP-AT**) 302
yotot poss. n. house (his/her/its) (**yo-OTOT, yo-OTOT-ti, yo-to-ti**).....................301, 303
yotot-ti prep. + poss. n. house (in his/her/its) (**yo-to-ta-ti**) 303
yoxat poss. n. scarred penis (his/its) (**yo-[xa]-AT-ti (?)**)....................................304
yu phonetic sign (**yu**) 304
yu pron. he/she/it; 3ʳᵈ pers. prevocalic pron. used with words beginning
    in *u* (**yu**)..304
yu pron. his/her/its; 3ʳᵈ pers. prevocalic poss. pron. used with words
    beginning in *u* (**yu**) 304
yub'te' n. tribute cloth (**yu-b'u-te'**) 304
yub'te' n. tribute mantle (**yu-b'u-te'**) 304
yuch'ab' poss. n. drinking vessel (his/her/its) (**yu-ch'a-b'a, yu-ch'a-b'i**) 304, 305
yunen poss. n. child (his); child [of father] (**yu-NE-{n}**) 305
yutal poss. n. beans (of cacao) (his/her/its) (**yu-ta-{l}, yu-ta-la**) 305, 306
yutal poss. adj. fruited (cacao) (his/her/its) (**yu-ta-{l}, yu-ta-la**) 305, 306
yutal poss. n. seeds (of cacao) (his/her/its) (**yu-ta-{l}, yu-ta-la**) 305, 306
yutzil poss. n. goodness (his/her/its) (**yu-tzi-li**) 306

ENGLISH INDEX

A

accede *joy*, tr. v. (**JOY, jo-JOY**) 117, 119
accede (did) *joyaj*, pass. v. (**jo-JOY-ja, JOY-ja**) 117, 119
acceded *joyajiy*, intr. com. v. (?) (**JOY-[ja]-ji-ya**) 120
acceded *chumwaniy*, pos. com. v. (**CHUM-[mu]-wa-ni-ya**) 68
acceded as ruler *joyaj ti ajawle*, pass. v. phr. (**jo-JOY-ja TI AJAW-le-{l}**) 117
acceded in lordship *joyaj ti ajawle*, pass. v. phr. (**jo-JOY-ja TI AJAW-le-{l}**) 117
acceded in lordship *chumwan ti ajawlel*, *ti*-construction v. phr.
    (**CHUM-wa-ni TI AJAW-le-{l}**) 68
accession *chum*, pos. v. (**CHUM, CHUM (?), CHUM-[mu]**) 66, 67
accession *chumlajiy*, pos. com. v. (**CHUM-la-ji-ya, CHUM-[mu]-la-ji-ya**) 67
accession house *k'al jun na*, n. (**K'AL JUN NA**) 146
administrator *aj sul*, title (**AJ su-lu**) 32
adorned (was) *nawaj*, pass. v. (**na-wa-ja**) 182
adorned (was) *tupaj*, pass. v. (**tu-pa-ja**) 239
again *xa*, adv. pref. (**xa/XA**) 275
already *xa*, adv. pref. (**xa/XA**) 275
all the gods (?) *olas k'u*, n. phr. (**o-la-si K'U**) 196
all the gods (?) *olis k'u*, n. phr. (**o-OL-si K'U**) 197
ancestor *mam*, relat. (**MAM**) 168
and then *i*, part. (**i/I**) 91
and then *wa*, part. (**wa/WA**) 261, 262
and then he/she saw/witnessed it *ilij*, part. + tr. v. (**I-IL-ji**) 93
Anterior Date Indicator *utiy*, intr. com. v. since it came to pass/since it
    happened/since it occurred (**u-ti-ya**) 257, 258
Anterior Date Indicator *utjiy*, intr. com. v. since it came to pass/since it
    happened/since it occurred (**u-ti-ji-ya**) 257
appear *tzak*, intr. v. (**tza-[ka]**) 241, 242
appear (make) *tzakaw*, tr. v. (**tza-[ka]-wa**) 242
appear (make god/divinity/holiness) *tzakaw ch'ul/tzakaw k'ul*, tr. v. phr.
    (**tza-[ka]-wa CH'UL/tza-[ka]-wa K'UL**) 242
arm *k'ab'*, n. (**k'a-[b'a]**) 142
armadillo *ib'ak'*, n. (**i-b'a-k'a**) 92
arrive *jul*, intr. v. (**JUL, ju-li, JUL-li**) 123, 124
arrive *tal*, intr. v. (**TAL, ta-li**) 226
arrived *juliy*, intr. com. v. (**ju-li-ya**) 125
arrived (was) *julaj*, pass. v. (**JUL-li-ja**) 124
arrived (they) *julob'*, intr. pl. v. (**ju-li-OB'**) 124
artist *itz'at*, n. (**ITZ'AT, i-tz'a-ta, ITZ'AT-ta**) 100, 101
artist *chuwen*, n. (**CHUWEN**) 69
ascend *nak*, intr. v. (**na-ku**) 180
ascend *tab'*, tr. v. (**TAB'**) 223
ascended *tab'iy*, intr. com. v. (**TAB'-[yi]**) 223, 224
as the . . . *tikil*, prep. phr. (**ti-ki-li**) 232
at *ta*, prep. (**ta/TA**) 221, 222
at *ti*, prep. (**ti/TI**) 231
auspices/authority (under the) *kab'ij*, relat. (**KAB'-ji**) 130
auspices/authority (under the) *kab'iy*, relat. (**KAB'-ya**) 131
axe (self-axe) *ch'akab'*, intr. v. (**CH'AK-ka-b'a**) 74, 75
axed (was) *ch'akaj*, pass. v. (**ch'a-ka-ja**) 74

B

back *pat*, n. body part (**PAT, pa-ti, PAT-ta**) 202, 203, 204
ball game *pitz*, n. (**pi-tzi**) 208

ball player *pitz*, n. (**pi-tzi**) 208
ball player *aj pitz*, title (**AJ pi-tzi**) 31
ball player *aj pitzlawal*, title (**AJ pi-tzi-la-wa-{l}**, **AJ pi-tzi-la-wa-la**) 31
banner *jasaw*, n. flap-staff (**ja-sa-wa**) 108
banner *lakam*, n. (**LAKAM, la-ka-ma**) 159
banner stone *lakam tun*, n. (**LAKAM TUN, LAKAM TUN-ni**) 160
bat *sutz'*, n. animal (**su-tz'i**) 219
bathe *yataj*, tr. v. (**ya-ta-ji**) 285
bathe *yatij*, tr. v. (**ya-ti-ji**) 285
bean, beans *b'ul*, n. (**b'u-la**) 46
beans (of cacao) (his/her/its) *yutal*, poss. n. component of the PSS
    (**yu-ta-{l}**, **yu-ta-la**)..305, 306
became the sky *och ta chaan/ok ta kaan*, tr. v. phr.
    (**OCH TA CHAAN-na/OK TA KAAN-na**) 195
before them *yichnal*, prep. phr. (**yi-chi-NAL, yi-[chi]-NAL**) 295
before you *awa ichnal*, declarative phr. (**AJ-wa-chi-NAL**) 33
being *b'a*, n. (**b'a/B'A**) 39
being *winik*, n. (**WINIK, wi-WINIK-ki**)...269, 271
beloved *jun tan*, adj. (**JUN TAN-na**) 127
below *yemal*, adv. (**ye-ma-la**) 292
betroth *mak*, tr. v. (**ma-ka**) 167
betroth *makax*, tr. v. (**ma-ka-xa**) 167
betrothed (was) *makaj*, pass. v. (**ma-ka-ja**) 167
big *lakam*, adj. (**LAKAM, la-ka-ma**) 159
big stone *lakam tun*, adj. + n. (**LAKAM TUN, LAKAM TUN-ni**) 160
bind *k'al*, tr. v. (**K'AL**)..144
bird *mut*, n. (**mu-ti**)..174
bird *mutul*, n. species unknown; main sign of the Tikal EG (**MUTUL**) 174, 175
bird *muwan*, n. mythological bird; type of sparrow hawk (?)
    (**mu-wa-ni, MUWAN-na, MUWAN-ni**) 175, 176
bird (mot-mot?) *xuk*, n. (**xu-[ku]**) 277
bird (mot-mot?) *xukpi*, n. (**xu-[ku]-pi**) 278
bird (quetzal) *k'uk'*, n. (**K'UK'**) 155
bird (with a) *ti'xukpi*, prep. phr.; preposition plus proper name of the
    dance-staff depicted at Yaxchilán (**ti xu-[ku]-pi**) 232
Bird Flower Lord *K'uy Nik Ajaw*, title (**k'u-yu NIK-ki AJAW**) 156
black *ek'*, adj. (**EK'**) 88, 89
black headband *ek' jun*, adj. + n. (**EK' JUN**) 89
black hole *ek' waynal*, adj. + n. (**EK' WAY-NAL**) 90
Black Hole Place *Ek' Waynal*, n. (**EK' WAY-NAL**) 90
blue *yax*, adj. (**YAX, ya-xa**) 286, 287
blue-green *yax*, adj. (**YAX, ya-xa**) 286, 287
bone *b'ak*, n. (**B'AK, b'a-ki**) 41
book *jun*, n. (**JUN, ju-na**) 125, 126
born (be) *si*, intr. v. (**SI**) 217
born *sij-ya*, intr. com. v. (**SI-ji-ya**) 217
born (was) *siyaj*, pass. v. (**SI-ya-ja**) 218
bound (was) *k'alaj*, pass. v. (**K'AL-ja**) 145
bound the deer hoof (was) *k'alaj mayij*, pass. v. phr. (**K'AL-ja MAY(?)-ji**) 145
bound the headband *k'al jun*, tr. v. phr. (**K'AL JUN-na**) 145
bound the white headband *k'al sak jun*, v. phr.
    (**K'AL SAK JUN, K'AL SAK ju-na**)..146
bound the white headband *k'al-jiy sak jun*, tr. v. phr. (**K'AL-ji-ya SAK JUN**) 145
bowl (ceramic) *jay*, n. (**ja-yi**) 109
bring down; war *jub'*, intr. v. (**JUB' (?)**) 121
bring down [a site/location/polity]; war *jub'-Emblem Glyph*, intr. v.
    (**JUB'-EMBLEM GLYPH**) 121

brother (older) *sukun*, n. (**su-ku-{n}**) 219
brother (younger) *itz'in*, n. (**i-tz'i-{n}**) 101
brother (his/her younger) *yitz'in*, poss. n. (**yi-tz'i-na**) 298
brother person (older) *sukun winik*, adj. + n. (**su-ku-{n} WINIK-ki**) 219
brother person (younger) *itz'in winik*, adj. + n. (**i-tz'i-{n} WINIK**) 101
brought down; war *jub'uy*, intr. v. (**ju-b'u-yi, JUB'(?)-yi, JUB'(?)-yi-ya**) 122
bullrush *pu*, n. (**pu/PU/PUJ**) 210
bullrush *puj*, n. (**pu/PU/PUJ**) 210
bundle *pi*, n. (**pi/PI/PIJ**) 207
bundle *pij*, n. (**pi-ji**) 208
bundle *piy*, n. (**PI-ya**) 209
burden *ikatz*, n. (**i-ka-tzi**) 93, 94
burden *ikitz*, n. (**i-ki-tzi**) 94
burden *kuch*, n. (**KUCH, ku-chu**) 138
burden stone *kuch tun*, adj. + n. (**KUCH TUN**) 138
buried (was) *mukaj*, pass. v. (**mu-ka-ja**) 173
burned *puliy*, intr. com. v. (**pu-lu-yi, PUL-[yi]**) 210
bury *muk*, tr. v. (**mu-ka**) 173

C

cacao *kakaw*, n. (**ka-ka-wa, ka-{ka}-wa**) 132
calabash tree *makom*, n. (**ma-ko-ma**) 168
came into being *aya?*, v. phr. (**a-ja-ya, a-ya, a-ya-ya**) 29, 37
came out *lok'iy*, intr. com. v. (**LOK-yi**) 163
came out from *lok'-ta*, intr. v. (**lo-k'u-ta**) 163
came to pass (since it) *utiy*, intr. com. v. Anterior Date Indicator (ADI)
    (**u-ti-ya**) 257, 258
came to pass (since it) *utjiy*, intr. com. v. Anterior Date Indicator (ADI)
    (**u-ti-ji-ya**) 257
capstone *mak*, n. (**ma-ka**) 167
captive *b'ak*, n. (**B'AK, b'a-ki**) 41
captor *chaan/kaan*, n. (**CHAAN/KAAN, CHAAN-na/KAAN-na**) 49, 50
captor *chan/kan*, n. (**cha-CHAN/ka-KAN, CHAN/KAN, cha-nu/ka-nu**) 52, 57, 58
capture *chuk*, tr. v. (**chu-ka, chu-[ku]**) 65
captured (was) *chukaj*, pass. v. (**chu-ka-ja, chu-[ku]-ja**) 65, 66
captured (was) *chukjiy*, intr. com. v. (**chu-[ku]-ji-ya**) 66
cargo *kuch*, n. (**KUCH, ku-chu**) 138
carried (was) *kuch-taj*, pass. v. (**KUCH-ta-ja**) 138
carry *kuch*, n. (**KUCH, ku-chu**) 138
carve *uxul*, intr. v. (**u-xu-[lu]**) 260
carving *uxul*, intr. v. (**u-xu-[lu]**) 260
cattail reed *pu*, n. (**pu/PU/PUJ**) 210
cattail reed *puj*, n. (**pu/PU/PUJ**) 210
cave *ch'en*, n. (**CH'EN, CH'EN-na**) 77, 78
center *ol*, n. (**OL**) 196
center (in the) (?) *chatan*, prep. phr. (**cha-TAN-na**) 58
center of (in the) *tan*, prep. phr. (**TAN, TAN-na**) 226, 228
centipede *chapat*, n. (**CHAPAT**) 58
Chaak *Chaak*, n. deity name, the Maya Rain God
    (**CHAAK, CHAAK-ki, cha-ki**) 48, 49, 53, 54
Chak Xib' Chaak *Chak Xib' Chaak*, n. deity name (**CHAK XIB' cha-ki**) 54
character *wojol*, n. (**wo-jo-li**) 272
chat name *chat k'ab'a*, n. phr. (**cha-te' K'AB'A**) 58
cherished *jun tan*, adj. (**JUN TAN-na**) 127
child (her) *yach'am*, poss. n. literally "her harvest"
    (**ya-CH'AM, ya-CH'AM-ma**) 282, 283
child (her) *yal*, poss. n. literally "her harvest" (**ya-AL**) 281, 282

child (his) *yunen*, poss. n. child of father (**yu-NE-{n}**) 305
child [of father] *unen*, n. (**u-ne-{n}**) 256
chocolate *kakaw*, n. (**ka-ka-wa, ka-{ka}-wa**)..132
choose *paj*, tr. v. (**pa/PAJ**) 199
chop *ch'ak*, tr. v. (**CH'AK, CH'AK-ka**) 74
chop (with a blow) *ch'ak*, tr. v. (**CH'AK, CH'AK-ka**) 74
chopped (was) *ch'akaj*, pass. v. (**ch'a-ka-ja**) 74
claw, jaguar *ich'ak*, n. (**ICH'AK, ICH'AK-ki**) 92, 93
claw, jaguar *mol*, n. (**MOL (?)**) 171
claw, jaguar (his/her/its) *yich'ak*, poss. n. (**yi-ch'a-ki**) 295
claw stone, jaguar *ich'ak tun*, n. (**ICH'AK TUN-ni**) 93
claw stone, jaguar *mol tun*, n. (**MOL (?) TUN-ni**) 171
clay *luk'*, n. (**lu-k'u**)..164
close *k'al*, tr. v. (**K'AL**) 144
close *mak*, tr. v. (**ma-ka**) 167
close *makax*, tr. v. (**ma-ka-xa**) 167
closed (was) *k'alaj*, pass. v. (**K'AL-ja**) 145
closed (was) *makaj*, pass. v. (**ma-ka-ja**) 167
closed the first stone *yax k'al tun*, v. phr. (**YAX K'AL TUN-ni**) 288
closed the first *tun yax k'al tun*, v. phr. (**YAX K'AL TUN-ni**) 288
closed the headband *k'al jun*, tr. v. (**K'AL JUN-na**) 145
closed the stone (was) *k'al tun*, pass. v. phr. (**K'AL TUN-ni**) 146
closed the white headband *k'al-jiy sak jun*, tr. v. phr. (**K'AL-ji-ya SAK JUN**) 145
closed the white headband *k'al sak jun*, v. phr.
    (**K'AL SAK JUN, K'AL SAK ju-na**)..146
closing *k'al*, tr. incom. v. (**k'a-li**) 144
clothes *b'uk*, pl. n. (**b'u-ku**)..45
cloud *muyal*, n. (**MUYAL**) 176
cloud *tok*, n. (**to-ko**)..233
cloud center *tok tan*, n. (**to-ko-TAN-na**)..234
Cloud Center Lord *Tok Tan Ajaw*, title (**to-ko TAN AJAW**) 234
Cloud Center Person *Tok Tan Winik*, title (**to-ko TAN WINIK-ki**) 234
co-essence *way*, n. *nawal* (**WAY, WAY-ya**) 266, 267
co-essence *wayab'*, n. (**wa-WAY-{a}-[b'i]**) 264
come *tal*, intr. v. (**TAL, ta-li**) 226
come (have) *takaj*, pass. v. (**ta-ki-ja**) 225
come (was) *takaj*, pass. v. (**ta-ki-ja**) 225
come to pass *ut*, intr. v. (**u-ti**) 257
come to pass (it will) *utom*, intr. incom. v. Future Date Indicator (FDI)
    (**u-to-ma**) 258, 259
coming back (someone) *pakax*, v. phr. (**pa-ka-xa**) 201
companions (his/her/its) *yataj*, poss. pl. n. (**ya-ta-ji**) 285
company of (in the) *yete'*, prep. phr. (**ye-te'**) 292, 293
company of (in the) *yete'j*, prep. phr. (**ye-te'-je**) 293
company of (in the) *yichnal*, prep. phr. (**yi-chi-NAL, yi-[chi]-NAL**) 295
company of (in the) *yitaj*, prep. phr. (**yi-ta, yi-ta-ji, yi-[ta]-ji**) 297
completion *k'al*, n. (**K'AL**) 144
conjure *tzak*, tr. v. (**tza-[ka]**) 241, 242
conjure *tzakaw*, tr. v. (**tza-[ka]-wa**) 242
conjure god/divinity/holiness *tzakaw ch'ul/tzakaw k'ul*, tr. v. phr.
    (**tza-[ka]-wa CH'UL/tza-[ka]-wa K'UL**) 242
conquer *nak*, tr. v. (**na-ku**) 180
Corn God *Jun Nal Ye*, n. Maize God (**JUN NAL YE**) 127
corn gruel *sa*, n. *atole* (**sa/SA**)..211
corn gruel *ul*, n. *atole* (**u-lu**) 256
count *tz'ak*, tr. v. (**TZ'AK**) 247
count *tz'ak b'ul*, tr. v. (**TZ'AK b'u-li**) 248
count *xok*, n. (**xo-ki**) 277

counted (was) *tz'akaj*, pass. v. (**TZ'AK-aj**) 247
Count of Captives *aj-X-b'ak*, title (**AJ-X-B'AK**) 34
count of years *tzik ja'ab'?/tzik ab'?*, intr. v. phr. the Initial Series
    Introductory Glyph (**tzi-ka JA'AB' (?)/tzi-ka AB' (?)**) 243
cover *mak*, tr. v. (**ma-ka**) 167
cover *mak*, n. (**ma-ka**) 167
cover *makax*, tr. v. (**ma-ka-xa**) 167
covered (was) *makaj*, pass. v. (**ma-ka-ja**) 167
crocodile *ayin*, n. (**AYIN**) 37
crown *nak*, n. (**na-ku**) 180
cut up (was) *susaj*, pass. v. (**su-sa-ja**) 219

D

dance *ak'ot*, n. (**ak'/AK'OT, AK'OT-ta, a-AK'OT-ta**) 26, 35
dance *ak'ot*, tr. v. (**ak'/AK'OT, AK'OT-ta**) 35
danced (was) *ak'otaj*, pass. v. (**AK'OT-ta-ja**) 35
dance object *chak'at*, n. name of the "basket staff" used in dances at
    Yaxchilán (**CHAK K'AT**) 54
dance object *xuk*, n. proper name of dance staff used at
    Yaxchilán (**xu-[ku]**) 277
dance object *xukpi*, n. proper name of dance staff used at
    Yaxchilán (**xu-[ku]-pi**) 278
darkness *ak'ab'*, n. (**AK'AB'**) 35
dawn *pas/pasaj*, n. (**PAS/PASAJ, pa-sa**) 202
dawn (first) *yax pas*, adj. + n. (**YAX PAS, YAX pa-{s}**) 289
day *k'in*, n. (**K'IN, K'IN (?), K'IN-ni**) 151, 152, 153
day *lat*, n. (**la-ta**) 161
days later *-lat*, temp. suf. (**la-ta**) 161
death *cham*, intr. v. (**CHAM, CHAM-mi**) 55, 56
death *chamil*, intr. v. (**CHAM-li**) 56
death *k'ay u sak nik ik'il/ch'ay u sak nich ik'il*, intr. incom. v. phr.
    (**k'a-yi U SAK NIK IK'-li/ch'a-yi U SAK NICH IK'-li**) 151
death *och b'i*, tr. v. phr. (**OCH B'I**) 192
death *och b'i-aj*, pass. v. phr. (**OCH B'I-ja**) 192
death *och b'ij-jiy*, tr. v. phr. (**OCH B'I-ji-ji-ya**) 193
death *och ja'*, tr. v. phr. (**OCH JA'**) 194
death *och ja'-aj*, pass. v. phr. "was entered the water" (**OCH JA'-ja**) 194
decapitate *ch'ak*, tr. v. (**CH'AK, CH'AK-ka**) 74
decapitate (self-decapitate) *ch'akab'*, intr. v. (**CH'AK-ka-b'a**) 74
decapitated (was) *ch'akaj*, pass. v. (**ch'a-ka-ja**) 74
dedication *och k'ak'*, tr. v. phr. (**OCH-chi K'AK', OCH K'AK'**) 193, 194
deer (white-tailed) *chij*, n. (**CHIJ**) 61
deer hoof *may?*, n. (**MAY (?)**) 169
deity name *yo-at*, n. (**YOP-AT-ti (?)**) 302
deity name *yop-at*, n. (**YOP a-AT-ta, YOP AT, YOP AT-ta**) 302
descend *em*, intr. v. (**EM**) 90
destroy *jom*, tr. v. (**JOM**) 118, 119
destroy *sat*, tr. v. (**sa-ta**) 216
destroyed *satay*, intr. com. v. (**sa-ta-yi**) 216
diadem *nak*, n. (**na-ku**) 180
did it *kab'ij*, tr. v. (**KAB'-ji**) 130
did it *kab'iy*, tr. v. (**KAB'-ya**) 131
did it *kab'jiy*, tr. v. (**KAB'-ji-ya**) 131
dies *chamiy*, intr. incom. v. (**CHAM-mi-ya**) 56
divine *ch'ul/k'ul, ch'ujul/k'ujul*, adj. (**CH'UL/K'UL (CH'UJUL/K'UJUL),
    CH'UL-lu/K'UL-lu (CH'UJUL-lu/K'UJUL-lu)**) 80, 81, 82, 84
divine *k'u*, adj. (**k'u/K'U**) 154, 155

Divine Cloud Center Lord *Ch'ul Tok Tan Ajaw/K'ul Tok Tan Ajaw,*
    Ch'ujul Tok Tan Ajaw/K'ujul Tok Tan Ajaw, title
    (**CH'UL to-{k} TAN AJAW/K'UL to-{k} TAN AJAW**
    (**CH'UJUL to-{k} TAN AJAW/K'UJUL to-{k} TAN AJAW**)) 85
divine flint *ch'ul tok'/k'ul tok', ch'ujul tok'/k'ujul tok',* adj. + n.
    (**CH'UL-lu to-k'a/K'UL-lu to-k'a**
    (**CH'UJUL-lu to-k'a/K'UJUL-lu to-k'a**)) 85
divine lord *ch'ul ajaw/k'ul ajaw, ch'ujul ajaw/k'ujul ajaw,* title
    (**CH'UL AJAW-wa/K'UL AJAW-wa**
    (**CH'UJUL AJAW-wa/K'UJUL AJAW-wa**)) 83
divine man *ch'ul winik/k'ul winik, ch'ujul winik/k'ujul winik,* adj. + n.
    (**CH'UL WINIK-ki/K'UL WINIK-ki**
    (**CH'UJUL WINIK-ki/K'UJUL WINIK-ki**)) 85
divine name *ch'ul k'ab'a/k'ul k'ab'a,* adj. + n. (**CH'UL K'AB'A/K'UL K'AB'A**) 84
divine person *ch'ul winik/k'ul winik, ch'ujul winik/k'ujul winik,* adj. + n.
    (**CH'UL WINIK-ki/K'UL WINIK-ki (CH'UJUL WINIK-ki/**
    K'UJUL WINIK-ki)) 85
divine woman *ch'ul ixik/k'ul ixik, ch'ujul ixik/k'ujul ixik,* adj. + n
    (**CH'UL IXIK-ki/K'UL IXIK-ki, CH'UJUL IXIK-ki/K'UJUL IXIK-ki**) 84
divinity *k'uj,* n. (**k'u-ju**) 155
divinity (in his/her/its) *tuk'ul,* prep. phr. (**TU K'U-li**) 236
divinity title *matawil,* title (**ma-ta-wi-la**) 168
dog *tzul,* n. (**tzu-lu**) 244
dog *tz'i,* n. (**TZ'I, tz'i-i**) 250, 252
doing (his/her/its) *u b'a,* poss. n. (**U B'A**) 255, 256
doing of (the) *u b'a,* poss. n. (**U B'A**) 255, 256
doorway *pasil,* n. (**pa-si-li**) 202
doubled over (was) *paklaj,* pos. v. (**pa-ka-la-ja**) 200
dove *mukuy,* n. (**mu-ku-yi**) 174
dove *tukun,* n. (**tu-ku-nu**) 236
dreamer *wayab',* n. (**wa-WAY-{a}-[b'i]**) 264
dreaming place (in his/her/its) *tu wayb'il,* prep. phr. (**TU WAY-[b'i]-li**) 239
drink *uch',* n. (**UCH'**) 256
drink *uch',* intr. v. (**UCH'**) 256
drink (type of) *ch'ajalte',* n. (**ch'a-ja-{l}-te'**) 72
drinking cup/vessel (his/her/its) *yuch'ab',* n. (**yu-ch'a-b'a, yu-ch'a-b'i**) 304, 305
dripper *ch'ajom,* title (**ch'a-jo-ma, ch'a-JOM**) 73
drop of water, urine, or other liquid *ch'a,* n. (**ch'a/CH'A**) 71
drop of water, urine, or other liquid *ch'aj,* n. (**ch'a-ji**) 73
drops, droplet *ch'a,* n. (**ch'a/CH'A**) 71
drops, droplet *ch'aj,* n. (**ch'a-ji**) 73
dwarf *ch'at,* n. (**ch'a-ti**) 76

E

earflare *tup,* n. (**tu-pa**) 238
ear-flared (was) *tupaj,* pass. v. (**tu-pa-ja**) 239
earlier today *samiy,* temp. phr. (**sa-mi-ya**) 216
earlier today *sajmiy,* temp. phr. (**sa-aj-mi-ya**) 212
earth *kab',* n. (**KAB'**) 129, 130
earth *lum,* n. (**lu-mi**) 164
earthly gods *kab'al k'u,* adj. + pl. n. (**KAB'-la K'U**) 131
east *lak'in,* n. cardinal direction (**LAK-K'IN-ni**) 160
eat *we',* intr. v. (**we'/WE'**) 267, 268
eaten (was) *k'uxaj,* pass. v. (**k'u-xa-ja**) 156
eating of (his/her/its) *u we'y,* tr. incom. v. phr. (**U we'-ya**) 259
eight *waxak,* n. cardinal number (**WAXAK**) 265

Eighteen [Snake/Centipede] Heads *Waxaklajun U B'a*, n. proper name of
   the scaled Vision Serpent/Centipede thought to derive from
   Teotihuacan imagery (**WAXAKLAJUN U B'A**) 265
Eighteen [Snake/Centipede] Heads *Waxaklajun U B'a*, n. proper name of
   the 13th ruler of Copán in the Yax K'uk' Mo' lineage
   (**WAXAKLAJUN U B'A**)..265
Eight First Chaak *Waxak Na Chaak*, n. proper name of God I (GI) of
   the Palenque Triad (**WAXAK NA CHAAK**) 265
elevate *nak*, intr. v. (**na-ku**) 180
eleven *b'uluk*, n. cardinal number (**B'ULUK**) 46
emerge *joy*, tr. v. (**JOY, jo-JOY**)...117, 119
emerge *joyajiy*, tr. v. (**JOY-[ja]-ji-ya**) 120
emerged *lok'iy*, intr. com. v. (**LOK'-yi**) 163
emerged from *lok'-ta*, intr. v. (**lo-k'u-ta**)...163
emergent (was) *joyaj*, pass. v. (**jo-JOY-ja, JOY-ja**) 117, 119
end *jil*, intr. v. (**ji-li**) 115
end *jom*, tr. v. (**JOM**)..118, 119
end *laj*, tr. v. (**la-ja**) 157
end *tzutz*, tr. v. (**TZUTZ**) 244, 245
ended *tzutziy*, intr. com. v. (**TZUTZ-yi**) 246
ended (was) *tzutzaj*, pass. v. (**TZUTZ-ja, tzu-tzu-ja**) 245
engraving *jul*, n. (**JUL**)...123
enter *och*, intr. v. (**OCH, OCH-chi**) 191, 192, 193
entered (was) *ochaj*, pass. v. (**OCH-ja/OK-ja**) 194
entered into the sky *och ta chaan/ok ta kaan*, tr. v. phr.
   (**OCH TA CHAAN-na/OK TA KAAN-na**) 195
entered the fire *och k'ak*, tr. v. phr. dedication (**OCH-chi K'AK', OCH K'AK'**) 193, 194
entered the road *och b'i*, tr. v. phr. (**OCH B'I**) 192
entered the road (was) *och b'i-aj*, pass. v. phr. (**OCH B'I-ja**) 192
entered the tree *och te'/ok te'*, tr. v. phr. (**OCH TE'/OK TE'**) 195
entered the water *och ja'*, tr. v. phr. death (**OCH JA'**)..............................194
entered the water (was) *och ja'-aj*, pass. v. phr. (**OCH JA'-ja**) 194
enter-treeship (at the) *ta ochlel*, prep. phr. (**TA OCH-le-{l}**) 228
entrance *way*, n. (**WAY, WAY-ya**) 266, 267
erect *wa*, pos. v. (**wa/WA**)..262
erected (something) *wak*, n. (**WAK**) 262, 263
erected sky *wak chaan/wak kaan*, n. (**WAK-ki CHAAN/WAK-ki KAAN**) 263
Erected Sky Lord *Wak Chaan Ajaw/Wak Kaan Ajaw*, title
   (**WAK CHAAN-na AJAW/WAK KAAN-na AJAW**) 263
erected thing *wawaan*, title (**wa-wa-aj-ni**) 264
escaped *lok'iy*, intr. com. v. (**LOK'-yi**) 163
essence *itz'*, n. (**ITZ'**) 99
expire *tzutz*, tr. v. (**TZUTZ**) 244, 245
expired *tzutziy*, intr. com. v. (**TZUTZ-yi**)..246
expired (was) *tzutzaj*, pass. v. (**TZUTZ-ja, tzu-tzu-ja**)................................245

F

face *nak*, n. (**na-ku**) 180
faced down (was) *paklaj*, pos. v. (**pa-ka-la-ja**) 200
father *chit*, n. (**CHIT, CHIT-ti**) 62, 63
fawn (?) *may?*, n. (**MAY (?)**)...169
female *ix*, fem. agentive pref. (**IX/IXIK**) 103
female *ixik*, fem. agentive pref. (**IX/IXIK**) 103
fiery water place *k'ak' naab'*, adj. + n. (**K'AK' NAAB'**) 144
fills up *najiy*, tr. incom. v. (**na-ja-yi**)..180
finish *laj*, tr. v. (**la-ja**) 157
fire *k'ak'*, n. (**K'AK', k'a-K'AK', K'AK'-k'a**) 143

fire [and] smoke *k'ak' b'utz'*, n. (**K'AK'-k'a B'UTZ'-tz'i**) 144
fire-entered *och k'ak'*, tr. v. phr. dedication (**OCH-chi K'AK', OCH K'AK'**) 193, 194
Fire Lord *Yajaw K'ak'*, poss. n. title (**ya-AJAW K'AK'**) 280
fire sea *k'ak' naab'*, adj. + n. (**K'AK' NAAB'**) 144
first *b'a*, adj. (**b'a/B'A**) 39
first *na*, adj. ordinal number (**na/NA/NAJ**)................................177, 178
first *naj*, adj. ordinal number (**na/NA/NAJ**) 177, 178
first *yax*, adj. (**YAX, ya-xa**) 286, 287
first born *b'a yal*, title (**B'A YAL**) 43
first dawn *yax pas*, adj. + n. (**YAX PAS, YAX pa-{s}**)...............................289
First Dawn *Yax Pas*, adj. + n. name of the sixteenth ruler of Copán in the
    Yax K'uk' Mo' lineage (**YAX PAS, YAX pa-{s}**)......................................289
first father (?) *yax chit*, adj. + n. (**YAX CHIT**)...................................287
first harvest *yax ch'am*, adj. + n. (**YAX CH'AM, YAX ch'a-CH'AM**) 288
first harvesting [of] K'awil *yax ch'am K'awil*, v. phr. (**YAX CH'AM K'AWIL**) 288
first image *yax k'oj*, adj. + n. (**YAX k'o-jo**)......................................289
first lineage member *b'a ch'ok*, title (**B'A ch'o-ko**)................................40
first lord *b'a ajaw*, title (**B'A AJAW**) 40
first receiving [of] K'awil *yax ch'am K'awil*, v. phr. (**YAX CH'AM K'AWIL**) 288
first sculptor *b'a uxul*, title (**B'A u-xu-[lu]**) 42
first sprout *b'a ch'ok*, title (**B'A ch'o-ko**)......................................40
first young person *b'a ch'ok*, title (**B'A ch'o-ko**)................................40
first youth *b'a ch'ok*, title (**B'A ch'o-ko**) 40
fish *chay/kay*, n. (**CHAY/KAY, cha-ya**)..59
five *jo*, n. cardinal number (**JO**) 116, 117
flap-staff *jasaw*, n. (**ja-sa-wa**)..108
flies *k'ay/ch'ay*, intr. incom. v. (**k'a-yi/ch'a-yi**) 150
flint *tok'*, n. (**TOK', to-k'a**) 234, 235
flint [and] shield *tok' pakal*, n. (**to-k'a pa-ka-la, TOK' PAKAL**) 235
flower *janaab'*, n. (**JANAAB', ja-na-b'i**) 106, 107
flower *nich*, n. (**NICH/NIK, NICH-li/NIK-li**) 183, 184
flower *nichil*, n. (**NICH-li/NIK-li**) 184
flower *nichim*, n. (**ni-chi-{m}**) 183
flower *nik*, n. (**NICH/NIK, NICH-li/NIK-li**) 183, 184
flower *nikil*, n. (**NICH-li/NIK-li**) 184
flower *nikte'*, n. possibly the mayflower (**NIKTE', NIKTE'-te'**) 184, 185
flower nectar *itz'*, n. (**ITZ'**) 99
flower-shield *janaab' pakal*, n. (**[JANAAB'] PAKAL, JANAAB' [PAKAL]-la**) 107
Flower-Shield *janaab' pakal*, n. name of several Late Classic kings of
    Palenque (**[JANAAB'] PAKAL, JANAAB' [PAKAL]-la**) 107
foot *och/ok*, n. (**OCH/OK**) 192
foot (his/her/its) *yok*, n. (**yo-ko, yo-OK-ki**) 299, 300
foot of (at the) *ta ochlel*, prep. phr. (**TA OCH-le-{l}**) 228
form *pat*, tr. v. (**PAT, pa-ti, PAT-ta**)...............................202, 203, 204
formed *pat b'uj*, tr. com. v. (**PAT-ta-b'u-ji**)...................................205
formed *pat b'uy*, tr. com. v. (**PAT-b'u-ya**) 204
formed *patlaj*, pos. com. v. (**PAT-[la]-ja**)......................................204
formed *patwan*, com. v. (**PAT-ta-wa-ni, PAT-wa-ni**) 205
formed in clay *pak'ajiy*, intr. com. v. phr. (**pa-k'a-ji-ya**) 201
form in clay *pak'*, tr. v. (**pa-k'a**) 201
four *chan/kan*, n. cardinal number (**CHAN/KAN**)................................56, 57
fresh *tzi*, adj. (**tzi/TZI**)..243
from *ti*, prep. (**ti/TI**) 231
front of (in) *tan*, prep. phr. (**TAN, TAN-na**) 226, 228
front of the cave (in) *tan ch'en*, double loc. phr. (**TAN CH'EN-na**) 227
front of the cave Three Hill Water (in) *tan ch'en ox witzaj*,
    double loc. phr. + n. (**TAN CH'EN OX WITZ-aj**) 227
fruited (for his/her) *ta yutal*, prep. phr. (**TA yu-ta-{l}**) 228

fruited (his/her/its) *yutal*, poss. adj. component of the PSS
(**yu-ta-{l}, yu-ta-la**)..305, 306
Future Date Indicator (FDI) *utom*, intr. incom. v. it will happen, it will occur,
it will come to pass (**u-to-ma**) 258, 259

G

get drunk on *tikal*, tr. v. (**ti-ka-la**) 232
give *tz'aj*, tr. v. (**tz'a/TZ'A**)...247
give *wa yak'aw*, tr. v. (**wa-ya-k'a-wa**) 266
giving (his/her/its) *yak'*, poss. n. (**ya-k'u**) 284
giving (his/her/its) *yak'aw*, poss. n. (**ya-k'a-wa**)............................283, 284
glutton *sitz winik*, n. (**si-tzi WINIK-ki**)..218
glyph *wojol*, n. (**wo-jo-li**) 272
go *xan*, intr. v. (**XAN-na, xa-XAN-na**) 275, 276
god *k'u*, n. (**k'u/K'U**) 155
god *k'uj*, n. (**k'u-ju**)...155
go down *kojoy*, intr. v. (**ko-jo-yi**) 137
gods, earthly *kab'al k'u*, adj. + n. (**KAB'-la K'U**) 131
goes *b'ixan*, incom. irreg. v. (**B'IXAN-na**)..44
goodness (his/her/its) *yutzil*, poss. n. (**yu-tzi-li**) 306
go up *tab'*, tr. v. (**TAB'**) 223
grab *tzak*, tr. v. (**tza-[ka]**) 241, 242
grab *tzakaw*, tr. v. (**tza-[ka]-wa**) 242
grandfather *mam*, n. (**MAM**) 168
grandson (his/her) *yab'il*, poss. n. (**ya-b'i-li**) 282
grasp *tzak*, tr. v. (**tza-[ka]**) 241, 242
grasp *tzakaw*, tr. v. (**tza-[ka]-wa**)..242
great *chak*, adj. (**CHAK**) 52, 53
great *lakam*, adj. (**LAKAM, la-ka-ma**) 159
great *noj*, adj. (**NOJ**) 185, 186
great *nuk*, adj. (**nu-ku**) 188
great holy lord *chak ch'ul ajaw/chak k'ul ajaw*, title (**CHAK CH'UL AJAW/
CHAK K'UL AJAW**) 53
great star *chak ek'*, n. (**CHAK EK'**) 53
great stone *lakam tun*, adj. + n. (**LAKAM TUN, LAKAM TUN-ni**)............160
great water *lakam ja'*, adj. + n. (**LAKAM JA'**) 160
green *yax*, adj. (**YAX, ya-xa**) 286, 287
grind *k'uxajiy*, tr. v. (**k'u-xa-ji-ya**) 156
ground (was) *k'uxaj*, pass. v. (**k'u-xa-ja**) 156
gruel (corn) *sa*, n. *atole* (**sa/SA**) 211
gruel (corn) *ul*, n. *atole* (**u-lu**) 256
guardians *kokonob'*, pl. n. (**ko-ko-no-OB'**) 137

H

half diminished *tan lam*, adj. "half period" (**[TAN] LAM**) 227
half diminished (was) *tan lamaj*, pass. v. "half period" (**[TAN] LAM-ja**) 227
hand *k'ab'*, n. (**K'AB', ka-[b'a]**) 142
happen *ut*, intr. v. (**u-ti**) 257
happen (it will) *utom*, intr. incom. v. Future Date Indicator (FDI) (**u-to-ma**) 258, 259
happened (since it) *utiy*, intr. com. v. Anterior Date Indicator (ADI)
(**u-ti-ya**) 257, 258
happened (since it) *utjiy*, intr. com. v. Anterior Date Indicator (ADI)
(**u-ti-ji-ya**) 257
happened (then it) *i-ut*, part. + intr. v. Posterior Date Indicator (PDI) (**i-u-ti**) 102
happened at (it) *utiy*, prep. phr. (**u-ti-ya**) 257, 258
happened at (it) *utjiy*, prep. phr. (**u-ti-ji-ya**) 257

harvest *ch'am*, tr. v. (**CH'AM, CH'AM-ma**) 75, 76
harvest *ch'am*, n. (**CH'AM, CH'AM-ma**) 75, 76
harvest K'awil *ch'am K'awil*, tr. v.
   (**CH'AM K'AWIL-la, CH'AM-ma K'AWIL-la**).....................................75, 76
he *aj*, masc. agentive pron. (**a/AJ**) 25, 26
he *u*, 3rd pers. pron. (**u/U**) 253, 254, 255
he *ya*, 3rd pers. prev. pron. used with words beginning in *a* (**ya**) 279, 280
he *ye*, 3rd pers. prev. pron. used with words beginning in *e* (**ye/YE**) 290, 291
he *yi*, 3rd pers. prev. pron. used with words beginning in *i* (**yi**) 294
he *yo*, 3rd pers. prev. pron. used with words beginning in *o* (**yo/YOP, yo**) 298
he *yu*, 3rd pers. prev. pron. used with words beginning in *u* (**yu**) 304
head *b'a*, n. (**b'a/B'A**) 39
head *jol*, n. (**JOL, JOL-lo**).....................................118
headband *junal*, n. (**ju-na-la**) 126
headdress *kojaw*, n. (**KOJAW, KOJAW-wa, ko-ja-wa**) 136, 137
headdress *pixom*, n. (**pi-xo-ma**) 209
heart *ol*, n. (**OL**) 196
heart *wol*, n. (**wo-la**) 273
heart (his/her/its) *yol*, poss. n. (**yo-OL-la**) 300
heart-center (his/her/its) *yol tan*, poss. n. (**yo-OL-la TAN-na**) 300
heavenly *chaanal/kaanal*, adj. (**CHAAN-na-NAL/KAAN-na-NAL**) 51
heavenly god, earthly god *ch'ul chaan ch'ul kab'/k'ul kaan k'ul kab', ch'ujul*
   chaan ch'ujul kab'/k'ujul kaan k'ujul kab', tit. + phr.
   (**CH'UL CHAAN CH'UL KAB'/K'UL KAAN K'UL KAB'**
   (**CH'UJUL CHAAN CH'UJUL KAB'/K'UJUL KAAN K'UJUL KAB'**)).................83
heavenly gods *chaanal k'u/kaanal k'u*, adj. + pl. n.
   (**[CHAAN]-NAL K'U/[KAAN]-NAL K'U**) 51
heavenly gods *chaan ch'ul/kaan k'ul*, adj. + pl. n.
   (**CHAAN-na CH'UL/KAAN-na K'UL**) 51
helmet *kojaw*, n. (**KOJAW, KOJAW-wa, ko-ja-wa**) 136, 137
helmet (war) *waxaklajun u b'a*, n. (**WAXAKLAJUN U B'A**) 265
he of *aj*, masc. agentive pron. (**a/AJ**) 25, 26
he of the ball game *aj pitzlawal* title, ballplayer
   (**AJ pi-tzi-la-wa-{l}, AJ pi-tzi-la-wa-la**).....................................31
he of the burnishing/
   scratching *aj uxul*, title (**AJ u-xu-[lu]**) 32
he of the sacred books *aj k'ujun*, title (**AJ k'u-{JUN}-na, AJ k'u-JUN-na**) 30
he of the sculpture *aj uxul*, title (**AJ u-xu-[lu]**) 32
he of the water *aj naab'*, title (**AJ na-b'i**) 30
he of the writing *aj tz'ib'*, title (**AJ tz'i-b'a**) 32
he of X-number of captives *aj-X-b'ak*, title; see Count of Captives
   (**AJ-X-B'AK**) 34
hers *u*, 3rd pers. poss. pron. (**u/U**) 253, 254, 255
her *ya*, 3rd pers. prev. poss. pron. used with words beginning in *a* (**ya**) 279, 280
her *ye*, 3rd pers. prev. poss. pron. used with words beginning in *e* (**ye/YE**) 290, 291
her *yi*, 3rd pers. prev. poss. pron. used with words beginning in *i* (**yi**) 294
her *yo*, 3rd pers. prev. poss. pron. used with words beginning in *o*
   (**yo/YOP, yo**) 298
her *yu*, 3rd pers. prev. poss. pron. used with words beginning in *u* (**yu**) 304
he the administrator *aj sul*, title (**AJ su-lu**) 32
he the ballplayer *aj pitz*, title (**AJ pi-tzi**) 31
he the leader *aj payal*, title (**AJ pa-ya-la**).....................................31
he the youthful *aj pitz*, title (**AJ pi-tzi**) 31
hill *witz*, n. (**WITZ, wi-tzi**) 270
his *u*, 3rd pers. poss. pron. (**u/U**).....................................253, 254, 255
his *ya*, 3rd pers. prev. poss. pron. used with words beginning in *a* (**ya**) 279, 280
his *ye*, 3rd pers. prev. poss. pron. used with words beginning in *e* (**ye/YE**).........290, 291
his *yi*, 3rd pers. prev. poss. pron. used with words beginning in *i* (**yi**) 294

his *yo*, 3rd pers. prev. poss. pron. used with words beginning in *o* (**yo/YOP, yo**) 298
his *yu*, 3rd pers. prev. poss. pron. used with words beginning in *u* (**yu**) 304
hoist *pak'*, tr. v. (**pa-k'a**) 201
hoist *tz'ap*, pos. v. (**tz'a-[pa]**) 248
hoist *tz'apwa*, pos. v. (**tz'a-[pa]-wa**) 249
hoisted *pak'ajiy*, intr. com. v. (**pa-k'a-ji-ya**) 201
hoisted *tz'apajiy*, intr. com. v. (**tz'a-pa-ji-ya**) 249
hoisted (something) *wak*, n. (**WAK**) 262, 263
hoisted (was) *tz'apaj*, pass. v. (**tz'a-pa-ja, tz'a-[pa]-ja**) 248, 249
hoisted sky *wak chaan/wak kaan*, n. (**WAK-ki CHAAN/WAK-ki KAAN**)....................263
Hoisted Sky Lord *Wak Chaan Ajaw/Wak Kaan Ajaw*, title
    (**WAK CHAAN-na AJAW/WAK KAAN-na AJAW**) 263
hole *way*, n. (**WAY, WAY-ya**) 266, 267
holy *ch'ul/k'ul, ch'ujul/k'ujul*, adj. (**CH'UL/K'UL (CH'UJUL/K'UJUL),
    CH'UL-lu/K'UL-lu (CH'UJUL-lu/K'UJUL-lu)**) 80, 81, 82, 84
Holy Cloud Center Lord *Ch'ul Tok Tan Ajaw/K'ul Tok Tan Ajaw, Ch'ujul
    Tok Tan Ajaw/K'ujul Tok Tan Ajaw*, title
    (**CH'UL to-{k} TAN AJAW/K'UL to-[k] TAN AJAW
    (CH'UJUL to-{k} TAN AJAW/K'UJUL to-{k} TAN AJAW)**) 85
holy flint *ch'ul tok'/k'ul tok', ch'ujul tok'/k'ujul tok'*, adj. + n.
    (**CH'UL-lu to-k'a/K'UL-lu to-k'a
    (CH'UJUL-lu to-k'a/K'UJUL-lu to-k'a)**) 85
holy lord *ch'ul ajaw/k'ul ajaw, ch'ujul ajaw/k'ujul ajaw*, title
    (**CH'UL AJAW-wa/K'UL AJAW-wa
    (CH'UJUL AJAW-wa/K'UJUL AJAW-wa)**) 83
holy man *ch'ul winik/k'ul winik, ch'ujul winik/k'ujul winik*, adj. + n.
    (**CH'UL WINIK-ki/K'UL WINIK-ki
    (CH'UJUL WINIK-ki/K'UJUL WINIK-ki)**) 85
holy name *ch'ul k'ab'a/k'ul k'ab'a*, adj. + n. (**CH'UL K'AB'A/K'UL K'AB'A**) 84
holy person *ch'ul winik/k'ul winik, ch'ujul winik/k'ujul winik*, adj. + n.
    (**CH'UL WINIK-ki/K'UL WINIK-ki
    (CH'UJUL WINIK-ki/K'UJUL WINIK-ki)**) 85
holy woman *ch'ul ixik/k'ul ixik, ch'ujul ixik/k'ujul ixik)*, adj. + n.
    (**CH'UL IXIK-ki/K'UL IXIK-ki
    (CH'UJUL IXIK-ki/K'UJUL IXIK-ki)**) 84
hoof (deer) *may?*, n. (**MAY (?)**) 169
horizontal? *k'a/ch'a*, pos. (**k'a/ch'a (K'A/CH'A?)**) 141
house *na*, n. (**na/NA/NAJ**) 177, 178
house *naj*, n. (**na/NA/NAJ**) 177, 178
house *na otot*, n. (**NA OTOT-ja**) 181
house *otot*, n. (**OTOT**) 197
house (his/her/its) *yotot*, poss. n. (**yo-OTOT, yo-OTOT-ti, yo-to-ti**) 301, 303
house (in his/her/its) *tu naj*, prep. phr. (**TU na-ja**) 238
house (in his/her/its) *yotot-ti*, prep. + poss. n. (**yo-to-ta-ti**) 303
housed (was) *ototaj*, pass. v. (**OTOT-ja**) 197
human *winik*, n. (**WINIK, wi-WINIK-ki**) 269, 271
hummingbird *tz'unun*, n. (**tz'u-nu-{n}**) 252
hunchback *ch'at*, n. (**ch'a-ti**) 76
hurling (his/her/its) *yalaj*, poss. n. (**ya-la-ja**) 284
hurt *k'uxajiy*, tr. v. (**k'u-xa-ji-ya**) 156
hurt (was) *k'uxaj*, pass. v. (**k'u-xa-ja**) 156

I

I *in*, 1st pers. pron. (**IN**) 98
I am your servant *a winiken*, declarative phr. (**AJ-wi-na-{i} ke-na**) 33
image *b'a*, n. (**b'a/B'A**) 39
image *b'aj*, n. (**b'a-ja**) 40
image *k'ob'a*, n. (**k'o-b'a**) 154

image *k'oj*, n. (**k'o-jo**) 154
image (his/her/its) *u b'a*, poss. n. (**U B'A**) 255, 256
image of (the) *u b'a*, poss. n. (**U B'A**) 255, 256
in *ta*, prep. (**ta/TA**) 221, 222
in *tan*, loc. prep. (**TAN, TAN-na**) 226, 228
in *ti*, prep. (**ti/TI**) 231
in (his/her/its) *tu*, prep. + pron. (**TU**) 236
incensario *sak lak tun*, n. (**SAK la-ka-TUN, SAK la-ka-TUN-ni**) 214
increase *tz'ak*, tr. v. (**TZ'AK**) 247
increase *tz'ak b'ul*, tr. v. (**TZ'AK b'u-li**) 248
increased (was) *tz'akaj*, pass. v. (**TZ'AK-aj**) 247
indeed *b'ajin*, adv. (**b'a-ji-ni**) 40
in (his/her/its) divinity *tu k'ul*, prep. phr. (**TU K'U-li**) 236
in (his/her/its) dreaming place *tu wayb'il*, prep. phr. (**TU WAY-[b'i]-li**)) 239
in (his/her/its) house *tu naj*, prep. phr. (**TU na-ja**) 238
Initial Series Introductory Glyph *tzik ja'ab'/tzik ab'*, intr. v. phr. literally
     "the count of years" (**tzi-ka JA'AB' (?)/tzi-ka AB' (?)**) 243
inkpot *kuch ab'ak*, n. (**KUCH AB'AK**) 138
in (his/her/its) sleeping place *tu wayb'il*, prep. phr. (**TU WAY-[b'i]-li**)) 239
in (his/her/its) structure *tu naj*, prep. phr. (**TU na-ja**) 238
interpreter *chi'lam*, n. (**chi-ji-la-ma**) 61
in the tongue *ti yak'il?*, prep. phr. (**TI ya-AK'-il**) 232
island *pet*, n. (**PET**) 206
it *u*, 3rd pers. pron. (**u/U**) 253, 254, 255
it *ya*, 3rd pers. prev. pron. used with words beginning in *a* (**ya**) 279, 280
it *ye*, 3rd pers. prev. pron. used with words beginning in *e* (**ye/YE**) 290, 291
it *yi*, 3rd pers. prev. pron. used with words beginning in *i* (**yi**) 294
it *yo*, 3rd pers. prev. pron. used with words beginning in *o* (**yo/YOP, yo**) 298
it *yu*, 3rd pers. prev. pron. used with words beginning in *u* (**yu**) 304
its *u*, 3rd pers. poss. pron. (**u/U**) 253, 254
its *ya*, 3rd pers. prev. poss. pron. used with words beginning in *a* (**ya**) 279, 280
its *ye*, 3rd pers. prev. poss. pron. used with words beginning in *e* (**ye/YE**) 290, 291
its *yi*, 3rd pers. prev. poss. pron. used with words beginning in *i* (**yi**) 294
its *yo*, 3rd pers. prev. poss. pron. used with words beginning in *o* (**yo/YOP, yo**) ...298
its *yu*, 3rd pers. prev. poss. pron. used with words beginning in *u* (**yu**) 304
Itz'amná *Itz'amná*, n. proper name of the principal god of the Maya
     pantheon (**itz'-am-{na}**) 99
Itz'am Yej *Itz'am Yej*, n. deity name; name of the Principal Bird Deity
     (**ITZ'AM ye-ji**) 100

J

jaguar *b'alam*, n. (**B'ALAM**) 42
jaguar *ix*, n. (**IX**) 102
jaguar *jix*, n. (**ji-IX, ji-JIX, JIX**) 114, 115
jaguar claw *ich'ak*, n. (**ICH'AK, ICH'AK-ki**) 92, 93
jaguar claw *mol?*, n. (**MOL (?)**) 171
jaguar claw (his/her/its) *yich'ak*, poss. n. (**yi-ch'a-ki**) 295
jaguar claw stone *ich'ak tun*, n. (**ICH'AK TUN-ni**) 93
jaguar paw *ich'ak*, n. (**ICH'AK, ICH'AK-ki**) 92, 93
jaguar paw *mol?*, n. (**MOL (?)**) 171
jaguar paw stone *ich'ak tun*, n. (**ICH'AK TUN-ni**) 93
jaguar paw stone *mol tun?*, n. (**MOL(?) TUN-ni**) 171
jaguar throne *ix tzam?*, n. (**IX TZ'AM(?)**) 103
Jaguar Throne Stone Place *Ix Tzam? Ku-aj*, n. (**IX TZ'AM(?) ku-aj**) 103
jewel *pet*, n. (**PET**) 206
join *tzutz*, tr. v. (**TZUTZ**) 244, 245
Jun Nal Ye *Jun Nal Ye*, n. deity name, proper name of the Maize God
     (**JUN NAL ye**) 127

K

K'awil *K'awil*, n. deity name; proper name of the god K'awil
    (**ka-K'AWIL, K'AWIL, K'AWIL-la, K'AWIL-li**) 143, 149
K'awilnal person *K'awinal winik*, n. (**k'a-wi-NAL WINIK**) 150
K'awilnals *K'awilnalob'*, n. deity name; K'awilnals (pl.) (**K'AWIL-NAL-OB'**) 149
K'awils *K'awilob'*, pl. n. (**K'AWIL-OB'**) 150
kingship *ajawlel*, n. (**AJAW-le-le**) 29
kingship (in) *ti ajawlel*, prep. phr. (**TI AJAW le-{l}**) 231
Knot-Mouth *mokoch*, n. proper name of lesser god (**mo-ko-chi**) 171

L

lady *na*, n. (**na/NA/NAJ**) 178
lady *naj*, n. (**na/NA/NAJ**) 178
lance *lom*, n. (**lo-mu**) 163
large *lakam*, adj. (**LAKAM, la-ka-ma**) 159
large *nuk*, adj. (**nu-ku**) 188
large stone *lakam tun*, adj. + n. (**LAKAM TUN, LAKAM TUN-ni**).............................160
leaf *yop*, n. (**yo/YOP**)...298
learned one *itz'at*, n. (**ITZ'AT, i-tz'a-ta, ITZ'AT-ta**) 100, 101
letter *wojol*, n. (**wo-jo-li**) 272
librarian *aj k'ujun*, title (**AJ k'u-{JUN}-na, AJ k'u-JUN-na**) 30
lid *mak*, n. (**ma-ka**)..167
lifted (something) *wak*, n. (**WAK**) 262, 263
Lifted Lord *Wak Chaan Ajaw/Wak Kaan Ajaw*, title
    (**WAK CHAAN-na AJAW/WAK KAAN-na AJAW**) 263
lifted sky *wak chaan/wak kaan*, n. (**WAK-ki CHAAN/WAK-ki KAAN**) 263
lifted thing *wawaan*, title (**wa-wa-aj-ni**) 264
lineage shrine *wayb'il*, n. (**WAY-b'i-li**) 267
lintel *pakab'*, n. (**pa-ka-b'a**) 200
lizard *ayin*, n. (**AYIN**) 37
load *ikatz*, n. (**i-ka-tzi**) 93, 94
load *ikitz*, n. (**i-ki-tzi**)..94
load *kuch*, n. (**KUCH, ku-chu**) 138
lord *ajaw*, title (**AJAW, a-ja-wa, AJAW-wa**) 27, 28, 29
lord (his/her/its) *yajaw*, poss. n. generally "underlord"
    (**ya-AJAW-wa, ya-ja-wa**) 280, 283
Lord of the Fire *Yajaw K'ak'*, poss. prep. phr. title (**ya-AJAW K'AK'**) 280
Lord of the Tree *yajaw te'*, poss. prep. phr. title (**ya-AJAW-wa TE'**) 281
Lord of the Tree (his/her/its) *yajaw te'*, poss. prep. phr. title
    (**ya-AJAW-wa TE'**) 281
Lord of the Tree (his/her/its) *u yajaw te'*, poss. prep. phr. title
    (**U ya-AJAW-wa TE'**) 260
lordship *ajawlel*, n. (**AJAW-le-le**) 29
lordship (in) *ti ajawlel*, prep. phr. (**TI AJAW le-{l}**) 231
lose *sat*, tr. v. (**sa-ta**) 216
lost *satay*, intr. com. v. (**sa-ta-yi**) 216
lying down *k'a/ch'a*, pos. (**k'a/ch'a (K'A/CH'A?)**)...141
lying down sky *k'a chaan*, pos. + n. (**K'A CHAAN-na**) 142

M

macaw *mo'*, n. (**mo/MO', MO'**) 171, 172
Macaw Mountain *Mo' Witz*, n. proper name of location (**MO' WITZ**) 172
Macaw Mountain Lord *Mo' Witz Ajaw*, n.
    (**mo-o WITZ AJAW, mo-o wi-tzi AJAW**) 172

made *pat b'uj*, tr. com. v. (**PAT-ta-b'u-ji**) 205
made *pat b'uy*, tr. com. v. (**PAT-b'u-ya**)..204
made *patlaj*, pos. com. v. (**PAT-[la]-ja**) 204
made *patwan*, com. v. (**PAT-ta-wa-ni, PAT-wa-ni**) 205
maize *nal*, n. (**NAL**) 180, 181
maize curl *nal*, n. (**NAL**) 180, 181
Maize God *Jun Nal Ye*, n. deity name (**JUN NAL YE**) 127
maize gruel *sa*, n. atole (**sa/SA**) 211
maize gruel *ul*, n. atole (**u-lu**) 256
make *pat*, tr. v. (**PAT, pa-ti, PAT-ta**) 202, 203, 204
make appear *tzakaw*, tr. v. (**tza-[ka]-wa**) 242
make appear god/divinity/holiness *tzakaw ch'ul/tzakaw k'ul*, tr. v. phr.
    (**tza-[ka]-wa CH'UL/tza-[ka]-wa K'UL**) 242
make round *wol*, tr. v. (**wo-la**) 273
man *winik*, n. (**WINIK, wi-WINIK-ki**) 269, 271
man *xib'*, n. (**XIB'**) 277
manifest *jal*, tr. v. (**JAL, ja'-li**) 106, 111
manifest *jal-jiy*, tr. v. (**JAL-ji-ya**) 106
manifest god/divinity/holiness *tzakaw ch'ul/tzakaw k'ul*, tr. v. phr.
    (**tza-[ka]-wa CH'UL/tza-[ka]-wa K'UL**) 242
many *ox*, adj. (**OX**) 197, 198
many *b'olon*, adj. (**B'OLON**)..44, 45
many strengths *b'olon iplaj*, adj. + n. (**B'OLON i-pi-[la]-ja**) 45
mask *k'ob'a*, n. (**k'o-b'a**) 154
mask *k'oj*, n. (**k'o-jo**) 154
mask *nak*, n. (**na-ku**) 180
matawil *matawil*, divinity title, specific meaning unknown (**ma-ta-wi-la**) 168
maternal grandfather *mam*, n. (**MAM**)..168
middle *ol*, n. (**OL**) 196
middle of (in the) *tan*, prep. phr. (**TAN, TAN-na**)......................................226, 228
mold *pak'*, tr. v. (**pa-k'a**) 201
molded *pak'ajiy*, intr. com. v. (**pa-k'a-ji-ya**) 201
monkey (howler) *b'atz'*, n. (**b'a-tz'u**) 42
monkey (spider) *max*, n. (**ma-xi**) 168, 169
month *winal*, n. month of twenty days in LC (**WINAL**)................................269
mother *na*, n. (**na/NA/NAJ**) 178
mother *naj*, n. (**na/NA/NAJ**) 178
mother (his/her) *yaxun?*, poss. n. (**ya-xu-na (?)**) 290
mot-mot bird (?) *xuk*, n. (**xu-[ku]**) 277
mot-mot bird (?) *xukpi*, n. (**xu-[ku]-pi**) 278
mountain *witz*, n. (**WITZ, wi-tzi**) 270
Mountain Macaw *Witz Mo'*, n. (**wi-tzi mo-o**) 270
Mountain Place (White Flowery) *Witz Sak Nik Nal*, n. proper name of the
    Kawak Monster on the Tablet of the Foliated Cross at Palenque
    (**wi-tzi SAK-NIK-ki NAL**) 271
mouth *chi*, n. (**chi/CHI**) 61
mud *luk'*, n. (**lu-k'u**) 164
Mutul Lords *Mutul Ajaw-tak*, pl. n. (**MUTUL AJAW-TAK**) 175
my *in*, 1st pers. poss. pron. (**IN**) 98
my cave *in ch'en*, poss. n. (**IN CH'EN**) 98
my clothes *in b'uk*, poss. n. (**IN-b'u-ku**) 98
my earspool *in tup*, poss. n. (**IN tu-pa**) 99
my earth, my land *in kab'*, poss. n. (**IN KAB'**) 98
my tribute *in pat*, poss. n. (**IN pa-ta**) 99

N

Na Kan *Na Kan*, n. deity name; part of the name of a Vision Serpent
(**NA ka-KAN**) 180
name *kab'a*, n. (**K'AB'A**) 142
namesake (of) *yete' k'ab'a-il*, poss. n. (**ye-te' k'a-b'a-li**).................293
negative marker *ma* (**ma/MA**) 165, 166
new *tzi*, adj. (**tzi/TZI**) 243
nine *b'olon*, n. cardinal number (**B'OLON**) 44, 45
no heart *mi ol*, negative marker + n. (**MI OL-la**) 170
north *nal*, n. cardinal direction (**NAL (?)**, **na-NAL**) 181
north *nojol*, n. cardinal direction (**NOJOL**) 186
north *xaman*, n. cardinal direction (**xa-ma-na**) 275
not *ma*, adv. (**ma/MA**) 165, 166
nothing *mi*, n. (**mi/MI**) 169, 170
not seen (was) *ma ilaj*, pass. v. (**MA-[IL]-aj**) 166
numerical classifier *nak*, for counts associated with titles (**na-ku**)..........180
numerical classifier *pik*, units/groups of 8,000 (**PIK**) 208
numerical classifier *pis*, "measure"; for counts of periods of time (**pi-si**) 208
numerical classifier *tal*, for ordinal numbers (**TAL**, **ta-li**) 226

O

obsidian *taj*, n. (**ta-ji**) 224
occur *ut*, intr. v. (**u-ti**) 257
occur (it will) *utom*, intr. incom. v. Future Date Indicator (FDI) (**u-to-ma**) 258, 259
occurred (since it) *utiy*, intr. com. v. Anterior Date Indicator (ADI) (**u-ti-ya**) 257, 258
occurred (since it) *utjiy*, intr. com. v. Anterior Date Indicator (ADI) (**u-ti-ji-ya**) 257
offering (his/her/its) *yak'*, poss. n. (**ya-k'u**) 284
offering (his/her/its) *yak'aw*, poss. n. (**ya-k'a-wa**) 283, 284
older brother *sukun*, n. (**su-ku-{n}**) 219
older brother person *sukun winik*, n. (**su-ku-{n} WINIK-ki**) 219
omen *mut*, n. (**mu-ti**) 174
on *ti*, prep. (**ti/TI**)..231
one *jun*, n. cardinal number (**JUN**) 125, 126
one *wi*, n. cardinal number (**wi/WI**).......................................268, 269
one who fears *sajal*, title (**sa-ja-la**) 213
open *pas/pasaj*, tr. v. (**PAS/PASAJ**, **pa-sa**) 202
opening *pasil*, n. (**pa-si-li**) 202
Ox B'olon Chaak *Ox B'olon Chaak*, n. deity name, proper name of deity;
possibly GI of the Palenque Triad (**OX B'OLON CHAAK**) 198

P

painting *tz'ib'*, n. (**tz'i-b'a**, **tz'i-b'i**) 251
paper *jun*, n. (**JUN**, **ju-na**) 125, 126
paper headband *jun*, n. (**JUN**, **ju-na**)...................................125, 126
particle suffix *-il*, for indicating possession (**-il**) 95, 96
paw, jaguar *ich'ak*, n. (**ICH'AK**, **ICH'AK-ki**) 92, 93
paw, jaguar *mol?*, n. (**MOL (?)**) 171
paw, jaguar (his/her/its) *yich'ak*, poss. n. (**yi-ch'a-ki**) 295
paw stone, jaguar *ich'ak tun*, n. (**ICH'AK TUN-ni**) 93
paw stone, jaguar *mol? tun*, n. (**MOL(?) TUN-ni**)............................171
payment *tojol*, n. (**to-jo-li**) 233
peccary *chitam*, n. (**CHITAM**) 62
pen (quill) *cheb'*, n. (**che-b'u**) 60
penance (do) *ch'ab'*, intr. v. (**CH'AB**, **ch'a-b'a**) 72

penis *ach*, n. (Ch'olan) (**ACH-(cha)**) 27
penis *at*, n. (Yucatec) (**AT, AT-ti**) 36, 37
penis (bled) *toxat*, n. (**to-[xa]-AT-ti, to-XAT**) 235, 236
penis (scarred) *yo-at*, adj. + n. (**yo-a-AT-ta, yo-AT, yo-AT-ta, yo-AT-ti**) 298, 299
penis (his/its) scarred *yoxat*, poss. n. (**yo-[xa]-AT-ti (?)**) 304
person *winik*, n. (**WINIK, wi-WINIK-ki**) 269, 271
pierce *ch'ab'*, intr. v. (**CH'AB, ch'a-b'a**) 72
pierce *jul*, tr. v. (**JUL, ju-li, JUL-li**) 123, 124
pierce (with a lance) *ch'ab'*, tr. v. (**CH'AB, ch'a-b'a**) 72
pigeon *mukuy*, n. (**mu-ku-yi**) 174
piled up *tz'apajiy*, intr. com. v. (**tz'a-pa-ji-ya**) 249
piled up (was) *tz'apaj*, pass. v. (**tz'a-pa-ja, tz'a-[pa]-ja**) 248, 249
pile up *tz'ap*, tr. v. (**tz'a-[pa]**) 248
pile up *tz'apwa*, pos. v. (**tz'a-[pa]-wa**) 249
pine torch *taj*, n. (**TAJ**) 224
place *nal*, loc. determinative suf. (**NAL**) 180, 181
plant *pak'*, tr. v. (**pa-k'a**) 201
planted *pak'ajiy*, intr. com. v. (**pa-k'a-ji-ya**) 201
planted upright *tz'apajiy*, intr. com. v. (**tz'a-pa-ji-ya**) 249
planted upright (was) *tz'apaj*, pass. v. (**tz'a-pa-ja, tz'a-[pa]-ja**) 248, 249
plant upright *tz'ap*, pos. v. (**tz'a-[pa]**) 248
plant upright *tz'apwa*, pos. v. (**tz'a-[pa]-wa**) 249
plate *lak*, n. (**LAK, la-ka**) 159
plate (tripod) *jawte'*, n. (**ja-wa-te'**) 108, 109
play ball *pitzal*, intr. v. (**pi-tzi-la**) 209
played ball *pitzalaj*, pos. com. v. (**pi-tzi-la-ja**) 209
plaza *naab'*, n. (**NAAB', na-b'i**) 178, 179
plural suffix *-tak* (**TAK, ta-ki, TAK-ki**) 225
portal *way*, n. (**WAY, WAY-ya**) 266, 267
Posterior Date Indicator (PDI) *I*, part. then, and then (**i/I**) 91
Posterior Date Indicator (PDI) *i-ut*, part. + intr. v. 102
precious *k'an*, adj. (**K'AN, K'AN-na**) 147
Precious Stair Place *K'anal Eb'*, n. (**K'AN-NAL-la e-b'u**) 148
precious stone *k'an tun*, adj. + n. (**K'AN TUN-ni**) 148
present *tab'*, tr. v. (**TAB'**) 223
presented *tab'iy*, intr. com. v. (**TAB'-[yi]**) 223, 224
primordial sea *k'ak' naab'*, n. (**K'AK' NAAB'**) 144
progressive aspect marker *i-yuwal*, for ongoing action (**i-yu-wa-la**) 104
progressive aspect marker? (on transitive verbs) *wa* (**wa/WA**)........................261, 262
pure *sak*, adj. (**SAK**) 213
pure artist *sak chuwen*, n. (**SAK CHUWEN**) 214
put in order *tz'ak*, tr. v. (**TZ'AK**) 247
put in order *tz'ak b'ul*, tr. v. (**TZ'AK b'u-li**) 248
put in order (was) *tz'akaj*, pass. v. (**TZ'AK-aj**) 247

Q

quarter *way*, n. room (**WAY, WAY-ya**) 266, 267
quetzal bird *k'uk'*, n. (**K'UK'**)..155
quill pen *cheb'*, n. (**che-b'u**) 60

R

rabbit *tul*, n. (**TUL**) 236
Rain God *Chaak*, n. deity name; the Maya Rain God
    (**CHAAK, CHAAK-ki, cha-ki**) 48, 49, 53, 54

Rain God Sky *Chaak Chaan/Chaak Kaan*, n. deity name
    (**cha-ki CHAAN-na/cha-ki KAAN-na**) 54
raised-up thing *wawaan*, title (**wa-wa-aj-ni**) 264
rasped (was) *susaj*, pass. v. (**su-sa-ja**) 219
receive *ch'am*, tr. v. (**CH'AM, CH'AM-ma**) 75, 76
receive K'awil *ch'am K'awil*, tr. v.
    (**CH'AM K'AWIL-la, CH'AM-ma K'AWIL-la**)..75, 76
red *chak*, adj. (**CHAK**) 52, 53
red holy lord *chak ch'ul ajaw/chak k'ul ajaw*, title
    (**CHAK CH'UL AJAW/CHAK K'UL AJAW**)..53
Red Man Rain God (?) *Chak Xib' Chaak*, n. deity name (**CHAK XIB' cha-ki**) 54
reed *pu*, n. (**pu/PU/PUJ**) 210
reed *puj*, n. (**pu/PU/PUJ**) 210
Reeds (Place of) *Pu*, n. proper name of Tollan in Mayan (**pu/PU/PUJ**) 210
resin *itz'*, n. (**ITZ'**) 99
resplendent *sak*, adj. (**SAK**) 213
resplendent artist *sak chuwen*, adj. + n. (**SAK CHUWEN**) 214
Resplendent Wind God Star (?) *Sak Ik' Ek'*, n. deity name; proper name
    of god with "wind" manifestations (**SAK IK' EK'**) 214
rest *jal*, intr. v. (**JAL, ja'-li**) 106, 111
rest *jal-jiy*, intr. v. (**JAL-ji-ya**) 106
rest *jil*, intr. v. (**ji-li**) 115
revealed *ye/yej*, adj. (**ye/YE**) 290, 291
rise *nak*, intr. v. (**na-ku**) 180
rise up *tab'*, tr. v. (**TAB'**) 223
road *b'e*, n. (**b'e/B'E**) 43
road *b'i*, n. (**b'i/B'I**) 43, 44
road-entered *och b'ij-jiy*, tr. v. phr. (**OCH B'I-ji-ji-ya**) 193
roll up *kotz'*, tr. v. (**ko-tz'o**) 137
room *way*, n. (**WAY, WAY-ya**) 266, 267
root *wi*, n. (**wi/WI**) 268, 269
Root-Sprout Tree House *Wi Ch'ok Te' Na*, n. the "Lineage Founder" glyph
    (**WI-CH'OK TE' NA**) 269
rose up *tab'iy*, intr. com. v. (**TAB'-[yi]**) 223, 224
rotate *pet*, intr. v. (**PET**) 206
rotated *petjiy*, intr. com. v. (**PET-ji-ya**) 206
round (make) *wol*, tr. v. (**wo-la**) 273
round (something) *wol*, n. (**wo-la**) 273
rulership *ajawlel*, n. (**AJAW-le-le**) 29
rulership (in) *ti ajawlel*, prep. phr. (**TI AJAW le-{l}**) 231

S

sacred *ch'ul/k'ul, ch'ujul/k'ujul*, adj. (**CH'UL/K'UL (CH'UJUL/K'UJUL),**
    CH'UL-lu/K'UL-lu (CH'UJUL-lu/K'UJUL-lu)) 80, 81, 82, 84
sacred *k'u*, n. (**k'u/K'U**) 154, 155
sacred Chatan person *ch'ul chatan winik/k'ul chatan winik, ch'ujul chatan*
    winik/k'ujul chatan winik, adj. + n. (**CH'UL cha-TAN WINIK/K'UL**
    cha-TAN WINIK (CH'UJUL cha-TAN WINIK/K'UJUL
    cha-TAN WINIK), CH'UL cha-TAN-na wi-WINIK-ki/K'UL
    cha-TAN-na wi-WINIK-ki (CH'UJUL cha-TAN-na wi-WINIK-ki/
    K'UJUL cha-TAN-na wi-WINIK-ki)) 83, 84
Sacred Cloud Center Lord *Ch'ul Tok Tan Ajaw/K'ul Tok Tan Ajaw, Ch'ujul*
    Tok Tan Ajaw/K'ujul Tok Tan Ajaw, title (**CH'UL to-{k} TAN**
    AJAW/K'UL to-[k] TAN AJAW (CH'UJUL to-{k}
    TAN AJAW/K'UJUL to-{k} TAN AJAW)) 85
sacred flint *ch'ul tok'/k'ul tok', ch'ujul tok'/k'ujul tok'*, adj. + n.
    (**CH'UL-lu to-k'a/K'UL-lu to-k'a (CH'UJUL-lu to-k'a/K'UJUL-lu to-k'a)**) 85

sacred lord *ch'ul ajaw/k'ul ajaw, ch'ujul ajaw/k'ujul ajaw*, title
(**CH'UL AJAW-wa/K'UL AJAW-wa (CH'UJUL AJAW-wa/K'UJUL
AJAW-wa))** 83
sacred man *ch'ul winik/k'ul winik, ch'ujul winik/k'ujul winik*, adj. + n. (**CH'UL
WINIK-ki/K'UL WINIK-ki (CH'UJUL WINIK-ki/K'UJUL WINIK-ki))** 85
sacred name *ch'ul k'ab'a/k'ul k'ab'a*, adj. + n. (**CH'UL K'AB'A/K'UL K'AB'A**) 84
sacred person *ch'ul winik/k'ul winik, ch'ujul winik/k'ujul winik*, adj. + n.
(**CH'UL WINIK-ki/K'UL WINIK-ki
(CH'UJUL WINIK-ki/K'UJUL WINIK-ki))** 85
sacred woman *ch'ul ixik/k'ul ixik, ch'ujul ixik/k'ujul ixik)*, adj. + n.
(**CH'UL IXIK-ki/K'UL IXIK-ki (CH'UJUL IXIK-ki/K'UJUL IXIK-ki))** 84
sacrifice *ch'ab'*, intr. v. (**CH'AB, ch'a-b'a**) 72
sage *itz'at*, n. (**ITZ'AT, i-tz'a-ta, ITZ'AT-ta**) 100, 101
said (it is) *aliy*, intr. v. (**a-li-ya**) 36
saw (he/she/it) *yilij*, pron. + intr. com. v. (**yi-IL-ji**) 296
saw (he/she/it) *yilajiy*, pron. + intr. com. v. (**yi-li-aj-ji-ya**) 297
saw it, then (he/she/it) *ilij*, part. + tr. v. (**I-IL-ji**) 93
say *aliy*, intr. v. (**a-li-ya**) 36
say *jal*, tr. v. (**JAL, ja'-li**) 106, 111
say *jal-jiy*, tr. v. (**JAL-ji-ya**) 106
say *wa yalaw*, tr. v. (**wa-ya-la-wa**) 266
saying (his/her/its) *yalajiy*, poss. n. (**ya-la-ji-ya**) 285
saying (his/her/its) *yalij*, poss. n. (**ya-la-ji**) 285
says (so he/she/it/they) *che'en*, quot. part. (**che-e-na, che-je-na**) 60
says on his/her/its bone (so it) *che'en tu b'ak*, v. phr. (**che-e-na TU b'a-ki**) 60
scatter *b'an*, tr. v. (**b'a-na**) 42
scatter *chok*, tr. v. (**CHOK**) 63
scatter drops *chokij*, tr. v. phr. (**CHOK-ji**) 63
scatter drops of liquid *chokaw ch'aj*, tr. v. phr. (**CHOK-ko-wa CH'A-ji,
CHOK-wa CH'A-ji)** 64
scatterer *ch'ajom*, title (**ch'a-jo-ma, ch'a-JOM**) 73
scribe *aj tz'ib'*, title (**AJ tz'i-b'a**) 32
sculpt *uxul*, intr. v. (**u-xu-[lu]**) 260
sculptor *aj uxul*, title (**AJ u-xu-[lu]**) 32
sculpture *uxul*, n. (**u-xu-[lu]**) 260
sea *naab'*, n. (**NAAB', na-b'i**) 178, 179
seasoned *tzi*, adj. (**tzi/TZI**) 243
seated *chumlajiy*, pos. com. v. (**CHUM-la-ji-ya, CHUM-[mu]-la-ji-ya**) 67
seated *chumwaniy*, pos. com. v. (**CHUM-[mu]-wa-ni-ya**) 68
seated (to be) *chum*, pos. v. (**CHUM, CHUM (?), CHUM-[mu]**) 66, 67
seated in lordship *chumwan ti ajawlel*, ti-construction v. phr.
(**CHUM-wa-ni TI AJAW le-{l}**) 68
seating of the stone *chum tun*, v. phr. (**CHUM-[mu] TUN-ni,
[CHUM] TUN-ni)** 68
seating of the *tun chum tun*, v. phr. (**CHUM-[mu] TUN-ni, [CHUM] TUN-ni**) 68
see *il*, tr. v. (**IL**) 96
seeds (of cacao) (for his/her) *ta yutal*, prep. phr. (**TA yu-ta-{l}**) 228
seeds/beans (his/her/its) *yutal*, poss. n. component of the PSS
(**yu-ta-{l}, yu-ta-la**) 305, 306
seen (was) *ilaj*, pass. v. (**IL-ja**) 97
seen (was not) *ma ilaj*, tr. v. (**MA-[IL]-aj**) 166
seen by he/she/it (was) *yilaj*, pass. v. phr. (**yi-IL-la-ja, yi-la-ji**) 296
seize *chuk*, tr. v. (**chu-ka, chu-[ku]**) 65
self *b'a*, refl. suf. (**b'a/B'A**) 39
serpent *chan/kan*, n. (**cha-CHAN/ka-KAN, CHAN/KAN**) 52, 57
set *k'al*, tr. v. (**K'AL**) 144
set (was) *k'alaj*, pass. v. (**K'AL-ja**) 145
set the stone (was) *k'al tun*, pass. v. phr. (**K'AL TUN-ni**) 146

seven *wuk*, n. cardinal number (**WUK**) 273
shark *xok*, n. (**xo-ki**) 277
she *ix/ixik*, fem. agentive pref. (**IX/IXIK, IXIK-ki**) 103
she *u*, 3ʳᵈ pers. pron. (**u/U**) 253, 254, 255
she *ya*, 3ʳᵈ pers. prev. pron. used with words beginning in *a* (**ya**) 279, 280
she *ye*, 3ʳᵈ pers. prev. pron. used with words beginning in *e* (**ye/YE**) 290, 291
she *yi*, 3ʳᵈ pers. prev. pron. used with words beginning in *i* (**yi**) 294
she *yo*, 3ʳᵈ pers. prev. pron. used with words beginning in *o* (**yo/YOP, yo**)................298
she *yu*, 3ʳᵈ pers. prev. pron. used with words beginning in *u* (**yu**) 304
shell *jub'*, n. (**JUB', JUB'-b'a**) 121
shell trumpet *jub'*, n. (**JUB', JUB'-b'a**) 121
shield *pakal*, n. name of several Palenque Classic Period kings
    (**PAKAL, pa-ka-la**) 200
shoot *jul*, tr. v. (**JUL, ju-li, JUL-li**) 123, 124
shot (was) *julaj*, pass. v. (**JUL-li-ja**) 124
shot (they) *julob'*, intr. pl. v. (**ju-li-OB'**) 124
shoulders *pat*, n. (**PAT, pa-ti, PAT-ta**) 202, 203, 204
since it happened/occurred *utiy*, intr. com. v. Anterior Date Indicator (ADI)
    (**u-ti-ya**) 257, 258
since it happened/occurred *utjiy*, intr. com. v. Anterior Date Indicator (ADI)
    (**u-ti-ji-ya**) 257
six *wak*, n. cardinal number (**WAK**) 262, 263
six sky *wak chaan/wak kaan*, n. (**WAK-ki CHAAN/WAK-ki KAAN**)..........................263
Six Sky Lord *Wak Chaan Ajaw/Wak Kaan Ajaw*, title
    (**WAK CHAAN-na AJAW/WAK KAAN-na AJAW**) 263
sky *chaan/kaan*, n. (**CHAAN/KAAN, CHAAN-na/KAAN-na**)..........................49, 50
sky cave *chaan ch'en/kaan ch'en*, n. (**CHAAN CH'EN-na/KAAN
    CH'EN-na, CHAAN-na CH'EN-na/KAAN-na CH'EN-na**) 50
sky-entered *och ta chaan/och ta kaan*, tr. v. phr.
    (**OCH TA CHAAN-na/OK TA KAAN-na**) 195
Sky K'awil *Chaan K'awil/Kaan K'awil*, n. deity name
    (**CHAAN-na K'AWIL-la/KAAN-na K'AWIL-la**) 51
sleep *way*, intr. v. (**WAY, WAY-ya**) 266, 267
sleeping place (in his/her/its) *tu wayb'il*, prep. phr. (**TU WAY-[b'i]-li**) 239
sleeping room *wayb'il*, n. (**WAY-b'i-li**) 267
smoke *b'utz'*, n. (**B'UTZ'**)...46
snake *chan/kan*, n. (**cha-CHAN/ka-KAN, CHAN/KAN**) 52, 57
son *nich*, n. relat. glyph (**NICH/NIK**) 183
son *nik*, n. relat. glyph (**NICH/NIK**) 183
son *nichil*, n. relat. glyph (**NICH-li/NIK-li**) 184
son *nikil*, n. relat. glyph (**NICH-li/NIK-li**) 184
son *nichim*, n. relat. glyph (**ni-chi-{m}**) 183
son (his) *yunen*, poss. n. child (of father) (**yu-NE-{n}**)..305
son of *unen*, n. child (of father) (**u-ne-{n}**) 256
son of *ya-ch'am*, poss. n. child (of mother); literally "her harvest"
    (**ya-CH'AM, ya-CH'AM-ma**)..282, 283
son of *yal*, poss. n. child (of mother); literally "her harvest" (**ya-AL**) 281, 282
speaker *chi'lam*, n. (**chi-ji-la-ma**) 61
spear *jul*, tr. v. (**JUL, ju-li, JUL-li**) 123, 124
speared (was) *julaj*, pass. v. (**JUL-li-ja**) 124
spider monkey *max*, n. (**ma-xi**) 168, 169
spirit *way*, n. nawal (**WAY, WAY-ya**) 266, 267
spirit *wayab'*, n. (**wa-WAY-{a}-[b'i]**) 264
split *jatz'ay*, tr. v. (**ja-tz'a-yi**) 108
sprinkled *puliy*, intr. com. v. (**pu-lu-yi, PUL-[yi]**) 210
sprout tree house *ch'ok te' na*, n. (**CH'OK TE' NA**) 80
stack *tz'ap*, tr. v. (**tz'a-[pa]**) 248
stack *tz'apwa*, pos. v. (**tz'a-[pa]-wa**) 249

stacked *tz'apajiy*, intr. com. v. (**tz'a-pa-ji-ya**) 249
stacked (was) *tz'apaj*, pass. v. (**tz'a-pa-ja, tz'a-[pa]-ja**)................................248, 249
staff *lom*, n. (**lo-mu**) 163
stairway (his/her/its) *yeb'al*, poss. n. (**ye-b'a-li**) 291
stairway, staircase *eb'*, n. (**e-b'u, EB'-[b'u]**) 88
stairway of *yeb'al*, poss. n. (**ye-b'a-li**)..291
standing one *b'akab'*, title (**b'a-ka-b'a**) 41
star *ek'*, n. (**EK'**) 89
statue *k'ob'a*, n. (**k'o-b'a**) 154
statue *k'oj*, n. (**k'o-jo**)..154
step on *tek'*, tr. v. phr. (**te'-k'a**)..230
stepped on (was) *tek'aj*, pass. v. phr. (**te'-k'a-ja**) 230
stingray spine *kix*, n. (**KIX (?)**))..135, 136
stone *tun*, n. (**TUN, TUN-ni**) 237, 238
stone-binding *k'al tun*, intr. v. phr. (**K'AL TUN-ni**) 146
stood up (something) *wak*, n. (**WAK**)..262, 263
stood-up sky *wak chaan/wak kaan*, n. (**WAK-ki CHAAN/WAK-ki KAAN**) 263
Stood-Up Sky Lord *Wak Chaan Ajaw/Wak Kaan Ajaw*, title
    (**WAK CHAAN-na AJAW/WAK KAAN-na AJAW**) 263
stood-up thing *wawaan*, title (**wa-wa-aj-ni**) 264
strike *jatz'ay*, tr. v. (**ja-tz'a-yi**) 108
strong *kelem*, adj. (**ke-KELEM, ke-le-ma**) 134
structure (in his/her/its) *tu naj*, prep. phr. (**TU na-ja**) 238
sun *k'in*, n. (**K'IN, K'IN-ni**) 151, 152, 153
sun-eyed *k'ina/k'inich*, adj. (**K'INA/K'INICH, K'INICH, K'INICH-ni**) 152
sun-faced *k'ina/k'inich*, adj. (**K'INA/K'INICH, K'INICH, K'INICH-ni**) 152
Sun-Faced Throne Stone *K'inich Tzam? Tun*, adj. + n. proper name of
    an altar (**K'IN-ni-chi TZAM(?) TUN-ni**) 153
Sun Lord *K'in Ajaw*, title (**K'IN-ni AJAW**) 153
Sun Water Place *K'in Ja'nal*, n. (**K'IN-ni JA'-NAL**) 154
surface [for writing] *jich*, n. (**ji-chi**) 114
surface [for writing] (its) *yich*, poss. n. (**yi-chi**) 294
sweat *itz'*, n. (**ITZ'**) 99
sweat bath *pib' naj*, n. *temescal* (**pi-b'i NA-aj**) 207
sweat bath *pib'nal*, n. *temescal* (**pi-b'i-NA-li**) 207

T

tail *ne*, n. (**ne/NE**) 182
take down; war *jub'*, intr. v. (**JUB' (?)**) 121
taken down; war *jub'uy*, intr. v. (**ju-b'u-yi, JUB'(?)-yi, JUB'(?)-yi-ya**) 122
tamale *wa*, n. (**wa/WA**) 261
tamale *waj*, n. (**wa-WA-ji**) 264
tapir *til*, n. (**TIL**) 232
temporal suffix *lat*, "X-number of days" (**la-ta**) 161
ten *lajun*, n. cardinal number (**LAJUN**) 158
terminate *jal*, intr. v. (**JAL, ja'-li**)..106, 111
terminate *jal-jiy*, intr. v. (**JAL-ji-ya**) 106
terminate *tzutz*, tr. v. (**TZUTZ**)..244, 245
terminated *tzutziy*, intr. com. v. (**TZUTZ-yi**) 246
terminated (was) *tzutzaj*, pass. v. (**TZUTZ-ja, tzu-tzu-ja**) 245
terminates *k'ay/ch'ay*, intr. incom. v. (**k'a-yi/ch'a-yi**) 150
terminates (his/her) resplendent soul *k'ay u sak nik ik'il/ch'ay u sak nich ik'il*,
    intr. incom. v. phr. (**k'a-yi U SAK NIK IK'-li/ch'a-yi U SAK NICH IK'-li**) 151
termination (his/her/its) *yajil*, poss. n. (**ya-ja-li**) 283
that, that one *ja'-i*, focus marker (**ja'-i**) 111
then, and then *i*, part. Posterior Date Indicator (PDI) (**i/I**) 91
then it happened *i-ut*, part. + intr. v. Posterior Date Indicator (PDI) (**i-u-ti**) 102

these *ja'ob'*, dem. pl. pron. (**ja'-o-b'a**) 111
these are *ja'ob'*, dem. pl. pron. (**ja'-o-b'a**) 111
they, they are *ja'ob'*, dem. pl. pron. (**ja'-o-b'a**) 111
thing *b'a*, refl. suf. (**b'a/B'A**) 39
this *ja'-i*, focus marker (**ja'-i**) 111
three *ox*, n. cardinal number (**OX**) 197, 198
threw (they) *julob'*, intr. pl. v. (**ju-li-OB'**) 124
thrice manifested *ox ajal*, v. phr. (**OX aj-ja-li**) 198
Thrice Manifested Chaak *Ox B'olon Chaak*, n. deity name; possibly GI of
    the Palenque Triad (**OX B'OLON CHAAK**) 198
thrice said *ox ajal*, v. phr. (**OX aj-ja-li**) 198
throne *tz'am?*, n. (**TZ'AM (?)**) 248
throne, jaguar *ix tz'am?*, n. (**IX TZ'AM(?)**) 103
throw *chok*, tr. v. (**CHOK**) 63
throw *jul*, tr. v. (**JUL, ju-li, JUL-li**) 123, 124
throw down *jom*, tr. v. (**JOM**) 118, 119
throw drops *chokij*, tr. v. phr. (**CHOK-ji**) 63
throw drops of liquid *chokaw ch'aj*, tr. v. phr.
    (**CHOK-ko-wa CH'A-ji, CHOK-wa CH'A-ji**) 64
throwing (his/her/its) *yalaj*, poss. n. (**ya-la-ja**) 284
thrown (was) *julaj*, pass. v. (**JUL-li-ja**) 124
tie *k'al*, tr. v. (**K'AL**) 144
tied (was) *k'alaj*, pass. v. (**K'AL-ja**) 145
tied the deer hoof (was) *k'alaj mayij?*, pass. v. phr. (**K'AL-ja MAY(?)-ji**).....................145
tied the headband *k'al jun*, tr. v. phr. (**K'AL JUN-na**)...145
tied the white headband *k'al-jiy sak jun*, tr. v. phr. (**K'AL-ji-ya SAK JUN**) 145
tied the white headband *k'al sak jun*, tr. v. phr.
    (**K'AL SAK JUN, K'AL SAK ju-na**)..146
title (unknown meaning) *kalomte'*, n.
    (**KALOMTE', ka-KALOMTE'-te', ka-lo-ma-te', KALOMTE'-te'**) 132, 133
title (unknown meaning) *yok k'in*, n. (**yo-OK [K'IN]-ni**) 300
to *ta*, prep. (**ta/TA**)..221, 222
to *ti*, prep. (**ti/TI**) 231
tobacco *may?*, n. (**MAY (?)**) 169
Tollan *Pu*, n. proper name of Tollan in Mayan (**pu/PU/PUJ**) 210
tongue *ak'*, n. (**ak'/AK'**) 34
tongue (in the) *ti yak'il*, prep. phr. (**TI ya-AK'-il**) 232
torch *taj*, n. (**TAJ**) 224
torch stone *taj tun*, n. (**TAJ TUN**) 225
tortilla *wa*, n. (**wa/WA**) 261, 262
tortilla *waj*, n. (**wa-WA-ji**) 264
travel *xan*, intr. v. (**XAN-na, xa-XAN-na**) 275, 276
travels *b'ixan*, incom. irreg. v. (**B'IXAN-na**) 44
tree *te'/che'*, n. (**te'/TE' (che'/CHE')**) 228, 229, 230
tree-entered *och te'/ok te'*, tr. v. phr. (**OCH TE'/OK TE'**) 195
tree-fresh *te'el*, adj. (**te'-TE'-le**) 231
Tree Lord *Ajaw Te'*, title (**AJAW-wa TE'**)...29
Tree Lord *yajaw*, title (**ya-AJAW-wa TE'**) 281
Tree Lord (his/her/its) *yajaw te'*, poss. n. title (**ya-AJAW-wa TE'**) 281
Tree Lord (his/her/its) *u yajaw te'*, poss. n. title (**U ya-AJAW-wa TE'**).....................260
tribute *ikatz*, n. (**i-ka-tzi**) 93, 94
tribute *ikitz*, n. (**i-ki-tzi**)...94
tribute *pat*, n. (**PAT, pa-ti, PAT-ta**) 202, 203, 204
tribute *patan*, n. (**pa-ta-{n}, pa-ta-na**)..203
tribute *tojol*, n. (**to-jo-li**) 233
tribute (his/her/its) *yikatz*, poss. n. (**yi-ka-tzo**) 296
tribute cloth *yub'te'*, n. (**yu-b'u-te'**) 304
tribute mantle *yub'te'*, n. (**yu-b'u-te'**) 304

trumpet (shell) *jub'*, n. (**JUB', JUB'-b'a**)...121
turkey (ocellated) *kutz'*, n. (**ku-tz'u**) 139
turn *pet*, intr. v. (**PET**) 206
turned *petjiy*, intr. com. v. (**PET-ji-ya**)..206
turtle *ak*, n. (**a-ku**)..34
twelve *chalajun/kalajun*, n. cardinal number (**CHALAJUN/KALAJUN**) 55
twenty *k'al*, n. cardinal number (**K'AL**)..144
twenty years *k'atun*, n. period of twenty years used in LC (**K'ATUN**) 148
two *cha/ka*, n. cardinal number (**CHA/KA**) 48

U

underlord *sajal*, title of unknown specific meaning (**sa-ja-la**) 213
underlord *yajaw*, title meaning "his/her/its lord" (**ya-AJAW-wa, ya-ja-wa**) 280, 283
under the auspices, under the authority *kab'ij*, relat. (**KAB'-ji**) 130
under the auspices, under the authority *kab'iy*, relat. (**KAB'-ya**) 131
under the auspices, under the authority *kab'jiy*, relat. (**KAB'-ji-ya**) 131
unripe *ch'ok*, adj. (**ch'o-ko, ch'o-[ko]**) 79
utterance (his/her/its) *yalajiy*, poss. n. (**ya-la-ji-ya**) 285
utterance (his/her/its) *yalij*, poss. n. (**ya-la-ji**) 285

V

valley *jem*, n. (**JEM**) 112
valley house *jem-na*, n. (**JEM NA**) 112
valley place *jemnal*, n. (**JEM-NAL**) 112
Venus (?) *Ek'*, n. (**EK'**)..89
vessel (thin-walled) *jay*, n. (**ja-yi**)..109
Vision Serpent *Na Kan*, n. (**NA ka-KAN**) 180
Vision Serpent *Waxaklajun U B'a*, n. (**WAXAKLAJUN U B'A**) 265

W

walk *xan*, intr. v. (**XAN-na, xa-XAN-na**) 275, 276
walks *b'ixan*, incom. irreg. v. (**B'IXAN-na**) 44
wall *paj*, n. (**pa/PAJ**) 199
war *jub'*, intr. v. bring down, take down (**JUB' (?)**) 121
war *jub'-Emblem Glyph*, intr. v. bring down [a site/location/polity]
   (**JUB'-EMBLEM GLYPH**) 121
war *jub'uy*, intr. v. brought down, taken down (**ju-b'u-yi, JUB'(?)-yi-ya**).........122
war helmet *waxaklajun u b'a*, n. (**WAXAKLAJUN U B'A**) 265
warrior *b'ate'*, n. (**b'a-te'**)..42
water *ja*, n. (**JA'**)..109, 110
water *naab'*, n. (**NAAB', na-b'i**)..178, 179
water *way*, n. (**WAY, WAY-ya**)..266, 267
water *yataj*, tr. v. (**ya-ta-ji**)..285
water *yatij*, tr. v. (**ya-ti-ji**)..286
water-entered *och ja'*, tr. v. phr. death (**OCH JA', OCH JA'-ja**) 194
water lily (?) *naab'*, n. (**NAAB', na-b'i**)..................................178, 179
watery stone *naab' tunich*, adj. + n. (**NAAB' TUN-chi**) 179
Waxak Na Chaak *Waxak Na Chaak*, n. proper name of God I (GI) of the
   Palenque Triad (**WAXAK NA CHAAK**) 265
went *b'ixan*, com. irreg. v. (**B'IXAN-na**) 44
went *b'ixaniy*, com. irreg. v. (**B'IXAN-ni-ya**).....................................44
went up *tab'iy*, intr. com. v. (**TAB'-[yi]**) 223, 224
west *chik'in*, n. cardinal direction (**chi-K'IN-ni**) 62
west *och k'in*, n. cardinal direction (**OCH K'IN**).................................195
west (in the) *chik'inil*, prep. phr. (**chi-[K'IN]-li**) 62

white *sak*, adj. (**SAK**) 213
white flowery *sak nik*, adj. (**SAK NIK**)..215
White Flowery Mountain Place *Witz Sak Nik Nal*, n. proper name of the
    Kawak Monster on the Tablet of the Foliated Cross at Palenque
    (**wi-tzi SAK-NIK-ki NAL**) 271
White Great House *Sak Nuk Naj*, n. proper name of building
    (**SAK nu-ku NAJ**) 215
White Tree Lord *Sak Te' Ajaw*, title (**SAK TE' AJAW-wa**) 215
whole *tz'ak*, adj. (**TZ'AK**) 247
whole (the) *olas*, adj. + n. (**o-la-si**) 196
whole (the) *olis*, adj. + n. (**o-OL-si**) 196, 197
whole set (the) *olas*, n. phr. (**o-la-si**) 196
whole set (the) *olis*, n. phr. (**o-OL-si**)...196, 197
whole set of gods (the) (?) *olas k'u*, n. phr. (**o-la-si K'U**) 196
whole set of gods (the) (?) *olis k'u*, n. phr. (**o-OL-si K'U**) 197
wide *nuk*, adj. (**nu-ku**) 188
wide water *lakam ja'*, adj. + n. (**LAKAM JA'**) 160
wife (his) *yatan*, poss. n. (**ya-ta-na**) 286
wife of *yatan*, poss. n. (**ya-ta-na**)..286
Wind God *Ik' K'u*, n. proper name of the Classic Maya Wind God (**IK' K'U**).................95
wise man *itz'at*, n. (**ITZ'AT, i-tz'a-ta, ITZ'AT-ta**) 100, 101
with *ta*, prep. (**ta/TA**) 221, 222
with *ti*, prep. (**ti/TI**) 231
with *yete'*, prep. (**ye-te'**) 292, 293
with *yitaj*, prep. (**yi-ta, yi-ta-ji, yi-[ta]-ji**) 297
with a bird *ti xukpi*, prep. phr. + proper name of dance staff (**ti-xu-[ku]-pi**) 232
within the cave *tan ch'en*, double loc. phr. (**TAN CH'EN-na**) 227
within the cave Three Hill Water *tan ch'en ox witzaj*, double loc. phr.
    (**TAN CH'EN OX WITZ-aj**)..227
Witik Lord *Witik Ajaw*, title (**wi-ti-ki AJAW**) 270
witnessed (he/she/it) *yilij*, pron. + intr. com. v. (**yi-IL-ji**) 296
witnessed (he/she/it) *yilajiy*, pron. + intr. com. v. (**yi-li-aj-ji-ya**) 297
witnessed, and then (he/she) *ilij*, part. + tr. v. (**I-IL-ji**) 93
witnessed by he/she/it (was) *yilaj*, pass. v. phr. (**yi-IL-la-ja, yi-la-ji**) 296
woman *ix/ixik*, n. (**IX/IXIK, IXIK-ki**) 103
wood *te'/che'*, n. (**te'/TE' (che'/CHE')**) 228, 229, 230
wound *jatz'ay*, tr. v. (**ja-tz'a-yi**)..108
wrap *k'al*, tr. v. (**K'AL**) 144
wrap *pixom*, tr. v. (**pi-xo-ma**) 209
wrapped (was) *k'alaj*, pass. v. (**K'AL-ja**) 145
wrapped the deer hoof (was) *k'alaj mayij?*, pass. v. phr.
    (**K'AL-ja MAY(?)-ji**) 145
wrapped the headband *k'al jun*, tr. v. phr. (**K'AL JUN-na**) 145
wrapped the white headband *k'al-jiy sak jun*, tr. v. phr.
    (**K'AL-ji-ya SAK JUN**) 145
wrapped the white headband *k'al sak jun*, v. phr.
    (**K'AL SAK JUN, K'AL SAK ju-na**)...146
wrap up *wol*, tr. v. (**wo-la**) 273
writing *tz'ib'*, n. (**tz'i-b'a, tz'i-b'i**) 251

Y

year *ab'*, n. (**AB'**) 26
year *ja'ab'*, n. (**JA'AB'**) 110
year *tun*, n. of 360 days; used in the Maya LC calendar and DNs
    (**TUN, TUN-ni**)...237, 238
yellow *k'an*, adj. (**K'AN, K'AN-na**) 147
yellow stone *k'an tun*, adj. + n. (**K'AN TUN-ni**).....................................148

SPANISH INDEX

Abreviaturas

ADI	marcador de fechas anteriores	ord.	ordinal
adj.	adjetivo	p.	persona
adv.	adverbio	part.	partícula
car.	cardinal	pas.	pasivo
cit.	citada	PDI	marcador de fechas posteriores
com.	completivo	pl.	plural
dec.	declarativo	pos.	de posición
dem.	demostrativo	poss.	posesivo
det.	determinativo	pref.	prefijo
dir.	dirección	prep.	preposición/frase de
EG	Glifo Emblema		preposición
FDI	marcador de fechas futuras	prev.	prevocálico
incom.	incompletivo	pron.	pronombre
intr.	intransitivo	ref.	reflexivo
irreg.	irregular	relac.	glifo de alguna relación
loc.	locativo	suf.	sufijo
n.	nombre (sustantivo)/frase de	tit.	título
	nombre	tr.	transitivo
num.	número	v.	verbo/frase de verbo

A

a *ta*, prep. (**ta/TA**) 221, 222
a *ti*, prep. (**ti/TI**) 231
abajo *yemal*, adv. (**ye-ma-la**) 292
abrir *pas/pasaj*, v. tr. (**PAS/PASAJ, pa-sa**) 202
abuelo materno *mam*, n. (**MAM**) 168
acceder *joy*, v. tr. (**JOY, jo-JOY**) 117, 119
accedió *joyajiy*, v. intr. com. (?) (**JOY-[ja]-ji-ya**) 120
accesión *chum*, v. pos. (**CHUM, CHUM (?), CHUM-[mu]**)..............................66, 67
accesión *chumlajiy*, v. pos. com. (**CHUM-la-ji-ya, CHUM-[mu]-la-ji-ya**) 67
accesión (fue) *chumwaniy*, v. pos. com. (**CHUM-[mu]-wa-ni-ya**) 68
accesión (fue) *joyaj*, v. pas. (**JOY-ja, jo-JOY-ja**) 119
accesión a poder *chumwan ti ajawlel*, construcción de v. con *ti*
    (**CHUM-wa-ni TI AJAW-le-{l}**) 68
accesión a poder *joyaj ti ajawlel*, construcción de v. con *ti*
    (**jo-JOY-ja TI AJAW-le-{l}**) 117
accesión en oficio *chumwan ti ajawlel*, construcción de v. con *ti*
    (**CHUM-wa-ni TI AJAW-le-{l}**) 68
accesión en oficio *joyaj ti ajawlel*, construcción de v. con *ti*
    (**jo-JOY-ja TI AJAW-le-{l}**) 117
acción (de él/ella/este) *u b'a*, n. poss. (**U B'A**) 255, 256
adentro de la cueva *tan ch'en*, loc. doble (**TAN CH'EN-na**) 227
adentro de la cueva Tres Cerro Agua *tan ch'en ox witzaj*, loc. doble
    (**TAN CH'EN OX WITZ-aj**)...227
administrador *aj sul*, tit. (**AJ su-lu**) 32
adornado (fue) *nawaj*, v. pas. (**na-wa-ja**) 182
adornado (fue) *tupaj*, v. pas. (**tu-pa-ja**) 239
agua *ja'*, n. (**JA'**) 109, 110
agua *naab'*, n. (**NAAB', na-b'i**) 178, 179

agua *way*, n. (**WAY, WAY-ya**) 266, 267
agua *yatij*, v. tr. (**ya-ti-ji**) 286
agua ancha *lakam ja'*, n. + adj. (**LAKAM JA'**) 160
agua grande *lakam ja'*, n. + adj. (**LAKAM JA'**) 160
agujerear *ch'ab'*, v. intr. (**CH'AB, ch'a-b'a**) 72
agujerear (con lanza) *ch'ab'*, v. intr. (**CH'AB, ch'a-b'a**) 72
a la *ta*, prep. (**ta/TA**) 221, 222
a la *ti*, prep. (**ti/TI**) 231
albardilla *mak*, n. (**ma-ka**) 167
amado *jun tan*, adj. (**JUN TAN-na**) 127
amanecer *pas/pasaj*, n. (**PAS/PASAJ, pa-sa**) 202
amaneciente (primer) *yax pas*, n. + adj. (**YAX PAS, YAX pa-{s}**) 289
amarillo *k'an*, adj. (**K'AN, K'AN-na**) 147
amarrado (fue) *k'alaj*, v. pas. (**K'AL-ja**) 145
amarrado a la pata del venado (fue) *k'alaj mayij?*, v. pas.
    (**K'AL-ja MAY(?)-ji**) 145
amarrar la faja blanca de la cabeza *k'al-jiy sak jun*, v. tr.
    (**K'AL-ji-ya SAK JUN**) 145
amarrar la faja blanca de la cabeza *k'al sak jun*, v.
    (**K'AL SAK JUN, K'AL SAK ju-na**) 146
amarrar la faja de la cabeza *k'al jun*, v. tr. (**K'AL JUN-na**) 145
amarrar la piedra *k'al tun*, v. intr. (**K'AL TUN-ni**) 146
amontonada (fue) *tz'apaj*, v. pas. (**tz'a-pa-ja, tz'a-[pa]-ja**) 248, 249
amontonar *tz'ap*, v. tr. (**tz'a-[pa]**) 248
amontonar *tz'apajiy*, v. intr. com. (**tz'a-pa-ji-ya**) 249
amontonar *tz'apwa*, v. pos. (**tz'a-[pa]-wa**) 249
ancho *nuk*, adj. (**nu-ku**) 188
antepasado *mam*, n. (**MAM**) 168
antorcha de pino *taj*, n. (**TAJ**) 224
año *ab'*, n. *ja'ab'* (**AB'**) 26
año *ja'ab'*, n. *ab'* (**JA'AB'**) 110
año *tun*, n. de 360 dias (**TUN, TUN-ni**) 237, 238
aparecer *tzak*, v. intr. (**tza-[ka]**) 241, 242
aparecido *aya*, v. (**a-ja-ya, a-ya, a-ya-ya**) 29, 37
apertura *pasil*, n. (**pa-si-li**) 202
aprehensor *chaan/kaan*, n. (**CHAAN/KAAN, CHAAN-na/KAAN-na**) 49, 50
aprehensor *chan/kan*, n. (**cha-CHAN/ka-KAN, CHAN/KAN, cha-nu/ka-nu**) 52, 57, 58
árbol *te'/che'*, n. (**te'/TE' (che'/CHE')**) 228, 229, 230
árbol-fresco *te'el*, adj. (**te'-TE'-le**) 231
arete *tup*, n. (**tu-pa**) 238
areteado (fue) *tupaj*, v. pas. (**tu-pa-ja**) 239
armadillo *ib'ak'*, n. (**i-b'a-k'a**) 92
arrojar *chok*, v. tr. (**CHOK**) 63
arrojar *jul*, v. intr. (**JUL, ju-li, JUL-li**) 123, 124
arrojar gotas *chokij*, v. tr. (**CHOK-ji**) 63
arrojar gotas de líquido *chokaw ch'aj*, v. tr.
    (**CHOK-ko-wa CH'A-ji, CHOK-wa CH'A-ji**) 64
arrojar por abajo *jom*, v. tr. (**JOM**) 118, 119
arrojó (ellos) *julob'*, v. intr. pl. (**ju-li-OB'**) 124
artista *itz'at*, n. (**ITZ'AT, i-tz'a-ta, ITZ'AT-ta**) 100, 101
artista *chuwen*, n. (**CHUWEN**) 69
artista puro *sak chuwen*, n. + adj. (**SAK CHUWEN**) 214
artista resplandeciente *sak chuwen*, n. + adj. (**SAK CHUWEN**) 214
ascender *nak*, v. intr. (**na-ku**) 180
ascender *tab'*, v. tr. (**TAB'**) 223
ascender *tab'iy*, v. intr. com. (**TAB'-[yi]**) 223, 224
asir *chuk*, v. tr. (**chu-ka, chu-[ku]**) 65
asir *tzak*, v. tr. (**tza-[ka]**) 241, 242

asir *tzakaw*, v. tr. (**tza-[ka]-wa**) 242
atado (fue) *k'alaj*, v. pas. (**K'AL-ja**) 145
atado a la faja blanca (de la cabeza) *k'al-jiy sak jun*, v. tr.
    (**K'AL-ji-ya SAK JUN**) 145
atado a la pata del venado (fue) *k'alaj mayij?*, v. pas. (**K'AL-ja MAY(?)-ji**) 145
atar *k'al*, v. tr. (**K'AL**) 144
atar la faja (de la cabeza) *k'al jun*, v. tr. (**K'AL JUN-na**) 145
atar la faja blanca (de la cabeza) *k'al sak jun*, v.
    (**K'AL SAK JUN, K'AL SAK ju-na**) 146
atole *sa*, n. (**sa/SA**) 211
atole *ul*, n. (**u-lu**) 256
augurio *mut*, n. (**mu-ti**) 174
avistó (fue) *ilaj*, v. pas. (**IL-ja**) 97
azul *yax*, adj. (**YAX, ya-xa**) 286, 287
azul-verde *yax*, adj. (**YAX, ya-xa**) 286, 287

B

bailado (fue) *ak'otaj*, v. pas. (**AK'OT-ta-ja**) 35
bailar *ak'ot*, v. tr. (**ak'/AK'OT, AK'OT-ta**) 35
baile *ak'ot*, n. (**ak'/AK'OT, a-AK'OT-ta, AK'OT-ta**) 26, 35
bajar *jub'*, v. intr. (**JUB' (?)**) 121
bajar *jub'uy*, v. intr. (**JUB(?)-yi, ju-b'u-yi, JUB'(?)-yi-ya**) 122
bajo la auspicia, bajo la autoridad *kab'ij*, relac. (**KAB'-ji**) 130
bajo la auspicia, bajo la autoridad *kab'iy*, relac. (**KAB'-ya**) 131
bajo la auspicia, bajo la autoridad *kab'jiy*, relac. (**KAB'-ji-ya**) 131
bandera *jasaw*, n. (**ja-sa-wa**) 108
bandera *lakam*, n. (**LAKAM, la-ka-ma**) 159
bañar *yataj*, v. tr. (**ya-ta-ji**) 285
bañar *yatij*, v. tr. (**ya-ti-ji**) 286
barro *luk'*, n. (**lu-k'u**) 164
beber *uch'*, v. intr. (**UCH'**) 256
bebida *uch'*, n. (**UCH'**) 256
bebida (tipo de) *ch'ajalte'*, n. (**ch'a-ja-{l}-te'**) 72
bibliotecario *aj k'ujun*, tit. (**AJ k'u-{JUN}-na, AJ k'u-JUN-na**) 30
blanco *sak*, adj. (**SAK**) 213
boca *chi*, n. (**chi/CHI**) 61
Boca del Nudo *mokoch*, n. nombre de un Dios (**mo-ko-chi**) 171
bondad (de él/ella/este) *yutzil*, n. poss. (**yu-tzi-li**) 306
borracho (de ser) *tikal*, v. tr. (**ti-ka-la**) 232
brazo *k'ab'*, n. (**k'a-[b'a]**) 142
brote casa de árbol *ch'ok te' na*, n. (**CH'OK TE' NA**) 80

C

cabeza *b'a*, n. (**b'a/B'A**) 39
cabeza *jol*, n. (**JOL, JOL-lo**) 118
cacao *kakaw*, n. (**ka-{ka}-wa, ka-ka-wa**) 132
calabacero *makom*, n. (**ma-ko-ma**) 168
caminar *b'ixan*, v. incom. irreg. (**B'IXAN-na**) 44
caminar *xan*, v. intr. (**XAN-na, xa-XAN-na**) 275, 276
camino *b'e*, n. (**b'e/B'E**) 43
camino *b'i*, n. (**b'i/B'I**) 43, 44
caña *pu*, n. (**pu/PU/PUJ**) 210
capturado (fue) *chukaj*, v. pas. (**chu-ka-ja, chu-[ku]-ja**) 65, 66
capturado (fue) *chukjiy*, v. intr. com. (**chu-[ku]-ji-ya**) 66
capturador *chaan/kaan*, n. (**CHAAN/KAAN, CHAAN-na/KAAN-na**) 49, 50
capturador *chan/kan*, n. (**cha-CHAN/ka-KAN, CHAN/KAN, cha-nu/ka-nu**) 52, 57, 58

capturar *chuk*, v. tr. (**chu-ka, chu-[ku]**) 65
cara *nak*, n. (**na-ku**) 180
cara del sol *k'ina/k'inich*, adj. (**K'INA/K'INICH, K'INICH, K'INICH-ni**) 152
carga *ikatz*, n. (**i-ka-tzi**) 93, 94
carga *ikitz*, n. (**i-ki-tzi**) 94
carga *kuch*, n. (**KUCH, ku-chu**) 138
cargamento *ikatz*, n. (**i-ka-tzi**) 93, 94
cargamento *ikitz*, n. (**i-ki-tzi**) 94
cargamento *kuch*, n. (**KUCH, ku-chu**) 138
casa *na*, n. (**na/NA/NAJ**) 177, 178
casa *naj*, n. (**na/NA/NAJ**) 177, 178
casa *na otot*, n. (**NA OTOT-ja**) 181
casa *otot*, n. (**OTOT**) 197
casa (de él/ella/este) *yotot*, n. poss. (**yo-OTOT, yo-OTOT-ti, yo-to-ti**) 301, 303
casa (de él/ella/este) *tu naj*, prep. (**TU-na-ja**) 238
casa de accesíon *k'al jun na*, n. (**K'AL JUN NA**) 146
casa del valle *jem na*, n. (**JEM-na**) 112
casco *kojaw*, n. (**KOJAW, KOJAW-wa, ko-ja-wa**) 136, 137
cautivo *b'ak*, n. (**B'AK, b'a-ki**) 41
celestial *chaanal/kaanal*, adj. (**CHAAN-na-NAL/KAAN-na-NAL**) 51
centro *ol*, n. (**OL**) 196
centro de la nube *tok tan*, n. (**to-ko-TAN-na**) 234
centro del corazón (de él/ella/este) *yol tan*, n. poss. (**yo-OL-la TAN-na**) 300
cero *mi*, n. (**mi/MI**) 169, 170
cerrado (fue) *k'alaj*, v. pas. (**K'AL-ja**) 145
cerrado (fue) *makaj*, v. pas. (**ma-ka-ja**) 167
cerrando *k'al*, v. incom. tr. (**k'a-li**) 144
cerrar *k'al*, v. tr. (**K'AL**) 144
cerrar *mak*, v. tr. (**ma-ka**) 167
cerrar *makax*, v. tr. (**ma-ka-xa**) 167
cerrar la faja blanca de la cabeza *k'al-jiy sak jun*, v. tr.
    (**K'AL-ji-ya SAK JUN**) 145
cerrar la faja blanca de la cabeza *k'al sak jun*, v.
    (**K'AL SAK JUN, K'AL SAK ju-na**) 146
cerrar la faja de la cabeza *k'al jun*, v. tr. (**K'AL JUN-na**) 145
cerrar la primera piedra *yax k'al tun*, v. (**YAX K'AL TUN-ni**) 288
cerrar la primera *tun* *yax k'al tun*, v. (**YAX K'AL TUN-ni**) 288
cerro *witz*, n. (**WITZ, wi-tzi**) 270
cervato *may*, n. (**MAY (?)**) 169
cielo *chaan/kaan*, n. (**CHAAN/KAAN, CHAAN-na/KAAN-na**) 49, 50
cielo-cueva *chaan ch'en/kaan ch'en*, n.
    (**CHAAN CH'EN-na/KAAN CH'EN-na, CHAAN-na
    CH'EN-na/KAAN-na CH'EN-na**) 50
Cielo del Dios de la Lluvia *Chaak Chaan/Chaak Kaan*, n.
    (**cha-ki CHAAN-na/cha-ki KAAN-na**) 54
cielo elevado *wak chaan/wak kaan*, n. (**WAK-ki CHAAN/WAK-ki KAAN**) 263
cielo enhiesto *wak chaan/wak kaan*, n. (**WAK-ki CHAAN/WAK-ki KAAN**) 263
cielo levantado *wak chaan/wak kaan*, n. (**WAK-ki CHAAN/WAK-ki KAAN**) 263
ciempiés *chapat*, n. (**CHAPAT**) 58
cinco *jo*, n. num. car. (**JO**) 116, 117
clasificador de num. *pik*, grupos de 8,000 (**PIK**) 208
clasificador de num. *pis*, "medida" para cuentas de tiempo (**pi-si**) 208
clasificador de num. *tal*, por números ordinales (**TAL, ta-li**) 226
cocodrilo *ayin*, n. (**AYIN**) 37
cola *ne*, n. (**ne/NE**) 182
colibrí *tz'unun*, n. (**tz'u-nu-{n}**) 252
colocado (fue) *k'alaj*, v. pas. (**K'AL-ja**) 145

comer *we'*, v. intr. (**we'/WE'**) 267, 268
comer (la acción de él/ella/este) *u we'y*, v. tr. incom. (**U we'-ya**) 259
comido (fue) *k'uxaj*, v. pas. (**k'u-xa-ja**) 156
comido (he) *k'uxajiy*, v. tr. (**k'u-xa-ji-ya**)...................................156
compañeros (de él/ella/este) *yataj*, n. poss. pl. (**ya-ta-ji**) 285
compañía de (en la) *yete'*, frase prep. (**ye-te'**)...................................292, 293
compañía de (en la) *yete'j*, frase prep. (**ye-te'-je**) 293
compañía de (en la) *yichnal*, frase prep. (**yi-chi-NAL, yi-[chi]-NAL**) 295
compañía de (en la) *yitaj*, frase prep. (**yi-ta, yi-ta-ji, yi-[ta]-ji**) 297
comprometido (fue) *makaj*, v. pas. (**ma-ka-ja**) 167
compromiso (en matrimonio) *mak*, v. tr. (**ma-ka**) 167
compromiso (en matrimonio) *makax*, v. tr. (**ma-ka-xa**) 167
con *ta*, prep. (**ta/TA**) 221, 222
con *ti*, prep. (**ti/TI**) 231
con *yete'*, prep. (**ye-te'**) 292, 293
con *yitaj*, prep. (**yi-ta, yi-ta-ji, yi-[ta]-ji**) 297
concha *jub'*, n. (**JUB', JUB'-b'a**) 121
concluido *tzutziy*, v. intr. com. (**TZUTZ-yi**) 246
concluido (fue) *tzutzaj*, v. pas. (**TZUTZ-ja, tzu-tzu-ja**)...................................245
concluir *k'ay/ch'ay*, v. intr. incom. (**k'a-yi/ch'a-yi**) 150
concluir *jal*, v. tr. (**JAL, ja'-li**) 106, 111
concluir *jal-jiy*, v. intr. (**JAL-ji-ya**) 106
concluir *tzutz*, v. tr. (**TZUTZ**) 244, 245
conejo *tul*, n. (**TUL**) 236
conjurar *tzak*, v. tr. (**tza-[ka]**) 241, 242
conjurar *tzakaw*, v. tr. (**tza-[ka]-wa**) 242
conjurar a Dios/divinidad/santidad *tzakaw ch'ul/tzakaw k'ul*, v. tr.
    (**tza-[ka]-wa CH'UL/tza-[ka]-wa K'UL**) 242
conquistar *nak*, v. tr. (**na-ku**) 180
contado (fue) *tz'akaj*, v. pas. (**TZ'AK-aj**) 247
contar *tz'ak*, v. tr. (**TZ'AK**) 247
contar *tz'ak b'ul*, v. tr. (**TZ'AK b'u-li**) 248
contar *xok*, n. (**xo-ki**) 277
con un pájaro *ti xukpi*, prep. + n. (**ti-xu-[ku]-pi**) 232
copa para beber (de él/ella/este) *yuch'ab'*, n. (**yu-ch'a-b'a, yu-ch'a-b'i**) 304, 305
corazón *ol*, n. (**OL**) 196
corazón *wol*, n. (**wo-la**) 273
corazón (de él/ella/este) *yol*, n. poss. (**yo-OL-la**) 300
corazón suyo *awol*, n. poss. (**AJ-wo-la**) 33
corona *nak*, n. (**na-ku**) 180
cosa *b'a*, suf. ref. (**b'a/B'A**).............................39
cosa elevada *wawaan*, tit. (**wa-wa-aj-ni**) 264
cosa enhiesta *wak*, n. (**WAK**) 262, 263
cosa enhiesta *wawaan*, tit. (**wa-wa-aj-ni**) 264
cosa levantada *wawaan*, tit. (**wa-wa-aj-ni**) 264
cosecha *ch'am*, n. (**CH'AM, CH'AM-ma**) 75, 76
cosechar K'awil *ch'am K'awil*, v. tr.
    (**CH'AM K'AWIL-la, CH'AM-ma K'AWIL-la**).............................75, 76
crecer *tz'ak*, v. tr. (**TZ'AK**).............................247
crecer *tz'ak b'ul*, v. tr. (**TZ'AK b'u-li**) 248
crecido (fue) *tz'akaj*, v. pas. (**TZ'AK-aj**) 247
cuando . . . *tikil*, prep. (**ti-ki-li**) 232
cuarto *way*, n. para dormir (**WAY, WAY-ya**) 266, 267
cuarto *wayb'il*, n. para dormir (**WAY-b'i-li**).............................267
cuarto (en lo de él/ella/este) *tu wayb'il*, frase prep. (**TU WAY-[b'i]-li**) 239
cuatro *chan/kan*, n. num. car. (**CHAN/KAN**) 56, 57
cubierto (fue) *makaj*, v. pas. (**ma-ka-ja**) 167

cubrir *mak*, v. tr. (**ma-ka**) 167
cubrir *makax*, v. tr. (**ma-ka-xa**)..167
Cuenta de Cautivos *aj-X-b'ak*, tit. (**AJ-X-B'AK**) 34
cuenta de los años *tzik ja'ab'?/tzik ab'?*, v. intr. el Glifo Introductorio
    del Serie Inicial (**tzi-ka JA'AB' (?)/tzi-ka AB' (?)**) 243
cueva *ch'en*, n. (**CH'EN, CH'EN-na**) 77, 78
culebra *chan/kan*, n. (**cha-CHAN/ka-KAN, CHAN/KAN, cha-nu/ka-nu**) 57, 58

CH

Chaak *Chaak*, n. nombre del Dios de la Lluvia
    (**CHAAK, CHAAK-ki, cha-ki**) 48, 49, 53, 54
Chak Xib' Chaak *Chak Xib' Chaak*, n. nombre de un Dios
    (**CHAK XIB' cha-ki**) 54
Chatan persona sagrada *ch'ul chatan winik/k'ul chatan winik, ch'ujul
    chatan winik/k'ujul chatan winik*, n. + adj. (**CH'UL cha-TAN
    WINIK/K'UL cha-TAN WINIK (CH'UJUL cha-TAN WINIK/K'UJUL
    cha-TAN WINIK), CH'UL cha-TAN-na wi-WINIK-ki/K'UL
    cha-TAN-na wi-WINIK-ki (CH'UJUL cha-TAN-na wi-WINIK-ki/K'UJUL
    cha-TAN-na wi-WINIK-ki**)) 83, 84
chocolate *kakaw*, n. (**ka-{ka}-wa, ka-ka-wa**)...132

D

dama *na*, n. (**na/NA/NAJ**) 178
dando (de él/ella) *yak'*, n. poss. (**ya-k'u**) 284
dando (de él/ella) *yak'aw*, n. poss. (**ya-k'a-wa**) 283, 284
danta *til*, n. (**TIL**) 232
dar *tz'a*, v. tr. (**tz'a/TZ'A**) 247
dar *wa yak'aw*, v. tr. (**wa-ya-k'a-wa**) 266
de *ti*, prep. (**ti/TI**) 231
decapitado (fue) *ch'akaj*, v. pas. (**ch'a-ka-ja**) 74
decapitar *ch'ak*, v. tr. (**CH'AK, CH'AK-ka**) 74
decapitarse (a uno mismo) *ch'akab'*, v. intr. (**CH'AK-ka-b'a**) 74, 75
decir *aliy*, v. intr. (**a-li-ya**)...36
decir *wa yalaw*, v. tr. (**wa-ya-la-wa**) 266
de él *u*, 3r p. pron. poss. (**u/U**) 253, 254, 255
de él *ya*, 3r p. pron. poss. por palabras que empiezan con *a* (**ya**) 279, 280
de él *ye*, 3r p. pron. poss. prev. por palabras que empiezan con *e*
    (**ye/YE**) 290, 291
de él *yi*, 3r p. pron. poss. prev. por palabras que empiezan con *i* (**yi**) 294
de él *yo*, 3r p. pron. poss. prev. por palabras que empiezan con *o*
    (**yo/YOP, yo**) 298
de él *yu*, 3r p. pron. poss. prev. por palabras que empiezan con *u* (**yu**) 304
de ella *u*, 3r p. pron. poss. (**u/U**) 253, 254, 255
de ella *ya*, 3r p. pron. poss. por palabras que empiezan con *a* (**ya**) 279, 280
de ella *ye*, 3r p. pron. poss. prev. por palabras que empiezan con *e*
    (**ye/YE**) 290, 291
de ella *yi*, 3r p. pron. poss. prev. por palabras que empiezan con *i* (**yi**) 294
de ella *yo*, 3r p. pron. poss. prev. por palabras que empiezan con *o*
    (**yo/YOP, yo**) 298
de ella *yu*, 3r p. pron. poss. prev. por palabras que empiezan con *u* (**yu**) 304
de ello, eso, esto *u*, 3r p. pron. poss. (**u/U**).................................253, 254, 255
de ello, eso, esto *ya*, 3r p. pron. poss. por palabras que empiezan
    con *a* (**ya**)..279, 280
de ello, eso, esto *ye*, 3r p. pron. poss. prev. por palabras que empiezan
    con *e* (**ye/YE**) 290, 291

de ello, eso, esto *yi*, 3r p. pron. poss. prev. por palabras que empiezan
   con *i* (**yi**) 294
de ello, eso, esto *yo*, 3r p. pron. poss. prev. por palabras que empiezan
   con *o* (**yo/YOP, yo**) 298
de ello, eso, esto *yu*, 3r p. pron. poss. prev. por palabras que empiezan
   con *u* (**yu**) 304
delante (de uno) *awa ichnal?*, dec. (**AJ-wa-chi-NAL**) 33
derribado (fue) *jub'uy*, v. intr. guerra (**ju-b'u-yi, JUB'(?)-yi, JUB'(?)-yi-ya**) 122
derribar; guerra *jub'*, v. intr. (**JUB' (?), ju-b'a**) 121
derribar [a un sitio, un lugar] *jub'-Emblem Glyph*, v. intr. guerra
   (**JUB'-EMBLEM GLYPH**) 121
derrumbamiento *kojoy*, v. intr. (**ko-jo-yi**) 137
descansar *jal*, v. intr. (**JAL, ja'-li**) 106, 111
descansar *jal-jiy*, v. intr. (**JAL-ji-ya**) 106
descansar *jil*, v. intr. (**ji-li**) 115
descender *em*, v. intr. (**EM**) 90
desde entonces *xa*, pref. adv. (**xa/XA**) 275
de ser borracho de *tikal*, v. tr. (**ti-ka-la**) 232
desmembrado (fue) *susaj*, v. pas. (**su-sa-ja**) 219
destruido (fue) *satay*, v. intr. com. (**sa-ta-yi**) 216
destruir *jom*, v. tr. (**JOM**) 118, 119
destruir *sat*, v. tr. (**sa-ta**) 216
día *k'in*, n. (**K'IN, K'IN (?), K'IN-ni**) 151, 152, 153
día *lat*, n. (**la-ta**) 161
diadema *nak*, n. (**na-ku**) 180
días después *-lat*, suf. temp. (**la-ta**) 161
dice *aliy*, v. intr. (**a-li-ya**) 36
dice *jal*, v. tr. (**JAL, ja'-li**) 106, 111
dice *jal-jiy*, v. tr. (**JAL-ji-ya**) 106
dices (entonces él/ella/este) *che'en*, part. cit. (**che-e-na, che-je-na**) 60
dices en el hueso de él/ella (entonces) *che'en tu b'ak*, part. cit.
   (**che-e-na TU b'a-ki**) 60
dicho *aliy*, v. intr. (**a-li-ya**) 36
dicho (de él/ella) *yalajiy*, n. poss. (**ya-la-ji-ya**) 285
dicho (de él/ella) *yalij*, n. poss. (**ya-la-ji**) 285
dicho tres veces *ox ajal*, v. (**OX aj-ja-li**) 198
Dieciocho Cabezas [de la Culebra/del Ciempiés] *Waxaklajun U B'a*,
   n. nombre de la Serpiente/del Ciempiés del arte Teotihuacano
   (**WAXAKLAJUN U B'A**)...265
Dieciocho Cabezas [de la Culebra/del Ciempiés] *Waxaklajun U B'a*, n.
   nombre de un rey de Copán del linaje de Yax K'uk' Mo'
   (**WAXAKLAJUN U B'A**)...265
diez *lajun*, n. num. car. (**LAJUN**) 158
dintel *pakab'*, n. (**pa-ka-b'a**) 200
Dios *k'u*, n. (**k'u/K'U**) 154, 155
Dios *k'uj*, n. (**k'u-ju**) 155
Dios (nombre de un) *yop-at*, n. (**YOP-a-AT-ta, YOP-AT, YOP-AT-ta**) 302
Dios celestial, Dios terrenal *ch'ul chaan ch'ul kab'/k'ul kaan k'ul kab'*,
   ch'ujul chaan ch'ujul kab'/k'ujul kaan k'ujul kab', tit.
   (**CH'UL CHAAN CH'UL KAB'/K'UL KAAN K'UL KAB'**
   (**CH'UJUL CHAAN CH'UJUL KAB'/K'UJUL KAAN K'UJUL KAB'**)) 83
Dios del Maíz *Jun Nal Ye*, n. nombre de un Dios (**JUN NAL YE**)...........................127
Dios del Viento *Ik' K'u*, n. nombre del Dios del Viento (**IK' K'U**) 95
Dioses celestiales *chaanal k'u/kaanal k'u*, n.
   (**[CHAAN]-NAL K'U/[KAAN]-NAL K'U**) 51
Dioses celestiales *chaan ch'ul/kaan k'ul*, n.
   (**CHAAN-na CH'UL/KAAN-na K'UL**) 51

Dioses terrenales *kab'al k'u*, n. + adj. (**KAB'-la K'U**) 131
disparar *jul*, v. intr. (**JUL, ju-li, JUL-li**) 123, 124
dispararon (ellos) *julob'*, v. intr. pl. (**ju-li-OB'**) 124
disparo (fue) *julaj*, v. pas. (**JUL-li-ja**) 124
divinidad *k'uj*, n. (**k'u-ju**) 155
divinidad (lo de él/ella/este) *tuk'ul*, frase prep. (**TU K'U-li**) 236
divino *ch'ul/k'ul, ch'ujul/k'ujul*, adj. (**CH'UL/K'UL (CH'UJUL/K'UJUL),**
        CH'UL-lu/K'UL-lu (CH'UJUL-lu/K'UJUL-lu)))..................................80, 81, 82, 84
divino *k'u*, adj. (**k'u/K'U**) 154, 155
Divino Señor del Centro de la Nube *Ch'ul Tok Tan Ajaw/K'ul Tok Tan Ajaw,*
        Ch'ujul Tok Tan Ajaw/K'ujul Tok Tan Ajaw, tit.
        (**CH'UL to-{k} TAN AJAW/K'UL to-{k} TAN AJAW**
        (**CH'UJUL to-{k} TAN AJAW/K'UJUL to-{k} TAN AJAW**))..................85
doblado (fue) *paklaj*, v. pos. (**pa-ka-la-ja**) 200
doce *chalajun/kalajun*, n. num. car. (**CHALAJUN/KALAJUN**)..................................55
dormir *way*, v. intr. (**WAY, WAY-ya**) 266, 267
dos *cha/ka*, n. num. car. (**CHA/KA**) 48

E

echarse *k'a/ch'a*, v. pos. (**k'a/ch'a (K'A/CH'A?)**)...141
él *aj*, pron. del hombre (**a/AJ**) 25, 26
él *u*, pron. de 3r p. (**u/U**) 253, 254, 255
él *ya*, 3r p. pron. prev. por palabras que empiezan con *a* (**ya**)..........................279, 280
él *ye*, 3r p. pron. prev. por palabras que empiezan con *e* (**ye/YE**) 290, 291
él *yi*, 3r p. pron. prev. por palabras que empiezan con *i* (**yi**) 294
él *yo*, 3r p. pron. prev. por palabras que empiezan con *o* (**yo/YOP, yo**) 298
él *yu*, 3r p. pron. prev. por palabras que empiezan con *u* (**yu**) 304
el administrador *aj sul*, tit. (**AJ su-lu**) 32
el de *aj*, pron. del hombre (**a/AJ**) 25, 26
el de la escritura *aj tz'ib'*, tit. (**AJ tz'i-b'a**)..32
el de la escultura *aj uxul*, tit. (**AJ u-xu-[lu]**) 32
el del agua *aj naab'*, tit. (**AJ na-b'i**) 30
el del juego de pelota *aj pitzlawal*, tit. (**AJ pi-tzi-la-wa-{I}, AJ pi-tzi-la-wa-la**) 31
el de los libros sagrados *aj k'ujun*, tit. (**AJ k'u-{JUN}-na, AJ k'u-JUN-na**) 30
el de X-num. de cautivos *aj-X-b'ak*, tit. Vea Cuenta de Cautivos
        (**AJ-X-B'AK**) 34
elevado (algo) *wak*, n. (**WAK**) 262, 263
elevar *nak*, v. intr. (**na-ku**)..180
el jefe *aj payal*, tit. (**AJ pa-ya-la**) 31
el jugador de pelota *aj pitz*, tit. (**AJ pi-tzi**) 31
ella *ix/ixik*, n. pref. agentivo de mujer (**IX/IXIK, IXIK-ki**) 103
ella *u*, pron. del 3r p. (**u/U**) 253, 254, 255
ella *ya*, 3r p. pron. prev. por palabras que empiezan con *a* (**ya**) 279, 280
ella *ye*, 3r p. pron. prev. por palabras que empiezan con *e* (**ye/YE**) 290, 291
ella *yi*, 3r p. pron. prev. por palabras que empiezan con *i* (**yi**) 294
ella *yo*, 3r p. pron. prev. por palabras que empiezan con *o* (**yo/YOP, yo**) 298
ella *yu*, 3r p. pron. prev. por palabras que empiezan con *u* (**yu**) 304
ello, lo, la, eso, esto *u*, pron. de 3r p. (**u/U**)..253, 254, 255
ello, lo, la, eso, esto *ya*, 3r p. pron. prev. por palabras que empiezan
        con *a* (**ya**)...279, 280
ello, lo, la, eso, esto *ye*, 3r p. pron. prev. por palabras que empiezan
        con *e* (**ye/YE**) 290, 291
ello, lo, la, eso, esto *yi*, 3r p. pron. prev. por palabras que empiezan
        con *i* (**yi**) 294
ello, lo, la, eso, esto *yo*, 3r p. pron. prev. por palabras que empiezan
        con *o* (**yo/YOP, yo**)...298

ello, lo, la, eso, esto *yu*, 3r p. pron. prev. por palabras que empiezan
con *u* (**yu**) 304
emerger *joy*, v. tr. (**JOY, jo-JOY**) 117, 119
emerger *joyajiy*, v. tr. (**JOY'-[ja]-ji-ya**) 120
emergió *lok'iy*, v. intr. com. (**LOK'-yi**) 163
emergido (fue) *joyaj*, v. pas. (**jo-JOY-ja, JOY-ja**) 117, 119
emergió de *lok'-ta*, v. intr. (**lo-k'u-ta**) 163
en *ta*, prep. (**ta/TA**) 221, 222
en *tan*, loc. prep. (**TAN, TAN-na**) 226, 228
en *ti*, prep. (**ti/TI**) 231
enano *ch'at*, n. (**ch'a-ti**) 76
en casa (de él/ella/este) *yotot-ti*, prep. + n. poss. (**yo-to-ta-ti**) 303
en casa (fue) *ototaj*, v. pas. (**OTOT-ja**) 197
en de él/ella/este *tu*, prep. + pron. (**TU**) 236
enfrente de *tan*, pos. (**TAN, TAN-na**) 226, 229
enfrente de ellos *yichnal*, prep. + pron. (**yi-chi-NAL, yi-[chi]-NAL**) 295
enfrente de la cueva *tan ch'en*, loc. doble (**TAN CH'EN-na**) 227
enfrente de la cueva Tres Cerro Agua *tan ch'en ox witzaj*, loc. doble
(**TAN CH'EN OX WITZ-aj**)..227
enfrutado (de él/ella) *yutal*, adj. poss. (**yu-ta-{l}, yu-ta-la**) 305, 306
Enhestador *Wak Chaan Ajaw/Wak Kaan Ajaw*, tit.
(**WAK CHAAN-na AJAW/WAK KAAN-na AJAW**) 263
en lugar de sueños (de él/ella/este) *tu wayb'il*, prep. (**TU WAY-[b'i]-li**) 239
enrollada la faja blanca de la cabeza *k'al-jiy sak jun*, v. tr.
(**K'AL-ji-ya SAK JUN**) 145
enrollada la faja blanca de la cabeza *k'al sak jun*, v.
(**K'AL SAK JUN, K'AL SAK ju-na**)..146
enrollada la faja de la cabeza *k'al jun*, v. tr. (**K'AL JUN-na**) 145
enrollada la pata del venado (fue) *k'alaj mayij*, v. pas. (**K'AL-ja MAY-ji**) 145
enrollado (fue) *k'alaj*, v. pas. (**K'AL-ja**) 145
enrollar *k'al*, v. tr. (**K'AL**) 144
enrollar *pixom*, v. tr. (**pi-xo-ma**) 209
entalladura *uxul*, n. (**u-xu-[lu]**) 260
ente *b'a*, n. (**b'a/B'A**) 39
ente *winik*, n. (**WINIK, wi-WINIK-ki**) 269, 271
entero *tz'ak*, adj. (**TZ'AK**) 247
entero (el) *olis*, frase n. (**o-OL-si**) 196, 197
entero (lo de) *olas*, frase n. (**o-la-si**) 196
enterrado (fue) *mukaj*, v. pas. (**mu-ka-ja**) 173
enterrar *muk*, v. tr. (**mu-ka**) 173
entonces ocurrió *i-ut*, part. + v. intr. (PDI) (**i-u-ti**) 102
entonces, y entonces *i*, part. (PDI) (**i/I**) 91
entrada *way*, n. (**WAY, WAY-ya**) 266, 267
entrar *och*, v. intr. (**OCH, OCH-chi**) 191, 192, 193
entrar al agua *och ja'*, v. tr. muerte (**OCH JA'**) 194
entrar a la oficina del arbol *ta ochlel*, prep. (**TA OCH-le-{l}**) 228
entrar al árbol *och te'/ok te'*, v. tr. (**OCH TE'/OK TE'**) 195
entrar al camino *och b'i*, v. tr. (**OCH B'I**) 192
entrar al cielo *och ta chaan/ok ta kaan*, v. tr.
(**OCH TA CHAAN-na/OK TA KAAN-na**) 195
entrar al fuego *och k'ak'*, v. tr. dedicación (**OCH-chi K'AK', OCH K'AK'**) 193, 194
entró al agua (fue) *och ja'-aj*, v. pas. (**OCH JA'-ja**) 194
entró al árbol *och te'/ok te'*, v. tr. (**OCH TE'/OK TE'**) 195
entró al camino (fue) *och b'i-aj*, v. pas. (**OCH-B'I-ja**) 192
entró al cielo *och ta chaan/ok ta kaan*, v. tr.
(**OCH TA CHAAN-na/OK TA KAAN-na**) 195
entró al fuego *och k'ak'*, v. tr. dedicación (**OCH-chi K'AK', OCH K'AK'**) 193, 194

envolver *kotz'*, v. tr. (**ko-tz'o**) 137
envolverse *wol*, v. tr. (**wo-la**) 273
erecto *wa*, pos. v. (**wa/WA**) 261, 262
escalera *eb'*, n. (**e-b'u, EB'-[b'u]**) 88
escalera (de él/ella/este) *yeb'al*, n. poss. (**ye-b'a-li**) 291
escalera de *yeb'al*, n. poss. (**ye-b'a-li**) 291
escapar *lok'iy*, v. intr. com. (**LOK'-yi**) 163
escoger *paj*, v. tr. (**pa/PAJ**) 199
escribano *aj tz'ib'*, tit. (**AJ tz'i-b'a**)...32
escribiente *aj tz'ib'*, tit. (**AJ tz'i-b'a**) 32
escrito *tz'ib'*, n. (**tz'i-b'a, tz'i-b'i**) 251
escudo *pakal*, n. nombre de algunos reyes de Palenque
    (**PAKAL, pa-ka-la**) 200
esculpir *uxul*, v. tr. (**u-xu-[lu]**) 260
escultor *aj uxul*, tit. (**AJ u-xu-[lu]**) 32
escultura *uxul*, n. (**u-xu-[lu]**) 260
esencia *itz'*, n. (**ITZ'**)...99
espadaña (caña de) *pu*, n. (**pu/PU/PUJ**) 210
espalda *pat*, n. (**PAT, pa-ti, PAT-ta**)..202, 203, 204
esparcidor *ch'ajom*, n. (**ch'a-JOM, ch'a-jo-ma**) 73
esparcir *b'an*, v. tr. (**b'a-na**) 42
esparcir *chok*, v. tr. (**CHOK**) 63
esparcir gotas *chokij*, v. tr. (**CHOK-ji**) 63
esparcir gotas de líquido *chokaw ch'aj*, v. tr.
    (**CHOK-ko-wa CH'A-ji, CHOK-wa CH'A-ji**) 64
espina de pastinaca *kix?*, n. (**KIX (?)**) 135, 136
espirado *tzutziy*, v. intr. com. (**TZUTZ-yi**) 246
espirado (fue) *tzutzaj*, v. pas. (**TZUTZ-ja, tzu-tzu-ja**) 245
espirar *tzutz*, v. tr. (**TZUTZ**) 244, 245
espíritu *way*, n. *nawal* (**WAY, WAY-ya**) 266, 267
espíritu *wayab'*, n. (**wa-WAY-{a}-[b'i]**) 264
esplendoroso *sak*, adj. (**SAK**) 213
esposa (de él) *yatan*, n. poss. (**ya-ta-na**) 286
esposa de *yatan*, n. poss. (**ya-ta-na**) 286
estandarte *jasaw*, n. (**ja-sa-wa**) 108
estatua *k'ob'a*, n. (**k'o-b'a**) 154
estatua *k'oj*, n. (**k'o-jo**) 154
este *ja'-i*, pron. dem. (**ja'-i**) 111
estimado *jun tan*, adj. (**JUN TAN-na**) 127
estos *ja'ob'*, pron. dem., pl. (**ja'-o-b'a**) 111
estos, estos son *ja'ob'*, pron. dem., pl. (**ja'-o-b'a**) 111
estrella *ek'*, n. (**EK'**) 89
estrella grande *chak ek'*, n. + adj. (**CHAK EK'**) 53
estructura (en lo de él/ella/este) *tu naj*, prep. (**TU na-ja**) 238
expresión (de él/ella) *yalajiy*, n. poss. (**ya-la-ji-ya**) 285
expresión (de él/ella) *yalij*, n. poss. (**ya-la-ji**)...285

F

faja de la cabeza *junal*, n. (**ju-na-la**) 126
faja de la cabeza de papel *jun*, n. (**JUN, ju-na**) 125, 126
faja negra (de la cabeza) *ek' jun*, n. + adj. (**EK' JUN**) 89
flor *janaab'*, n. (**JANAAB', ja-na-b'i**) 106, 107
flor *nich/nik*, n. (**NICH/NIK**)..183
flor *nichil/nikil*, n. (**NICH-li/NIK-li**)..184
flor *nichim*, n. (**ni-chi-{m}**)...183
flor *nikte'*, n. posiblemente flor de mayo (**NIKTE', NIKTE'-te'**) 184, 185

flor-escudo *janaab' pakal*, n. (**[JANAAB'] PAKAL, [JANAAB'] PAKAL-la**) 107
florida blanca *sak nik*, adj. (**SAK NIK**) 215
forma *pat*, v. tr. (**PAT, pa-ti, PAT-ta**) 202, 203, 204
formado *pat b'uj*, v. tr. com. (**PAT-ta-b'u-ji**) 205
formado *pat b'uy*, v. tr. com. (**PAT-b'u-ya**) 204
formado *patwan*, v. com. (**PAT-ta-wa-ni, PAT-wa-ni**)...............................205
formado (fue) *patlaj*, v. pos. com. (**PAT-[la]-ja**) 204
formado en barro *pak'*, v. tr. (**pa-k'a**) 201
formado en barro *pak'ajiy*, v. intr. com. (**pa-k'a-ji-ya**) 201
fresco *tzi*, adj. (**tzi/TZI**) 243
frijol *b'ul*, n. (**b'u-la**) 46
frijol (de cacao) (de él/ella/este) *yutal*, n. poss. (**yu-ta-{l}, yu-ta-la**) 305
frutado (de él/ella) *ta yutal*, prep. (**TA yu-ta-{l}**) 228
fue desde *utjiy*, v. intr. com. (**u-ti-ji-ya**) 257
fuego *k'ak'*, n. (**K'AK', k'a-K'AK', K'AK'-k'a**) 143
fuego [y] humo *k'ak' b'utz'*, n. (**K'AK'-k'a B'UTZ'-tz'i**) 144
fuerte *kelem*, adj. (**ke-KELEM, ke-le-ma**) 134
fuiste *b'ixan*, v. com. irreg. (**B'IXAN-na**) 44
fuiste *b'ixaniy*, v. com. irreg. (**B'IXAN-ni-ya**) 44
fuiste por arriba *tab'iy*, v. intr. com. (**TAB'-[yi]**) 223, 224

G

garra de jaguar *ich'ak*, n. (**ICH'AK, ICH'AK-ki**) 92, 93
garra de jaguar *mol?*, n. (**MOL (?)**)...171
garra de jaguar (de él/ella/este) *yich'ak*, n. (**yi-ch'a-ki**) 295
girado *petjiy*, v. intr. com. (**PET-ji-ya**) 206
girar *pet*, v. intr. (**PET**) 206
glotón *sitz winik*, n. (**si-tzi WINIK-ki**) 218
golpear *jatz'ay*, v. tr. (**ja-tz'a-yi**) 108
gotas *ch'a*, n. (**ch'a/CH'A**) 71
gotas, gotita *ch'aj*, n. (**ch'a-ji**) 73
gotas de agua, orina u otro líquido *ch'a*, n. (**ch'a/CH'A**) 71
gotas de agua, orina u otro líquido *ch'aj*, n. (**ch'a-ji**) 73
goteador (alguien que gotea) *ch'ajom*, tit. (**ch'a-JOM, ch'a-jo-ma**) 73
gran *chak*, adj. (**CHAK**)..52, 53
gran *lakam*, adj. (**LAKAM, la-ka-ma**) 159
gran *noj*, adj. (**NOJ**) 185, 186
gran *nuk*, adj. (**nu-ku**) 188
Gran Casa Blanca *Sak Nuk Naj*, n. nombre de un edificio (**SAK nu-ku NAJ**) 215
grande *lakam*, adj. (**LAKAM, la-ka-ma**)..159
grande *nuk*, adj. (**nu-ku**) 188
Gran Señor del Santidad *chak ch'ul ajaw/chak k'ul ajaw*, tit.
      (**CHAK CH'UL AJAW/CHAK K'UL AJAW**) 53
grupo entero (el) *olas*, n. + adj. (**o-la-si**) 196
grupo entero (el) *olis*, n. + adj. (**o-OL-si**) 196, 197
grupo entero de los Dioses (el) (?) *olas k'u*, frase n. (**o-la-si K'U**) 196
grupo entero de los Dioses (el) (?) *olis k'u*, frase n. (**o-OL-si K'U**) 197
guacamaya *mo'*, n. (**mo/MO', MO'**) 171, 172
Guacamaya de Montaña *Witz Mo'*, n. (**wi-tzi mo-o**) 270
guardianes *kokonob'*, n. pl. (**ko-ko-no-OB'**) 137
guerra *jub'*, v. intr. (**JUB' (?)**) 121
guerra *jub'-Emblem Glyph*, v. intr. guerra contra un sitio o lugar
      (**JUB'-EMBLEM GLYPH**) 121
guerra *jub'uy*, v. intr. (**ju-b'u-yi, JUB(?)-yi, JUB'(?)-yi-ya**) 122
guerrillero *b'ate'*, n. (**b'a-te'**) 42

H

habitación *way*, n. (**WAY, WAY-ya**) 266, 267
hacer *pat*, v. tr. (**PAT, pa-ti, PAT-ta**) 202, 203, 204
hacer aparecer *tzakaw*, v. tr. (**tza-[ka]-wa**) 242
hacer aparecer a Dios/divinidad/santidad *tzakaw ch'ul/tzakaw k'ul*, v. tr.
    (**tza-[ka]-wa CH'UL/tza-[ka]-wa K'UL**) 242
hacerlo *kab'ij*, v. tr. (**KAB'-ji**) 130
hacerlo *kab'iy*, v. tr. (**KAB'-ya**)...131
hacerlo *kab'jiy*, v. tr. (**KAB'-ji-ya**) 131
hacer redonda *wol*, v. tr. (**wo-la**) 273
hacinado *tz'apajiy*, v. intr. com. (**tz'a-pa-ji-ya**) 249
hacinado (fue) *tz'apaj*, v. pas. (**tz'a-pa-ja, tz'a-[pa]-ja**) 248, 249
hacinar *tz'ap*, v. tr. (**tz'a-[pa]**) 248
hacinar *tz'apwa*, pos. v. (**tz'a-[pa]-wa**) 249
haz *pij*, n. de 400 años cada uno de 360 días; B'aktun (**pi/PI/PIJ, pi-ji**)...............207, 208
hecho *pat b'uj*, v. tr. com. (**PAT-ta-b'u-ji**) 205
hecho *pat b'uy*, v. tr. com. (**PAT-b'u-ya**) 204
hecho *patwan*, v. com. (**PAT-ta-wa-ni, PAT-wa-ni**)...205
hecho (fue) *patlaj*, v. pos. com. (**PAT-[la]-ja**) 204
hender *jatz'ay*, v. tr. (**ja-tz'a-yi**) 108
herida *jatz'ay*, v. tr. (**ja-tz'a-yi**) 108
hermano (mayor) *sukun*, n. (**su-ku-{n}**) 219
hermano (mayor) *sukun winik*, n. + adj. (**su-ku-{n} WINIK-ki**) 219
hermano (menor) *itz'in*, n. (**i-tz'i-{n}**) 101
hermano (menor) *itz'in winik*, n. + adj. (**i-tz'i-{n} WINIK, i-tz'i-{n} wi-WINIK-ki**) 101
hermano (menor) (de él/ella) *yitz'in*, n. poss. (**yi-tz'i-na**) 298
hijo (de él) *yunen*, n. poss. hijo de padre (**yu-NE-{n}**)...305
hijo (de madre) *ya-ch'am*, n. poss. literalmente "cosecha de ella"
    (**ya-CH'AM-ma, ya-CH'AM**)...282, 283
hijo (de madre) *yal*, n. poss. literalmente "cosecha de ella"
    (**ya-AL, ya-la**)...281, 282, 284
hijo (de padre) *nich*, n. relac. (**NICH/NIK**) 183
hijo (de padre) *nichil*, n. relac. (**NICH-li/NIK-li**) 184
hijo (de padre) *nichim*, n. relac. (**ni-chi-{m}**) 183
hijo (de padre) *nik*, n. relac. (**NICH/NIK**) 183
hijo (de padre) *nikil*, n. relac. (**NICH-li/NIK-li**) 184
hijo (de padre) *unen*, n. (**u-ne-{n}**) 256
hombre *winik*, n. (**WINIK, wi-WINIK-ki**)...269, 271
hombre *xib'*, n. (**XIB'**)...277
hombre de K'awilnal *K'awinal winik*, n. (**k'a-wi-NAL WINIK**) 150
hombre divino *ch'ul winik/k'ul winik, ch'ujul winik/k'ujul winik*, n. + adj.
    (**CH'UL WINIK-ki/K'UL WINIK-ki**
    (**CH'UJUL WINIK-ki/K'UJUL WINIK-ki**)) 85
hombre sagrado *ch'ul winik/k'ul winik, ch'ujul winik/k'ujul winik*, n. + adj.
    (**CH'UL WINIK-ki/K'UL WINIK-ki (CH'UJUL WINIK-ki/K'UJUL**
    WINIK-ki)) 85
hombros *pat*, n. (**PAT, pa-ti, PAT-ta**) 202, 203, 204
horizontal *k'a/ch'a*, pos. (**k'a/ch'a (K'A/CH'A?)**) 141
hoy mas temprano *sajmiy*, temp. (**sa-aj-mi-ya**) 212
hoyo *way*, n. (**WAY, WAY-ya**)...266, 267
hoyo negro *ek' waynal*, n. + adj. (**EK' WAY-NAL**) 90
hueso *b'ak*, n. (**B'AK, b'a-ki**) 41
huido su resplandeciente alma florida *k'ay u sak nik ik'il/ch'ay u sak nich
    ik'il*, v. intr. incom. (**k'a-yi U SAK NIK IK'-li/ch'a-yi U SAK NICH IK'-li**) 151
humano *winik*, n. (**WINIK, wi-WINIK-ki**) 269, 271
humo *b'utz'*, n. (**B'UTZ'**) 46

I

imagen *b'a*, n. (**b'a/B'A**) 39
imagen *b'aj*, n. (**b'a-ja**) 40
imagen *k'ob'a*, n. (**k'o-b'a**) 154
imagen *k'oj*, n. (**k'o-jo**) 154
imagen (de él/ella/este) *u b'a*, n. poss. (**U B'A**) 255, 256
imagen de (él) *u b'a*, n. poss. (**U B'A**) 255, 256
incensario *sak lak tun*, n. (**SAK la-ka-TUN, SAK la-ka-TUN-ni**) 214
inmaduro *ch'ok*, adj. (**ch'o-ko, ch'o-[ko]**) 79
intérprete *chi'lam*, n. (**chi-ji-la-ma**) 61
ir *b'ixan*, v. incom. irreg. (**B'IXAN-na**) 44
ir *xan*, v. intr. (**XAN-na, xa-XAN-na**) 275, 276
Itz'amná *Itz'amná*, n. nombre del Dios principal de los Mayas (**itz'-am-{na}**) 99
Itz'am Yej *Itz'am Yej*, n. nombre del Dios Pájaro Principal (**ITZ'AM ye-ji**) 100

J

jaguar *b'alam*, n. (**B'ALAM**) 42
jaguar *ix*, n. (**IX**) 102
jaguar *jix*, n. (**ji-IX, ji-JIX, JIX**) 114, 115
joroba *ch'at*, n. (**ch'a-ti**) 76
joven *ch'ok*, n. (**ch'o-ko, ch'o-[ko]**) 79
joven *kelem*, n. (**ke-KELEM, ke-le-ma**) 134
joven *pitz*, adj. (**pi-tzi**) 208
joven *pitzal*, adj. (**pi-tzi-la**) 209
joven (fue) *pitzalaj*, adj. (**pi-tzi-la-ja**) 209
jovencito *ch'ok*, n. (**ch'o-ko, ch'o-[ko]**) 79
juego de pelota *pitz*, n. (**pi-tzi**) 208
jugador de pelota *pitz*, n. (**pi-tzi**) 208
jugador de pelota *aj pitz*, tit. (**AJ pi-tzi**) 31
jugador de pelota *aj pitzlawal*, tit. (**AJ pi-tzi-la-wa-{l}, AJ pi-tzi-la-wa-la**) 31
jugar pelota *pitzal*, v. intr. (**pi-tzi-la**) 209
jugué pelota *pitzalaj*, v. com. pos. (**pi-tzi-la-ja**) 209
Jun Nal Ye *Jun Nal Ye*, n. nombre del Dios del Maíz (**JUN NAL YE**) 127
juntar *tzutz*, v. tr. (**TZUTZ**) 244, 245
juventud *ch'ok*, adj. (**ch'o-ko, ch'o-[ko]**) 79

K

K'awil *K'awil* n. nombre del Dios K'awil
   (**ka-K'AWIL, K'AWIL, K'AWIL-la, K'AWIL-li**) 143, 149
K'awil del Cielo *Chaan K'awil/Kaan K'awil*, n. nombre de un Dios
   (**CHAAN-na K'AWIL-la/KAAN-na K'AWIL-la**) 51
K'awilnalob' *K'awilnalob'*, n. pl. nombre de un Dios; K'awilnales (pl.)
   (**K'AWIL-NAL-OB'**) 149
K'awilob' *K'awilob'*, n. pl. (**K'AWIL-OB'**) 150

L

labrar *uxul*, v. intr. (**u-xu-[lu]**) 260
lagarto *ayin*, n. (**AYIN**) 37
lanza *lom*, n. (**lo-mu**) 163
lanzar *jul*, v. tr. (**JUL, ju-li, JUL-li**) 123, 124
lápiz de pluma de ave *cheb'*, n. (**che-b'u**) 60
lastimado (fue) *k'uxaj*, v. pas. (**k'u-xa-ja**) 156
lastimar *k'uxajiy*, v. tr. (**k'u-xa-ji-ya**) 156
lengua *ak'*, n. (**ak'/AK'**) 34

lengua (en la) *ti yak'il*, prep. (**TI ya-AK'-li**) 232
levantado *pak'ajiy*, v. intr. com. (**pa-k'a-ji-ya**) 201
levantado *tz'apajiy*, v. intr. com. (**tz'a-pa-ji-ya**) 249
levantado (algo) *wak*, n. (**WAK**) 262, 263
levantado (fue) *tz'apaj*, v. pas. (**tz'a-pa-ja, tz'a-[pa]-ja**) 248, 249
levantar *pak'*, v. tr. (**pa-k'a**) 201
levantar *tz'ap*, v. pos. (**tz'a-[pa]**) 248
levantar *tz'apwa*, v. pos. (**tz'a-[pa]-wa**) 249
libro *jun*, n. (**JUN, ju-na**) 125, 126
llegar *jul*, v. intr. (**JUL, ju-li**) 123, 124
llegar *tal*, v. intr. (**TAL, ta-li**) 226
llegaron (ellos) *julob'*, v. intr. pl. (**ju-li-OB'**) 124
llegó *juliy*, v. intr. com. (**ju-li-ya**) 125
llegó (fue) *julaj*, v. pas. (**JUL-li-ja**)` 124
llegó (fue) *takaj*, v. pas. (**ta-ki-ja**) 225
llenar *najiy*, v. tr. incom. (**na-ja-yi**) 180
llevado (fue) *kuch-taj*, v. pas. (**KUCH-ta-ja**) 138
llevar *kuch*, v. tr. (**KUCH, ku-chu**) 138
lodo *luk'*, n. (**lu-k'u**) 164
lugar *-nal*, suf. loc. det. (**NAL**) 180, 181
Lugar de Hoyo Negro *Ek' Waynal*, n. (**EK' WAY-NAL**) 90
Lugar de la Escalera Preciosa *K'anal Eb'*, n. + adj. (**K'AN-NAL-la e-b'u**) 148
Lugar de la Montaña de la Flor Blanca *Witz Sak Nik Nal*, n. nombre
    del monstruo Kawak de la Tableta de la Cruz Foliada de Palenque
    (**wi-tzi SAK-NIK-ki NAL**) 271
lugar del mar de fuego *k'ak' naab'*, n. + adj. (**K'AK' NAAB'**) 144
Lugar del Sol y del Agua *K'in Ja'nal*, n. (**K'IN-ni JA'-NAL**) 154
Lugar del trona de Piedra del Jaguar *Ix Tzam? Ku-aj*, n. (**IX TZ'AM(?) ku-aj**) 103
Lugar del Valle *Jemnal*, n. (**JEM-NAL**) 112

M

madera *te'/che'*, n. (**te'/TE' (che'/CHE')**) 228, 229, 230
madre *na*, n. (**na/NA/NAJ**) 178
madre (de él/ella) *yaxun?*, n. poss. (**ya-xu-na (?)**) 290
maíz *nal*, n. (**NAL**) 180, 181
manifestación tres veces *ox ajal*, v. (**OX aj-ja-li**) 198
manifestar *jal*, v. tr. (**JAL, ja'-li**) 106, 111
manifestar *jal-jiy*, v. tr. (**JAL-ji-ya**) 106
manifestar Dios/divinidad/santidad *tzakaw ch'ul/tzakaw k'ul*, v. tr.
    (**tza-[ka]-wa CH'UL/tza-[ka]-wa K'UL**) 242
mano *k'ab'*, n. (**K'AB', k'a-[b'a]**) 142
mar *naab'*, n. (**NAAB', na-b'i**) 178, 179
marcador del aspecto progresivo *i-yuwal* (**i-yu-wa-la**) 104
marcador del aspecto progresivo (?) *wa*, (**wa/WA**) 261, 262
marcador negativo *ma* (**ma/MA**) 165, 166
mar del fuego *k'ak' naab'*, n. + adj. (**K'AK' NAAB'**) 144
mar primordial *k'ak' naab'*, n. + adj. (**K'AK' NAAB'**) 144
máscara *k'ob'a*, n. (**k'o-b'a**) 154
máscara *k'oj*, n. (**k'o-jo**) 154
máscara *nak*, n. (**na-ku**) 180
matawil *matawil*, tit. de Dioses (**ma-ta-wi-la**) 168
media (en) (?) *chatan*, prep. (**cha-TAN-na**) 58
medio *ol*, n. (**OL**) 196
medio de (en el) *tan*, prep. (**TAN, TAN-na**) 226, 228
mi *in*, pron. poss. del 1r p. (**IN**) 98
mi arete *in tup*, n. poss. (**IN tu-pa**) 99

mi cueva *in ch'en*, n. poss. (**IN CH'EN**) 98
mi ropa *in b'uk*, n. poss. (**IN-b'u-ku**) 98
mismo *b'a*, suf. ref. (**b'a/B'A**) 39
mi tierra *in kab'*, n. poss. (**IN KAB'**) 98
mi tributo *in pat*, n. poss. (**IN pa-ta**) 99
molde *pak'*, v. tr. (**pa-k'a**) 201
moldurado *pak'ajiy*, v. intr. com. (**pa-k'a-ji-ya**) 201
moler *k'uxajiy*, v. tr. (**k'u-xa-ji-ya**) 156
molido (fue) *k'uxaj*, v. pas. (**k'u-xa-ja**) 156
mono (tipo araña) *max*, n. (**ma-xi**) 168, 169
mono (tipo saraguate) *b'atz'*, n. (**b'a-tz'u**) 42
montaña *witz*, n. (**WITZ, wi-tzi**) 270
Montaña de Guacamaya *Mo' Witz*, n. nombre de un local (**MO' WITZ**) 172
morirse *chamiy*, v. intr. incom. (**CHAM-mi-ya**) 56
muchas fuerzas *b'olon iplaj*, n. (**B'OLON i-pi-[la]-ja**) 45
muchos *ox*, adj. (**OX**) 197, 198
muchos *b'olon*, adj. (**B'OLON**) 44, 45
muerte *cham*, v. intr. (**CHAM, CHAM-(mi)**) 55, 56
muerte *chamil*, v. intr. (**CHAM-li**) 56
muerte *k'ay u sak nik ik'il/ch'ay u sak nich ik'il*, v. intr. incom.
   (**k'a-yi U SAK NIK IK'-li/ch'a-yi U SAK NICH IK'-li**) 151
muerte *och b'i*, v. tr. (**OCH B'I**) 192
muerte *och b'i-aj*, v. pas. (**OCH B'I-ja**) 192
muerte *och b'ij-jiy*, v. tr. (**OCH B'I-ji-ji-ya**) 193
muerte *och ja'*, v. tr. (**OCH JA'**) 194
mujer *ix*, n. (**IX/IXIK, IXIK-ki**) 103
mujer *ixik*, n. (**IX/IXIK, IXIK-ki**) 103
mujer divina *ch'ul ixik/k'ul ixik, ch'ujul ixik/k'ujul ixik*, adj. + n.
   (**CH'UL IXIK-ki/K'UL IXIK-ki, CH'UJUL IXIK-ki/K'UJUL IXIK-ki**) 84
mujer sagrada *ch'ul ixik/k'ul ixik, ch'ujul ixik/k'ujul ixik*, adj. + n.
   (**CH'UL IXIK-ki/K'UL IXIK-ki, CH'UJUL IXIK-ki/K'UJUL IXIK-ki**) 84
murciélago *sutz'*, n. animal (**su-tz'i**) 219

N

nacer *si*, v. intr. (**SI**) 217
nacido (fue) *siyaj*, v. pas. (**SI-ya-ja**) 218
nada *mi*, n. (**mi/MI**) 169, 170
Na Kan *Na Kan*, n. nombre de un Dios; nombre de una Serpiente de la
   Visión (**NA ka-KAN**) 180
nawal *way*, n. (**WAY, WAY-ya**) 266, 267
nawal *wayab'*, n. (**wa-WAY-{a}-[b'i]**) 264
néctar de flor *itz'*, n. (**ITZ'**) 99
negro *ek'*, adj. (**EK'**) 88, 89
nieto (de él/ella) *yab'il*, n. poss. (**ya-b'i-li**) 282
ninfa (?) *naab'*, n. (**NAAB', na-b'i**) 178, 179
no, ni *ma*, adv. (**ma/MA**) 165, 166
no hay corazón *mi ol*, marcador negativo + n. (**MI OL-la**) 170
nombre *k'ab'a*, n. (**K'AB'A**) 142
nombre del *chat chat k'ab'a*, tit. (**cha-te' K'AB'A**) 58
nombre divino *ch'ul k'ab'a/k'ul k'ab'a*, n. + adj.
   (**CH'UL K'AB'A/K'UL K'AB'A**) 84
nombre juvenil *ch'ok k'ab'a*, n. + adj. (**ch'o-[ko] K'AB'A**) 80
nombre sagrado *ch'ul k'ab'a/k'ul k'ab'a*, n. + adj.
   (**CH'UL K'AB'A/K'UL K'AB'A**) 84
norte *nal*, n. dir. car. (**NAL (?), na-NAL (?)**) 181

norte *nojol*, n. dir. car. (**NOJOL**) 186
norte *xaman*, n. dir. car. (**xa-ma-na**) 275
no vió *ma ilaj*, v. pas. (**MA-[IL]-aj**) 166
nube *muyal*, n. (**MUYAL**) 176
nube *tok*, n. (**to-ko**) 233
nueve *b'olon*, n. num. car. (**B'OLON**)...44, 45
nuevo *tzi*, adj. (**tzi/TZI**) 243

O

objeto del baile *xuk*, n. nombre de un objeto del baile usado a Yaxchilán
    (**xu-[ku]**) 277
objeto del baile *xukpi*, n. nombre de un objeto del baile usado a Yaxchilán
    (**xu-[ku]-ab**) 278
obscuridad *ak'ab'*, n. (**AK'AB'**) 35
obsidiana *taj*, n. (**ta-ji**) 224
occidente *chik'in*, n. dir. car. (**chi-K'IN-ni**) 62
occidente *och k'in*, n. dir. car. (**OCH K'IN**)..195
occidente (en el) *chik'inil*, prep. (**chi-[K'IN]-li**)..62
ocurrido (desde lo fui) *utiy*, v. intr. com.; ADI (**u-ti-ya**) 257, 258
ocurrido (desde lo fui) *utjiy*, v. intr. com.; ADI (**u-ti-ji-ya**) 257
ocurrido a la (fue) *utiy*, prep. (**u-ti-ya**) 257, 258
ocurrido a la (fue) *utjiy*, prep. (**u-ti-ji-ya**) 257
ocurrió *ut*, v. intr. (**u-ti**) 257
ocurrió (desde) *utiy*, v. intr. com.; ADI (**u-ti-ya**) 257, 258
ocurrió (desde) *utjiy*, v. intr. com.; ADI (**u-ti-ji-ya**) 257
ocurrir (en seguida) *utom*, v. intr. incom.; FDI (**u-to-ma**) 258, 259
ocurrirá (será) *utom*, v. intr. incom.; FDI (**u-to-ma**) 258, 259
ocho *waxak*, n. num. car. (**WAXAK**) 265
oeste *chik'in*, n. dir. car. (**chi-K'IN-ni**) 62
oeste *och k'in*, n. dir. car. (**OCH K'IN**) 195
oeste (en él) *chik'inil*, prep. (**chi-[K'IN]-li**) 62
ofrecimiento (de él/ella) *yak'*, n. poss. (**ya-k'u**) 284
ofrecimiento (de él/ella) *yak'aw*, n. poss. (**ya-k'a-wa**) 283, 284
ojos del sol *k'ina*, adj. (**K'INA/K'INICH, K'INICH, K'INICH-ni**) 152
ojos del sol *k'inich*, adj. (**K'INA/K'INICH, K'INICH, K'INICH-ni**) 152
once *b'uluk*, n. num. car. (**B'ULUK**) 46
orador *chi'lam*, n. (**chi-ji-la-ma**) 61
oriente *lak'in*, n. dir. car. (**LAK-K'IN-ni**) 160
otra vez *xa*, pref. adv. (**xa/XA**) 275
Ox B'olon Chaak *Ox B'olon Chaak*, n. nombre de un Dios; probablemente
    GI de la Tríada de Palenque (**OX B'OLON CHAAK**) 198

P

padre *chit*, n. (**CHIT, CHIT-ti**) 62, 63
pago *tojol*, n. (**to-jo-li**) 233
pájaro *mut*, n. (**mu-ti**)..174
pájaro *mutul*, n. glifo principal del EG de Tikal (**MUTUL**) 174, 175
pájaro *muwan*, n. pájaro mitológico; tipo gavilán (?)
    (**MUWAN-ni, MUWAN-na, mu-wa-ni**) 175, 176
pájaro mot-mot (?) *xuk*, n. (**xu-[ku]**) 277
pájaro mot-mot (?) *xukpi*, n. (**xu-[ku]-pi**) 278
palo *lom*, n. (**lo-mu**) 163
paloma *mukuy*, n. (**mu-ku-yi**) 174
paloma *tukun*, n. (**tu-ku-nu**) 236

paño de tributo *yub'te'*, n. (**yu-b'u-te'**) 304
papel *jun*, n. (**JUN**, **ju-na**) 125, 126
pared *paj*, n. (**pa/PAJ**) 199
pasó (desde) *utiy*, v. intr. com.; ADI (**u-ti-ya**) 257, 258
pasó (desde) *utjiy*, v. intr. com.; ADI (**u-ti-ji-ya**) 257
pata de venado *may?*, n. (**MAY (?)**) 169
pavo *kutz'*, n. (**ku-tz'u**) 139
peccarí *chitam*, n. (**CHITAM**) 62
pedernal *tok'*, n. (**TOK'**, **to-k'a**) 234, 235
pedernal divino *ch'ul tok'/k'ul tok'*, *ch'ujul tok'/k'ujul tok'*, adj. + n.
     (**CH'UL-lu to-k'a/K'UL-lu to-k'a**
     (**CH'UJUL-lu to-k'a/K'UJUL-lu to-k'a)**) 85
pedernal sagrado *ch'ul tok'/k'ul tok'*, *ch'ujul tok'/k'ujul tok'*, adj. + n.
     (**CH'UL-lu to-k'a/K'UL-lu to-k'a**
     (**CH'UJUL-lu to-k'a/K'UJUL-lu to-k'a)**) 85
pedernal y escudo *tok' pakal*, n. (Ch'olan) (**to-k'a pa-ka-la**, **TOK' PAKAL**) 235
pene *ach*, n. (Ch'olan) (**ACH-cha**)..27
pene *at*, n. (Yucatec) (**AT**, **AT-ti**) 36, 37
pene (ensangrado) *toxat*, n. (**to-[xa]-AT-ti**, **to-XAT**) 235, 236
pene con cicatriz *yo-at*, n. + adj. (**yo-a-AT-ta**, **yo-AT**, **yo-AT-ta**, **yo-AT-ti**) 298, 299
pene con cicatriz (de él/este) *yoxat*, n. poss. (**yo-[xa]-AT-ti (?)**) 304
penitencia (hacer) *ch'ab'*, v. intr. (**CH'AB**, **ch'a-b'a**) 72
perder *sat*, v. tr. (**sa-ta**) 216
perdido (fue) *satay*, v. intr. com. (**sa-ta-yi**) 216
perforar *jul*, v. tr. (**JUL**, **ju-li**, **JUL-li**) 123, 124
perro *tzul*, n. (**tzu-lu**) 244
perro *tz'i*, n. (**TZ'I**, **tz'i-i**) 250, 252
persona *winik*, n. (**WINIK**, **wi-WINIK-ki**) 269, 271
Persona del Centro de la Nube *Tok Tan Winik*, tit. (**to-ko TAN WINIK-ki**) 234
persona en pie *b'akab'*, tit. (**b'a-ka-b'a**) 41
pescado *chay/kay*, n. (**CHAY/KAY**, **cha-ya**) 59
pie *och/ok*, n. (**OCH/OK**) 192
pie (de él/ella/este) *yok*, n. poss. (**yo-ko**, **yo-OK-ki**) 299, 300
pie de (al) *ta ochlel*, prep. (**TA OCH-le-{l}**) 228
piedra *tun*, n. (**TUN**, **TUN-ni**) 237, 238
piedra acuosa *naab' tunich*, n. + adj. (**NAAB' TUN-chi**)..179
piedra amarilla *k'an tun*, n. + adj. (**K'AN TUN-ni**) 148
piedra de antorcha *taj tun*, n. (**TAJ TUN**) 225
piedra de bandera *lakam tun*, n. + adj. (**LAKAM TUN**, **LAKAM TUN-ni**) 160
piedra de carga *kuch tun*, n. (**KUCH TUN**) 138
piedra de garra de jaguar *ich'ak tun*, n. (**ICH'AK TUN-ni**) 93
piedra grande *lakam tun*, n. + adj. (**LAKAM TUN**, **LAKAM TUN-ni**) 160
piedra preciosa *k'an tun*, n. + adj. (**K'AN TUN-ni**) 148
pintura *tz'ib'*, n. (**tz'i-b'a**, **tz'i-b'i**) 251
pisado en (fue) *tek'aj*, v. pas. (**te'-k'a-ja**) 230
pisar *tek'*, v. tr. (**te'-k'a**) 230
plantado *pak'ajiy*, v. intr. com. (**pa-k'a-ji-ya**) 201
plantado recto *tz'apajiy*, v. intr. com. (**tz'a-pa-ji-ya**)..249
plantado recto (fue) *tz'apaj*, v. pas. (**tz'a-pa-ja**, **tz'a-[pa]-ja**)..................................248, 249
plantar *pak'*, v. tr. (**pa-k'a**)..201
plantar recto *tz'ap*, v. pos. (**tz'a-[pa]**) 248
plantar recto *tz'apwa*, v. pos. (**tz'a-[pa]-wa**) 249
plato *lak*, n. (**LAK**, **la-ka**) 159
plato (de tipo trípode) *jawte'*, n. (**ja-wa-te'**) 108, 109
plaza *naab'*, n. (**NAAB'**, **na-b'i**) 178, 179
poner *k'al*, v. tr. (**K'AL**) 144

poner en orden *tz'ak*, v. tr. (**TZ'AK**) 247
poner en orden *tz'ak b'ul*, v. tr. (**TZ'AK b'u-li**) 248
poner en orden *tz'akaj*, v. pas. (**TZ'AK-aj**)...247
portal *pasil*, n. (**pa-si-li**) 202
portal *way*, n. (**WAY, WAY-ya**) 266, 267
precioso *k'an*, adj. (**K'AN, K'AN-na**) 147
presentado *tab'iy*, v. intr. com. (**TAB'-[yi]**) 223, 224
presentar *tab'*, v. tr. (**TAB'**) 223
primera cosecha *yax ch'am*, n. + adj. (**YAX CH'AM, YAX ch'a-CH'AM**) 288
primera cosecha [de] K'awil *yax ch'am K'awil*, v. (**YAX CH'AM K'AWIL**) 288
primera imagen *yax k'oj*, n. + adj. (**YAX k'o-jo**) 289
primer amanecer *yax pas*, n. + adj. (**YAX PAS, YAX pa-{s}**) 289
primer brote *b'a ch'ok*, tit. (**B'A ch'o-ko**) 40
primer escultor *b'a uxul*, tit. (**B'A u-xu-[lu]**) 42
primer joven *b'a ch'ok*, tit. (**B'A ch'o-ko**) 40
primer miembro del linaje *b'a ch'ok*, tit. (**B'A ch'o-ko**) 40
primer nacido *b'a yal*, tit. (**B'A YAL**) 43
primero *b'a*, adj. (**b'a/B'A**) 39
primero *na*, adj.; num. ord. (**na/NA/NAJ**) 177, 178
primero *yax*, adj. (**YAX, ya-xa**) 286, 287
primer padre (?) *yax chit*, n. + adj. (**YAX CHIT**) 287
primer recibiendo [del] K'awil *yax ch'am K'awil*, v. (**YAX CH'AM K'AWIL**) 288
primer señor *b'a ajaw*, tit. (**B'A AJAW**) 40
prometer en matrimonio *mak*, v. tr. (**ma-ka**) 167
prometer en matrimonio *makax*, v. tr. (**ma-ka-xa**) 167
prometida en matrimonio (fue) *makaj*, v. pas. (**ma-ka-ja**) 167
Pu *Pu*, n. nombre en Maya del lugar mitológico de Tollan (**pu/PU/PUJ**).....................210

Q

quemado *puliy*, v. intr. com. (**pu-lu-yi, PUL-[yi]**) 210
querido *jun tan*, adj. (**JUN TAN-na**) 127
quetzal *k'uk'*, n. pájaro (**K'UK'**) 155

R

raíz *wi*, n. (**wi/WI**) 268, 269
Raíz-Brote Casa de Árbol *Wi Ch'ok Te' Na*, n. glifo del
   "Fundador del Linaje" (**WI CH'OK TE' NA**) 269
raspado (fue) *susaj*, v. pas. (**su-sa-ja**) 219
recibir *ch'am*, v. tr. (**CH'AM, CH'AM-ma**) 75, 76
recibir K'awil *ch'am K'awil*, v. tr. (**CH'AM K'AWIL-la, CH'AM-ma K'AWIL-la**) 75, 76
redondo (algo) *wol*, n. (**wo-la**) 273
reducido a la mitad (fue) *tan lamaj*, v. pas. "de la mitad del período"
   (**[TAN] LAM-ja**) 227
regresado (alguien) *pakax*, v. (**pa-ka-xa**) 201
reinado *ajawlel*, n. (**AJAW-le-le**) 29
reino (en) *ti ajawlel*, prep. (**TI AJAW le-{l}**) 231
relicario del linaje *wayb'il*, n. (**WAY-b'i-li**) 267
resina *itz'*, n. (**ITZ'**) 99
revelado *yej*, adj. (**ye/YE**)..290, 291
rizo de maíz *nal*, n. (**NAL**) 180, 181
rociado *puliy*, v. intr. com. (**pu-lu-yi, PUL-[yi]**) 210
rojo *chak*, adj. (**CHAK**) 52, 53
ropa *b'uk*, pl. n. (**b'u-ku**) 45
rotar *pet*, v. intr. (**PET**) 206

S

sabio *itz'at*, n. (**ITZ'AT, i-tz'a-ta, ITZ'AT-ta**) 100, 101

sacrificio *ch'ab'*, v. intr. (**CH'AB', ch'a-b'a**) 72

sagrado *ch'ul/k'ul, ch'ujul/k'ujul*, adj. (**CH'UL/K'UL (CH'UJUL/K'UJUL),
   CH'UL-lu/K'UL-lu (CH'UJUL-lu/K'UJUL-lu)**) 80, 81, 82, 84

sagrado *k'u*, adj. (**k'u/K'U**) 154, 155

Sak Ik' Ek' *Sak Ik' Ek'*, n. nombre de un Dios con manifestaciones
   del viento; Dios Resplandeciente del Viento? (**SAK IK' EK'**) 214

salir *lok'iy*, v. intr. com. (**LOK'-yi**) 163

salir de *lok'-ta*, v. intr. (**lo-k'u-ta**) 163

sangrador *ch'ajom*, tit. (**ch'a-jo-ma, ch'a-JOM**) 73

santidad (manifestar, conjurar) *tzakaw ch'ul/tzakaw k'ul*, v. tr.
   (**tza-[ka]-wa CH'UL/tza-[ka]-wa K'UL**) 242

saraguate (mono, tipo de) *b'atz'*, n. (**b'a-tz'u**) 42

sazonado *tzi*, adj. (**tzi/TZI**) 243

seis *wak*, n. num. car. (**WAK**) 262, 263

seis cielos *wak chaan/wak kaan*, n. (**WAK-ki CHAAN/WAK-ki KAAN**) 263

semillas (de él/ella/este) *ta yutal*, frase prep. (**TA yu-ta-{l}**) 228

semillas (de él/ella/este) *yutal*, n. poss. (**yu-ta-{l}, yu-ta-la**) 305, 306

señor *ajaw*, tit. (**AJAW, AJAW-wa, a-ja-wa**) 27, 28, 29

señor (de él/ella/este) *yajaw*, n. poss. generalmente "subordinado"
   (**ya-AJAW-wa, ya-ja-wa**) 280, 283

Señor Blanco del Árbol *Sak Te' Ajaw*, tit. (**SAK TE' AJAW-wa**) 215

Señor de la Flor-Pajaro *K'uy Nik Ajaw*, tit. (**k'u-yu NIK-ki AJAW**) 156

Señor de la Montaña Guacamaya *Mo' Witz Ajaw*, tit.
   (**mo-o WITZ AJAW, mo-o wi-tzi AJAW**) 172

Señor del Árbol *ajaw te'*, tit. (**AJAW-wa TE'**) 29

Señor del Árbol *yajaw te'*, n. poss. tit. (**ya-AJAW-wa TE'**) 281

Señor del Árbol (de él/ella) *yajaw te'*, n. poss. tit. (**ya-AJAW-wa TE'**) 281

Señor del Árbol (de él/ella/este) *u yajaw te'*, n. poss. tit. (**U ya-AJAW-wa TE'**) 260

Señor del Centro de la Nube *Tok Tan Ajaw*, n. poss. tit. (**to-ko TAN AJAW**) 234

Señor del Centro de la Nube Sagrada *Ch'ul Tok Tan Ajaw/K'ul Tok Tan Ajaw,
   Ch'ujul Tok Tan Ajaw/K'ujul Tok Tan Ajaw*, tit.
   (**CH'UL to-{k} TAN AJAW/K'UL to-{k} TAN AJAW
   (CH'UJUL to-{k} TAN AJAW/K'UJUL to-{k} TAN AJAW)**) 85

Señor del Fuego *Yajaw K'ak'*, n. poss. tit. (**ya-AJAW K'AK'**) 280

Señor de los Seis Cielos *Wak Chaan Ajaw/Wak Kaan Ajaw*, n. poss. tit.
   (**WAK CHAAN-na AJAW/WAK KAAN-na AJAW**) 263

Señor del Sol *K'in Ajaw*, tit. (**K'IN-ni AJAW**) 153

Señor de Witik *Witik Ajaw*, tit. (**wi-ti-ki AJAW**) 270

señor divino *ch'ul ajaw/k'ul ajaw, ch'ujul ajaw/k'ujul ajaw*, tit.
   (**CH'UL AJAW-wa/K'UL AJAW-wa
   (CH'UJUL AJAW-wa/K'UJUL AJAW-wa)**) 83

Señor Elevado del Cielo *Wak Chaan Ajaw/Wak Kaan Ajaw*, tit.
   (**WAK CHAAN-na AJAW/WAK KAAN-na AJAW**) 263

Señores de Mutul *Mutul Ajaw-tak*, pl. n. poss. tit. (**MUTUL AJAW-TAK**) 175

señoría (en) *ti ajawlel*, frase prep. (**TI AJAW LE-{l}**) 231

Señor Lavantado *Wak Chaan Ajaw/Wak Kaan Ajaw*, tit.
   (**WAK CHAAN-na AJAW/WAK KAAN-na AJAW**) 263

señor rojo sagrado *chak ch'ul ajaw/chak k'ul ajaw*, tit.
   (**CHAK CH'UL AJAW/CHAK K'UL AJAW**) 53

señor sagrado *ch'ul ajaw/k'ul ajaw, ch'ujul ajaw/k'ujul ajaw*, título
   (**CH'UL AJAW-wa/K'UL AJAW-wa
   (CH'UJUL AJAW-wa/K'UJUL AJAW-wa)**) 83

sentado *chum*, v. pos. (**CHUM, CHUM (?), CHUM-[mu]**) 66, 67

sentado *chumlajiy*, v. pos. com. (**CHUM-la-ji-ya, CHUM-[mu]-la-ji-ya**) 67

sentado *chumwaniy*, v. pos. com. (**CHUM-[mu]-wa-ni-ya**) 68
sentado en señoría *chumwan ti ajawlel*, v. (**CHUM-wa-ni TI AJAW LE-{l}**) 68
sentamiento de la piedra *chum tun*, v.
   (**CHUM-[mu] TUN-ni, [CHUM] TUN-ni**) 68
sentamiento del *tun chum tun*, v. (**CHUM-[mu] TUN-ni, [CHUM] TUN-ni**) 68
ser del cielo *och ta chaan/ok ta kaan*, v. tr.
   (**OCH TA CHAAN-na/OK TA KAAN-na**) 195
serpiente *chan/kan*, n. (**cha-CHAN/ka-KAN, CHAN/KAN**) 52, 57
siete *wuk*, n. num. car. (**WUK**) 273
sobre, encima *ti*, prep. (**ti/TI**) 231
sol *k'in*, n. (**K'IN, K'IN-ni**) 151, 152, 153
soñador *wayab'*, n. (**wa-WAY-{a}-[b'i]**) 264
soy su serviente *a winiken*, dec. (**AJ-wi-na-{i} ke-na**) 33
subir *nak*, v. intr. (**na-ku**) 180
subir *tab'*, v. tr. (**TAB'**) 223
subir *tab'iy*, v. intr. com. (**TAB'-[yi]**) 223, 224
subordinado *sajal*, tit. (**sa-ja-la**) 213
sudadero *pib' naj*, n. *temescal* (**pi-b'i NA-aj**) 207
sudadero *pib'nal*, n. *temescal* (**pi-b'i-NA-li**) 207
sudor *itz'*, n. (**ITZ'**)..99
sufijo plural *-tak* (**TAK, ta-ki, TAK-ki**) 225
superficie [para escribir] *jich*, n. (**ji-chi**) 114
superficie [para escribir] (de este) *yich*, poss. n. (**yi-chi**) 294
suyo *a*, pron. de 2o p. poss. (**a/AJ**) 25

T

tabaco *may?*, n. (**MAY (?)**) 169
tajado (fue) *ch'akaj*, v. pas. (**ch'a-ka-ja**) 74
tajar (a uno mismo) *ch'akab'*, v. intr. (**CH'AK-ka-b'a**) 74, 75
tajar (con hacha) *ch'ak*, v. tr. (**CH'AK, CH'AK-ka**) 74
tamale *wa*, n. (**wa/WA**) 261
tamale *waj*, n. (**wa-WA-ji**) 264
tapadera *mak*, n. (**ma-ka**) 167
tapir *til*, n. (**TIL**) 232
tela de tributo *yub'te'*, n. (**yu-b'u-te'**) 304
temescal *pib' naj*, n. (**pi-b'i NA-aj**) 207
temescal *pib'nal*, n. (**pi-b'i-NA-li**)...207
terminación *k'al*, n. (**K'AL**) 144
terminación (de él/ella) *yajil*, n. poss. (**ya-ja-li**) 283
terminado *tzutziy*, v. intr. com. (**TZUTZ-yi**) 246
terminado (fue) *tzutzaj*, v. pas. (**TZUTZ-ja, tzu-tzu-ja**) 245
terminar *jal*, v. intr. (**JAL, ja'-li**) 106, 111
terminar *jil*, v. intr. (**ji-li**) 115
terminar *jom*, v. tr. (**JOM**) 118, 119
terminar *-laj*, v. tr. (**-la-ja**) 157
terminar *tzutz*, v. tr. (**TZUTZ**) 244, 245
testificado (por él/ella/este) *yilij*, pron. + v. tr. com. (**yi-IL-ji**) 295, 296
testificado (por él/ella/este) *yilajiy*, pron. + v. tr. com. (**yi-li-aj-ji-ya**) 297
testificado por él/ella/este (fue) *yilaj*, v. pas. (**yi-IL-la-ja, yi-la-ji**) 296
tiburón *xok*, n. (**xo-ki**) 277
tierra *kab'*, n. (**KAB'**) 129, 130
tierra *lum*, n. (**lu-mi**) 164
tina de sudadero *pib' naj*, n. *temescal* (**pi-b'i NA-aj**) 207
tina de sudadero *pib'nal*, n. *temescal* (**pi-b'i-NA-li**) 207
tintero *kuch ab'ak*, n. (**KUCH AB'AK**) 138

tirado (fue) *julaj*, v. pas. (**JUL-li-ja**) 124
tirando (de él/ella) *yalaj*, n. poss. (**ya-la-ja**) 284
tirando (fue) *julaj*, v. pas. (**JUL-li-ja**) 124
tirar *jul*, v. tr. (**JUL, ju-li, JUL-li**) 123, 124
tiró (ellos) *julob'*, v. intr. pl. (**ju-li-OB'**)......................124
título (sin descifrar) *kalomte'*
    (**KALOMTE', ka-KALOMTE'-te', ka-lo-ma-te', KALOMTE'-te'**) 132, 133
tocado *kojaw*, n. (**KOJAW, KOJAW-wa, ko-ja-wa**) 136, 137
tocado *pixom*, n. (**pi-xo-ma**)..209
tocayo *yete' k'ab'a-il*, poss. n. (**ye-te' k'a-b'a-li**) 293
todos los Dioses (?) *olas k'u*, frase n. (**o-la-si K'U**) 196
todos los Dioses (?) *olis k'u*, frase n. (**o-OL-si K'U**) 197
tomar *tzak*, v. tr. (**tza-[ka]**) 241, 242
tomar *tzakaw*, v. tr. (**tza-[ka]-wa**) 242
tortilla *wa*, n. (**wa/WA**) 261, 262
tortilla *waj*, n. (**wa-WA-ji**) 264
tortuga *ak*, n. (**a-ku**) 34
trago *uch'*, n. (**UCH'**) 256
traste (de barro) *jay*, n. (**ja-yi**) 109
tres *ox*, n. num. car. (**OX**)..197, 198
tributo *ikatz*, n. (**i-ka-tzi**) 93, 94
tributo *ikitz*, n. (**i-ki-tzi**)..94
tributo *pat*, n. (**PAT, pa-ti, PAT-ta**) 202, 203, 204
tributo *patan*, n. (**pa-ta-{n}, pa-ta-na**) 203
tributo *tojol*, n. (**to-jo-li**) 233
tributo (de él/ella/este) *yikatz*, n. poss. (**yi-ka-tzo**) 296
trono *tz'am?*, n. (**TZ'AM (?)**) 248
trono de jaguar *ix tzam?*, n. (**IX TZ'AM(?)**) 103
Trono de Piedra Cara del Sol *K'inich Tzam? Tun*, n. + adj. nombre
    de clase de monumentos "altares" (**K'IN-ni-chi TZAM(?) TUN-ni**) 153
trompeta (de concha) *jub'*, n. (**JUB', JUB'-b'a**) 121

U

uno *jun*, n. num. car. (**JUN**) 125
uno que tiene miedo *sajal*, tit. (**sa-ja-la**)..........................213
usted *a*, pron. de 2o p. (**a/AJ**) 25
usted (de) *a*, pron. de 2o p. poss. (**a/AJ**)..........................25

V

valle *jem*, n. (**JEM**) 112
vasija (de pared delgada) *jay*, n. (**ja-yi**) 109
venado *chij*, n. (**CHIJ**) 61
venido *utom*, v. intr. incom.; FDI (**u-to-ma**) 258, 259
venir *tal*, v. intr. (**TAL, ta-li**) 226
venir a pasar *ut*, v. intr. (**u-ti**) 257
vente *k'al*, n. num. car. (**K'AL**) 144
Venus (?) *Ek'*, n. (**EK'**) 89
verdaderamente *b'ajin*, adv. (**b'a-ji-ni**) 40
verde *yax*, adj. (**YAX, ya-xa**) 286, 287
viajar *b'ixan*, v. incom. irreg. (**B'IXAN-na**) 44
viajar *xan*, v. intr. (**XAN-na, xa-XAN-na**) 275, 276
vio (él/ella/este) *yilij*, pron. + v. intr. com. (**yi-IL-ji**).............295, 296
vio (él/ella/este) *yilajiy*, pron. + v. intr. com. (**yi-li-aj-ji-ya**) 297
vió (no) *ma ilaj*, v. pas. (**MA-[IL]-aj**) 166

visto por él/ella/este (fue) *yilaj*, v. pas. (**yi-IL-la-ja**, **yi-la-ji**) 296
volado *k'ay/ch'ay*, v. intr. incom. (**k'a-yi/ch'a-yi**) 150
volteado *petjiy*, v. intr. com. (**PET-ji-ya**) 206
volver *pet*, v. intr. (**PET**)..206

W
Waxak Na Chaak *Waxak Na Chaak*, n. nombre del Dios I (GI)
    de la Tríada Palenque (**WAXAK NA CHAAK**) 265

Y
y entonces *wa*, part. (**wa/WA**)..261, 262
y entonces él/ella lo vio *ilij*, part. + v. tr. (**I-IL-ji**) 93
yo *in*, pron. de 1r p. (**IN**) 98

INDEX OF VISUAL ELEMENTS

A

animal head, unidentified
    (**ch'a**, Tnn; **JOM**, Tnn; **K'IN**, T544hv) 71, 119, 152
artist, with writing instrument in headband
    (**ITZ'AT**, Tnn) 100
axe (**CH'AK**, T190) 74

B

baby K'awil (**k'a-K'AWIL**, T1030f) 143
bat, head of
    (**SOTZ'**, T756; **tz'i**, T756b;
    xu, T756b) 218, 251, 277
bat, head of, upside-down
    (**TZUTZ**, T756inv) 245
bearded man, head of
    (**B'OLON**, TIXhv) 45
bird, full figure (**CHAAN/KAAN**, T746ff) 50
bird, full figure, with flower in eye
    (**JANAAB'**, 624ff) 107
bird, head of (**am**, Tnn and T1047a;
    CHAAN/KAAN, T746;
    K'ATUN, T1034v;
    K'UK', T744a; **MEN**, T1017v?;
    MUWAN-ni, T744:116;
    o, T1034v?; **pi/PI/PIJ**, T1033v;
    ti/TI, T747; **TUN**, T1034) 36, 49, 148, 155, 169, 176, 191, 207, 231, 238
bird, head of, with flower in eye
    (**JANAAB'**, 624hv) 106
bird, head of, with trifoliate eye
    (**CH'EN**, T598hv and Tnn.598hv;
    ki, T100hv)..78, 135
bird, plucking eye from animal head
    (**i**, T237v; **i-tz'i-{n}**, T237v:752) 92, 101
bird, with worm (**li**, Tnn) 162
blood, droplets of
    (**CH'UL/K'UL (CH'UJUL/K'UJUL)**,
    T32, T36, T37, T38, T40, and T41) 80, 81, 82
bloodletter (**CH'AB**, T712) 72
bone (**AJ-X-B'AK**, T12.II:570;
    B'AK, T570 and T111;
    CHAK, T109 and T590v) 34, 41, 52

book (**JUN**, T609) 125
bracket (**u/U**, T1 and T3) 253

C

celt belt assemblage (**nu**, T151) 187
centipede, head of (**CHAPAT**, Tnn) 58
circle (**OL**, T774; **PET**, T511v) 196, 206
circle, of dots (**mo**, T582; **MOL**, T581;
    MUYAL, T632v)..170, 171, 176
circle, with cross-hatching
    (**pa/PAJ**, T586 and T602) 199
circlets and curls (**to**, T44)..233
codex (**JUN**, T609) 125
comb (**ka**, T25) 129
comb, double (**sa**, T630 and T630v) 211
crocodile (**AYIN**, T844) 37
cross (**K'AN**, T281ms) 147
crossed bands (**at**, T552; **JAL**, T153;
    sa, T278:552; **ta/TA**, T565;
    tz'i, T563b) 36, 106, 212, 222, 250
curl (**b'u**, T21; **mu**, T19; **yi**, T17,
    T17hv, T18, and T575) 45, 172, 294
curls, opposed (**ta/TA**, T776.776 and T645;
    wo, T67) 222, 272

D

"dangler" god (**to-XAT**, T1030j) 236
darkness (**AKB'AL**, T504; **AK'AB'**, T504)................................34, 35
deer (**CHIJ**, T291.nn) 61
deer hoof (**MAY (?)**, Tnn) 169
dog, head of (**OCH/OK**, T765 and T765v;
    OK, T765a; **TZ'I**, T752 and T753) 192, 195, 250
"down balls" (**je**, T69) 111
drum, wooden (**AB'**, T548;
    AB'-[b'i], T548[585]; **JA'AB'**, T548;
    TUN, T548) 26, 110, 237

E

earflare (**po**, T687a) 209
earth (**KAB'**, T526; **KAB'AN**, T526) 130
eye, eyeball (**IL**, T618v; **IX**, T524)...................................96, 102
eyes (**ch'o**, T287) 78, 79

F

feather (**o**, T99 and T279)..189, 190
finger (**JUN**, T329) 125
fire (**K'AK'**, T122) 143
fish, full figure (**CHAY/KAY**, T738;
    ka, T203; **tz'u**, T203v) 59, 129, 252
fish, head of (**ka**, T738; **u/U**, T204 and T738v) 129, 254, 255
fist (**JOM**, T672) 118
flint blade (**ETZ'NAB'**, T527; **TOK'**, T257)......................90, 234, 235
flower (**K'IN**, T544; **NIKTE'**, T646 and T646v) 151, 184
flower, with stamen (**ITZ'**, T152)...99

flower and shield (**[JANAAB']** **PAKAL**, T624) 107
footprint, human (**b'e/B'E**, T301 and T301v) 43
footprint on staircase (**TAB'**, T32:843v;
　　TAB'-[yi], T32:843v-[17]) 223
frog (?), head of, upended
　　(**ju**, T740; **SI**, T740; **WINAL**, T741v) 120, 217, 269

G

god, reclining (**k'a-K'AWIL**, T1030f) 143
god head, smoking axe, mirror
　　(**K'AWIL**, T1030b; **K'AWIL-la**,
　　T1030b:178) 149
god head, unidentified
　　(**WUK**, TVIIhv; **ye/YE**, T1073) 273, 291
god head, with axe in hand
　　(**KALOMTE'-te'**, T1030mv) 133
gopher (?) (**b'a/B'A**, T757) 39

H

hair, tied (**MUTUL**, T569 and T778) 174, 175
hand, down-turned (**k'o**, T220;
　　ye/YE, T710 and T710v) 154, 290, 291
hand, grasping (**tza**, T714v) 241
hand, grasping blade (**OCH**, T361) 192
hand, grasping fish (**tza-[ka]**, T714) 241
hand, grasping writing instrument
　　(**AJ tz'i-b'a**, T12.nn:501:314; **tz'i**, Tnn) 32, 250
hand, outstretched leftward (**CH'AM**, T670) 75
hand, outstretched rightward (**K'AL**, T713a) 144
hand, over jaw (**cha-ki CHAAN-na/cha-ki KAAN-na**,
　　T520hv.561hv:23; **mi**, Tnn) 54, 170
hand, scattering (**CHOK**, T33v.710v) 63
hand, spread (**K'AB'**, T671) 142
hand, upright (**CHA/KA**, TIIhv; **chi/CHI**, T671;
　　ke, T220; **MANIK'**, T671; **mi**, T217v) 48, 61, 134, 168, 170
hand, upright, with crossed bands (**yo**, T673) 298
hand, with bauble (**JOM**, T218; **TZUTZ**, T218) 118, 244
hand, with celt (**OCH**, T361) 192
head, of bearded man (**B'OLON**, TIXhv) 45
head, of deceased man (?) (**u/U**, T1008v) 255
head, of elderly man (**ye/YE**, T1073) 291
head, of young man (**XIB'**, T1008) 277
head, with axe in eye (**WAK**, T1087v) 263
head, with earflare (**ye/YE**, T1073 and
　　T32:nn:115.1073) 291
head, zoomorphic, with curl in eye
　　(**WUK**, TVIIhv) 273
head, zoomorphic, with T585 infixed
　　(**b'i/B'I**, T1029) 44
helmet (**KOJAW**, T678; **KOJAW-wa**, T678.130) 136, 137
hole (**WAY**, T769a) 266
house (**OTOT**, T614:514v:59;
　　OTOT-ja, T221:115v:514v.181) 197
human body, sitting (**CHUM**, T644;
　　CHUM (?), T700 and T702v) 66, 67
human body, upside-down (**EM**, T227) 90

human head, with cross-hatching
(**pa/PAJ**, T586hv) 199
human head, with headdress (**OX**, TIIIhv) 198

I

impinged bone (**CH'EN**, T571 and T598v) 77
impinged eye (**CH'EN**, T598v) 77

J

jaguar, head of (**B'ALAM**, T751; **ji-JIX**, T60:762v) 42, 115
jaguar paw or claw of (**ICH'AK**, T5; **MOL (?)**, T5) 92, 171
jaguar pelt, over **AJAW** (**WAY**, T539v) 266
jaguar tail (**ne/NE**, Tnn) 182
jawbone (**cho**, T590; **CH'EN**, T598v) 63, 77
Jester God (**AJAW**, Tnn; **ju**, T1030o;
  ju-na, T1030o:23) 28, 120, 126

K

knot (**ji**, T60; **JUN**, T60; **TAJ**, T60) 112, 113, 125, 224
knot, of hair (**che**, T145 and T148) 59
knot, with cloth band (**JOY**, Tnn) 119

L

leaf (**OCH**, T213v; **yo/YOP**, T115) 191, 298
lizard (**AYIN**, T844) 37

M

macaw, beak of a (**a/AJ**, T238) 25
macaw, head of a (**a/AJ**, T743;
  ak'/AK'OT, T743[516b];
  mo/MO', T743v)...26, 35, 171
maize curl (**NAL**, T84 and T86;
  wi/WI, T86, T86v, and T117) 180, 181, 268, 269
maize kernel (**K'AN**, T506; **wa/WA**, T506) 147, 261
maize kernel, dotted (**tzi**, T507b) 243
man, head of (**AJAW**, T1000d; **XIB'**, T1008) 28, 277
man, head of, deceased (?) (**u/U**, T1008v) 255
man, head of, with blindfold (**JOM**, Tnn) 119
man, head of, with closed eye (**u/U**, T1008v) 255
man, head of, with "earth" over mouth
  (**sa**, T1004v)..212
man, head of, with fat lips (**u/U**, T231) 254
mirror (**li**, T24) 161
monkey face (?) (**k'u/K'U**, T1016) 155
moon (**ja**, T181 and T683; **JUL**, T683v;
  K'AL, T683a) 105, 123, 144
mountain (**WITZ**, T529) 270

O

obsidian (**CH'AB**, T712) 72
old man, head of (**MAM**, T1014v)..168
old man, head of, with net headdress
  (**TAB'-[yi]**, T1014a[17]) 223

P

parrot, beak of (**a/AJ**, T238) 25
parrot, head of (**a/AJ**, T743;
    ak'/AK'OT, T743[516b]; **mo/MO'**, T743v)...26, 35, 171
peccary, head of (**CHITAM**, T753v) 62
penis (**ACH-cha**, T761b:520; **AT**, T761b;
    AT-ti, T761b:59) 27, 36, 37
plate, with sun flower (**LAK**, T183) 159

Q

quetzal bird, head of (**K'UK'**, T744a) 155
quincunx (**b'i/B'I**, T585 and T1029;
    LAMAT, T510) 43, 44, 161

R

rabbit, head of (**TUL**, T758v; **tz'o**, T758v) 236, 252
rain clouds and rainbow (**KAWAK**, T528;
    ku, T528; **pi**, T177; **pi/PI/PIJ**, T528.528;
    pi-ji, T528.528:60; **PIK**, T528.528;
    TUN, T528) 133, 137, 206, 207, 208, 237
Rain God, portrait of (**CHAAK**, T1011) 48, 49
rattlesnake tail (**OCH**, T207v) 191
reed (**pu/PU/PUJ**, T854) 210
reptile, head of (?) (**b'u**, T21.741v; **e**, T741v;
    mu, T19.741v; **PAX**, T549hv).....................................45, 87, 173, 206
ribs, of a dog (**tzu**, T560v) 244
rodent, head of (**AJAW**, Tnn; **ch'o**, T758;
    ch'o-[ko], T758; **ji**, T758b;
    KAB', T758c)...28, 79, 114, 129

S

seeds (**nu**, T149)...186
shell (**jo**, T607; **JUB'**, T579v; **K'IN (?)**, T574) 116, 121, 151
shield (**PAKAL**, T624v)..200
skull (**B'AK**, T1045; **CHAM**, T736v;
    EB', T1045v[528]; **KIMI**, T1045v;
    LAJUN, TXhv; **u/U**, T232; **u-ti-ya**,
    T846[520].59:125; **xi**, T736v;
    ya, T126hv).........................41, 55, 88, 135, 158, 254, 258, 276, 280
skull-fist (**k'a/ch'a**, T669a and T669b)..141, 142
smoke (**B'UTZ'**, T122:563a and T1035a) 46
Snaggle Tooth Dragon (**wa/WA**, T130hv) 262
snake/serpent, full figure
    (**CHAN/KAN**, T206; **LOK'-yi**,
    T327:575) 57, 163
snake/serpent, head of
    (**cha-CHAN/ka-KAN**, T108:764;
    CHAN/KAN, T764; **CHIKCHAN**, T764) 52, 57, 62
snake/serpent, markings and belly scales
    (**AKB'AL**, T504; **AK'AB'**, T504; **ak'/AK'**,
    T504; **ma**, T566; **ta/TA**, T565) 34, 35, 166, 222
S-shape (**WAK**, T367) 263
staircase, stairway (**EB'-[b'u]**, T843[21.741]) 88
stingray spine (**KIX (?)**, T212) 135, 136

stone (**KAWAK**, T528; **ku**, T528;
    pi, T177; **pi/PI/PIJ**, T528.528;
    pi-ji, T528.528:60; **PIK**, T528.528;
    TUN, T528) 133, 137, 206, 207, 208, 237
Sun God, head of (**CHAN/KAN**, T1010) 57
swastika (**TZ'AK**, T573) 247

T
tail (**IN**, T116; **ne/NE**, T120, T856v, and
    Tnn; **ni**, T116) 98, 182, 183
tapir, head of (**TIL**, T758v)..232
teeth (**wa/WA**, T335) 261
throne (**TZ'AM (?)**, T150) 248
torch (**TAJ**, T122:150) 224
tree (**te'/TE' (che'/CHE')**, T87 and T513;
    tzu/TZU, T559) 228, 229, 244
tree (?), with flower/sun (**TAK**, T559[544]) 225
tripod stand (**ya**, T125 and T126)..279
T-shape (**IK'**, T503) 94
turtle (?), head of a
    (**a/AJ**, T743; **ak'/AK'OT**, T743[516b])......................................26, 35

V
vulture, head of a (**AJAW**, T747a; **ti/TI**, T747) 28, 231

W
water lily (**b'a/B'A**, T501; **IMIX**, T501;
    JA', T501v; **ma/MA**, T502;
    NAAB', T501v)...................................39, 97, 109, 166, 178
water lily-fist (**k'a-[b'a]**, T669[501])...142
wing, of a bird (**k'a/ch'a**, T76 and T77) 141
woman, head of (**IX/IXIK**, T1000b;
    JUN, T1000a; **na/NA/NAJ**, T1000a;
    tzi/TZI, T1000v) 103, 126, 178, 243
wood (**te'/TE' (che'/CHE')**, T87 and T513) 228, 229
worm-bird (**-il**, Tnn; **li**, Tnn)...96, 162
woven mat (**POP**, T551:130)..210

Y
"yin-yang" (**TAL**, T676) 226
young man, as Maize God (**WAXAK**, T1006) 265
young man, head of (**AJAW**, T1000d; **OX**, TIIIhv).................................28, 198
young man, head of, facing right (**wa/WA**, Tnn) 262
young man, head of, with curl (**yi**, T17hv)...294
young man, head of, with flower and smoke
    (**PUL-[yi]**, T122:1010c[17]) 210
young man, head of, with writing instrument
    in headband (**ITZ'AT**, Tnn) 100

SUBJECT INDICES

NUMBERS

Cardinals

one (**JUN, wi/WI**) 125, 126, 268, 269
two (**CHA/KA**) 48
three (**OX**) 197, 198
four (**CHAN/KAN**) 56, 57
five (**JO**) 116, 117
six (**WAK**)...262, 263
seven (**WUK**) 273
eight (**WAXAK**) 265
nine (**B'OLON**) 44, 45
ten (**LAJUN**)...158
eleven (**B'ULUK**) 46
twelve (**CHALAJUN/KALAJUN**)...55
twenty (**K'AL**) 144
eight thousand (**PIK**) 208

Ordinals

first (**b'a/B'A**) 39
first (**na/NA**) 177, 178
first (**YAX, ya-xa**) 286, 287

DAYS

All entries are given in the order of their occurrence in the Tzolk'in calendar, and correspond to their traditional Yucatec names.

1.　　Imix (**IMIX**) 97
2.　　Ik' (**IK'**) 94
3.　　Akb'al (**AKB'AL**) 34
4.　　K'an (**K'AN**) 147
5.　　Chicchan (**CHIKCHAN**) 61, 62
6.　　Kimi (**KIMI**) 135
7.　　Manik' (**MANIK'**) 168
8.　　Lamat (**LAMAT**) 161
9.　　Muluk (**MULUK**) 174
10.　　Ok (**OK**) 195
11.　　Chuwen (**CHUWEN**) 69
12.　　Eb' (**EB'**) 88
13.　　B'en (**B'EN**) 43
14.　　Ix (**IX**) 102
15.　　Men (**MEN**) 169
16.　　Kib' (**KIB'**) 135
17.　　Kab'an (**KAB'AN**) 130
18.　　Etz'nab' (**ETZ'NAB'**) 90
19.　　Kawak (**KAWAK**) 133
20.　　Ajaw (**AJAW**) 27

MONTHS

All entries are given in the order of their occurrence in the Ja'ab' calendar, and correspond to their traditional Yucatec names.

1.　　Pop (**POP**) 210
2.　　Wo (**WO**) 272
3.　　Sip (**CHAK K'AT, SIP**) 54, 218
4.　　Sotz' (**SOTZ'**) 218
5.　　Sek (**SEK**) 216
6.　　Xul (**XUL**) 278
7.　　Yaxk'in (**YAXK'IN**) 289
8.　　Mol (**MOL**) 171
9.　　Ch'en (**CH'EN**) 77
10.　　Yax (**YAX**) 287
11.　　Sak (**SAK**) 213
12.　　Kej (**KEJ**) 134
13.　　Mak (**MAK, ma-ka**) 167
14.　　K'ank'in (**K'ANK'IN**) 147
15.　　Muwan (**mu-wa-ni, MUWAN-na, MUWAN-ni**) 175, 176
16.　　Pax (**PAX**) 205, 206
17.　　K'ayab' (**K'AYAB'**) 150
18.　　Kumk'u (**KUMK'U**) 139
19.　　Wayeb' (**WAYEB'**) 267

LONG COUNT

1. B'aktun (**pi/PI/PIJ**, **pi-ji**, **PI-ya**) 207, 208, 209
2. K'atun (**K'ATUN**) 148
3. Tun (**TUN**, **TUN-ni**) 237, 238
4. Winal (**WINAL**) 269
5. K'in (**K'IN**, **K'IN (?)**, **K'IN-ni**) 151, 152, 153

PHONETIC SIGNS

a	vowel *a* (**a/AJ**)	25, 26
aj	phonetic sign (**a/AJ**)	25, 26
ak'	phonetic sign (**ak'/AK'**, **ak'/AK'OT**)	34, 35
am	phonetic sign (**am**)	36
at	phonetic sign (**at**)	36
b'a	phonetic sign (**b'a**, **b'a/B'A**)	39
b'e	phonetic sign (**b'e/B'E**)	43
b'i	phonetic sign (**b'i/B'I**)	43, 44
b'o	phonetic sign (**b'o**)	44
b'u	phonetic sign (**b'u**)	45
cha/ka	phonetic sign (**cha/ka**)	47, 48
che	phonetic sign (**che**)	59
chi	phonetic sign (**chi/CHI**)	61
cho	phonetic sign (**cho**)	63
chu	phonetic sign (**chu**)	64, 65
ch'a	phonetic sign (**ch'a/CH'A**, **ch'a**, **k'a/ch'a**)	71, 141, 142
ch'o	phonetic sign (**ch'o**)	78, 79
e	vowel *e* (**e**)	87
i	vowel *i* (**i/I**, **i**)	91, 92
ja	phonetic sign (**ja**)	105
ja'	phonetic sign (**ja'**)	109
je	phonetic sign (**je**)	111, 112
ji	phonetic sign (**ji**)	112, 113, 114
jo	phonetic sign (**jo**)	116
ju	phonetic sign (**ju**)	120
ka	phonetic sign (**ka**)	129
ke	phonetic sign (**ke**)	134
ki	phonetic sign (**ki**)	134, 135
ko	phonetic sign (**ko**)	136
ku	phonetic sign (**ku**)	137
k'a/ch'a	phonetic sign (**k'a/ch'a**, **k'a/ch'a (K'A/CH'A?)**)	141, 142
k'o	phonetic sign (**k'o**)	154
k'u	phonetic sign (**k'u**, **k'u/K'U**)	154, 155
la	phonetic sign (**la**)	157
le	phonetic sign (**le**)	161
li	phonetic sign (**li**)	161, 162
lo	phonetic sign (**lo**)	163
lu	phonetic sign (**lu**)	163, 164
ma	phonetic sign (**ma/MA**, **ma**)	165, 166
mi	phonetic sign (**mi/MI**)	169, 170
mo	phonetic sign (**mo**, **mo/MO'**)	170, 171
mu	phonetic sign (**mu**)	172, 173

na	phonetic sign (**na/NA/NAJ**)	177, 178
ne	phonetic sign (**ne/NE**)	182
ni	phonetic sign (**ni**)	183
no	phonetic sign (**no**)	185
nu	phonetic sign (**nu**)	186, 187
o	vowel *o* (**o**)	189, 190, 191
pa	phonetic sign (**pa/PAJ**)	199
pi	phonetic sign (**pi, pi/PI/PIJ**)	206, 207
po	phonetic sign (**po**)	209
pu	phonetic sign (**pu/PU/PUJ**)	210
sa	phonetic sign (**sa/SA, sa**)	211, 212
se	phonetic sign (**se**)	216
si	phonetic sign (**si**)	217
su	phonetic sign (**su**)	218
ta	phonetic sign (**ta/TA**)	221, 222
te'/che'	phonetic sign (**te'/TE' (che'/CHE')**)	228, 229, 230
ti	phonetic sign (**ti/TI**)	231
to	phonetic sign (**to**)	233
tza	phonetic sign (**tza**)	241
tzi	phonetic sign (**tzi, tzi/TZI**)	242, 243
tzo	phonetic sign (**tzo**)	243, 244
tzu	phonetic sign (**tzu/TZU, tzu**)	244
tz'a	phonetic sign (**tz'a/TZ'A**)	247
tz'i	phonetic sign (**tz'i**)	249, 250, 251
tz'o	phonetic sign (**tz'o**)	252
tz'u	phonetic sign (**tz'u**)	252
u	vowel *u* (**u/U**)	253, 254, 255
wa	phonetic sign (**wa/WA**)	261, 262
we'	phonetic sign (?) (**we'/WE'**)	267, 268
wi	phonetic sign (**wi/WI**)	268, 269
wo	phonetic sign (**wo**)	272
xa	phonetic sign (**xa/XA**)	275
xi	phonetic sign (**xi**)	276
xo	phonetic sign (**xo**)	277
xu	phonetic sign (**xu**)	277
-xul	phonetic signs (**xu-[lu]**)	278
ya	phonetic sign (**ya**)	279, 280
ye	phonetic sign (**ye/YE**)	290, 291
yi	phonetic sign (**yi**)	294
yo	phonetic sign (**yo/YOP, yo**)	298
yu	phonetic sign (**yu**)	304

VERBS/VERBAL PHRASES

A

ak'ot tr. v. dance (**ak'/AK'OT, AK'OT-ta, a-AK'OT-ta**) 35
ak'otaj pass. v. was danced (**AK'OT-ta-ja**) 35
aliy intr. v. say (**a-li-ya**) 36
aliy intr. v. it is said (**a-li-ya**) 36
aya v. phr. came into being (**a-ja-ya, a-ya, a-ya-ya**) 29, 37

B'

b'an tr. v. scatter (**b'a-na**) 42
b'ixan incom. irreg. v. goes (**B'IXAN-na**) 44
b'ixan incom. irreg. v. walks (**B'IXAN-na**) 44
b'ixan incom. irreg. v. travels (**B'IXAN-na**) 44
b'ixan com. irreg. v. went (**B'IXAN-na**) 44
b'ixaniy com. irreg. v. went (**B'IXAN-ni-ya**) 44

CH

cham intr. v. die (**CHAM, CHAM-mi**) 55, 56
chamil intr. v. die (**CHAM-li**) 56
chamiy intr. incom. v. dies (**CHAM-mi-ya**) 56
che'en tu b'ak v. phr. so it says on his/her/its bone (**che-e-na TU b'a-ki**) 60
chok tr. v. scatter (**CHOK**) 63
chok tr. v. throw (**CHOK**) 63
chokaw ch'aj tr. v. phr. scatter drops of liquid
      (**CHOK-ko-wa CH'A-ji, CHOK-wa CH'A-ji**) 64
chokaw ch'aj tr. v. phr. throw drops of liquid
      (**CHOK-ko-wa CH'A-ji, CHOK-wa CH'A-ji**) 64
chokij tr. v. phr. scatter drops (**CHOK-ji**) 63
chokij tr. v. phr. throw drops (**CHOK-ji**) 63
chuk tr. v. seize (**chu-ka, chu-[ku]**) 65
chuk tr. v. capture (**chu-ka, chu-[ku]**) 65
chukaj pass. v. captured (was); "capture" (**chu-ka-ja, chu-[ku]-ja**) 65, 66
chukjiy intr. com. v. captured (was); "capture" (**chu-[ku]-ji-ya**) 66
chum pos. v. be seated; "accession" (**CHUM, CHUM (?), CHUM-[mu]**) 66, 67
chumlajiy pos. com. v. seated; "accession"
      (**CHUM-la-ji-ya, CHUM-[mu]-la-ji-ya**) 67
chum tun v. phr. seating of the stone, seating of the *tun*
      (**CHUM-[mu] TUN-ni, [CHUM] TUN-ni**) 68
chumwaniy pos. com. v. seated; "accession" (**CHUM-[mu]-wa-ni-ya**) 68
chumwan ti ajawlel *ti*-construction v. phr. seated in lordship; "accession"
      (**CHUM-wa-ni TI AJAW le-{l}**) 68

CH'

ch'ab' intr. v. do penance, sacrifice (**CH'AB, ch'a-b'a**) 72
ch'ab' intr. v. pierce, lancing (**CH'AB, ch'a-b'a**) 72
ch'ak tr. v. chop (**CH'AK, CH'AK-ka**) 74
ch'ak tr. v. decapitate (**CH'AK, CH'AK-ka**) 74
ch'akab' intr. v. self-decapitate, self-axe; "self-sacrifice" (**CH'AK-ka-b'a**) 74, 75
ch'akaj pass. v. axed, chopped (was) (**ch'a-ka-ja**) 74
ch'akaj pass. v. decapitated (was) (**ch'a-ka-ja**) 74
ch'am tr. v. receive (**CH'AM, CH'AM-ma**) 75, 76
ch'am tr. v. harvest (**CH'AM, CH'AM-ma**) 75, 76

ch'am K'awil tr. v. receive K'awil
   (**CH'AM K'AWIL-la, CH'AM-ma K'AWIL-la**)..75, 76
ch'am K'awil tr. v. harvest K'awil
   (**CH'AM K'AWIL-la, CH'AM-ma K'AWIL-la**)..75, 76

E

em intr. v. descend (**EM**) 90

I

il tr. v. see (**IL**) 96
ilaj pass. v. seen (was) (**IL-ja**) 97
ilij part. + tr. v. then he/she saw/witnessed it (**I-IL-ji**) 93
i-ut part. + intr. v. and then it happened/occurred;
   Posterior Date Indicator (PDI) (**i-u-ti**) 102

J

jal tr. v. say (**JAL, ja'-li**) 106, 111
jal tr. v. manifest (**JAL, ja'-li**) 106, 111
jal intr. v. rest (**JAL, ja'-li**) 106, 111
jal intr. v. terminate (**JAL, ja'-li**) 106, 111
jal-jiy tr. v. say (**JAL-ji-ya**)..106
jal-jiy tr. v. manifest (**JAL-ji-ya**) 106
jal-jiy intr. v. rest (**JAL-ji-ya**) 106
jal-jiy intr. v. terminate (**JAL-ji-ya**) 106
jatz'ay tr. v. strike (**ja-tz'a-yi**) 108
jatz'ay tr. v. split (**ja-tz'a-yi**) 108
jatz'ay tr. v. wound (**ja-tz'a-yi**) 108
jil intr. v. rest (**ji-li**) 115
jil intr. v. end (**ji-li**) 115
-jiy intr. com. verbal suffix pattern (**-ji-ya**) 115
jom tr. v. end (**JOM**) 118, 119
jom tr. v. destroy/demolish (**JOM**) 118, 119
jom tr. v. throw down (**JOM**) 118, 119
joy tr. v. accede (**jo-JOY, JOY**) 117, 119
joy tr. v. emerge/come out (**jo-JOY, JOY**) 117, 119
joyaj pass. v. put in office (was) (**jo-JOY-ja, JOY-ja**) 117, 119
joyaj pass. v. emergent/come out (was) (**jo-JOY-ja, JOY-ja**) 117, 119
joyajiy intr. com. v. (?), acceded (**JOY-[ja]-ji-ya**) 120
joyajiy tr. v. emerge/come out (**JOY-[ja]-ji-ya**) 120
joyaj ti ajawlel pass. v. phr. acceded in lordship, acceded as ruler
   (**jo-JOY-ja TI AJAW-le-{l}**) 117
jub' intr. v. take down; "war" (**JUB' (?)**) 121
jub' intr. v. bring down; "war" (**JUB' (?)**) 121
jub'-Emblem Glyph intr. v. bring down [a site/location/polity];
   "war" (**JUB'-EMBLEM GLYPH**) 121
jub'uy intr. v. taken down/brought down; "war"
   (**ju-b'u-yi, JUB'(?)-yi, JUB'(?)-yi-ya**) 122
jul intr. v. arrive (**JUL, ju-li, JUL-li**) 123, 124
jul tr. v. throw (**JUL, ju-li, JUL-li**) 123, 124
jul tr. v. shoot (**JUL, ju-li, JUL-li**) 123, 124
jul tr. v. spear (**JUL, ju-li, JUL-li**) 123, 124
jul tr. v. pierce (**JUL, ju-li, JUL-li**) 123, 124
julaj pass. v. arrived (was) (**JUL-li-ja**)..124

julaj pass. v. thrown (was) (**JUL-li-ja**) 124
julaj pass. v. shot (was) (**JUL-li-ja**) 124
julaj pass. v. speared (was) (**JUL-li-ja**) 124
juliy intr. com. v. arrived (**ju-li-ya**) 125
julob' intr. pl. v. arrived (they) (**ju-li-OB'**) 124
julob' intr. pl. v. threw (they) (**ju-li-OB'**) 124
julob' intr. pl. v. shot (they) (**ju-li-OB'**) 124

K

kab'ij tr. v. did it (**KAB'-ji**) 130
kab'iy tr. v. did it (**KAB'-ya**) 131
kab'jiy tr. v. did it (**KAB'-ji-ya**) 131
kojoy intr. v. go down (**ko-jo-yi**) 137
kotz' tr. v. roll up (**ko-tz'o**) 137
kuch tr. v. carry (**KUCH, ku-chu**) 138
kuch-taj pass. v. carried (was) (**KUCH-ta-ja**) 138

K'

k'al tr. v. bind/tie/wrap (**K'AL**) 144
k'al tr. v. close (**K'AL**) 144
k'al tr. v. set (**K'AL**) 144
k'al tr. incom. v. closing (**k'a-li**) 144
k'alaj pass. v. bound/tied/wrapped (was) (**K'AL-ja**) 145
k'alaj pass. v. closed (was) (**K'AL-ja**) 145
k'alaj pass. v. set (was) (**K'AL-ja**) 145
k'alaj mayij? pass. v. phr. bound/tied/wrapped the deer hoof (was)
    (**K'AL-ja MAY-ji**) 145
k'al-jiy sak jun tr. v. phr. bound/tied/wrapped/closed the white headband
    (**K'AL-ji-ya SAK JUN**) 145
k'al jun tr. v. phr. bound/tied/wrapped/closed the headband (**K'AL JUN-na**) 145
k'al sak jun v. phr. bound/tied/wrapped/closed the white headband
    (**K'AL SAK JUN, K'AL SAK ju-na**) 146
k'al tun intr. v. phr. "stone-binding" (**K'AL TUN-ni**) 146
k'al tun pass. v. phr. closed/set (was) the stone (**K'AL TUN-ni**) 146
k'ay/ch'ay intr. incom. v. terminates (**k'a-yi/ch'a-yi**) 150
k'ay/ch'ay intr. incom. v. flies (**k'a-yi/ch'a-yi**) 150
k'ay u sak nik ik'il/ch'ay u sak nich ik'il intr. incom. v. phr. terminates his/her
    resplendent soul (**k'a-yi U SAK NIK IK'-li/ch'a-yi U SAK NICH IK'-li**) 151
k'uxaj pass. v. eaten (was) (**k'u-xa-ja**) 156
k'uxaj pass. v. ground (was) (**k'u-xa-ja**) 156
k'uxaj pass. v. hurt (was) (**k'u-xa-ja**) 156
k'uxajiy tr. com. v. ate (**k'u-xa-ji-ya**) 156
k'uxajiy tr. v. grind (**k'u-xa-ji-ya**) 156
k'uxajiy tr. v. hurt (**k'u-xa-ji-ya**) 156

L

-laj pos. com. verbal suffix pattern (**-la-ja, -[la]-ja, -la-ji**) 157, 158
-laj/laj tr. v. end/finish (**-la-ja**) 157
lok'iy intr. com. v. came out (**LOK'-yi**) 163
lok'iy intr. com. v. emerged (**LOK'-yi**) 163
lok'iy intr. com. v. escaped (**LOK'-yi**) 163
lok'-ta intr. v. came out from (**lo-k'u-ta**) 163
lok'-ta intr. v. emerged from (**lo-k'u-ta**) 163

M

ma ilaj pass. v. not seen (was) (**MA-[IL]-aj**) 166
mak tr. v. close (**ma-ka**) 167
mak tr. v. cover (**ma-ka**) 167
mak tr. v. betroth (**ma-ka**) 167
makaj pass. v. closed (was) (**ma-ka-ja**) 167
makaj pass. v. covered (was) (**ma-ka-ja**) 167
makaj pass. v. betrothed (was) (**ma-ka-ja**) 167
makax tr. v. close (**ma-ka-xa**) 167
makax tr. v. cover (**ma-ka-xa**) 167
makax tr. v. betroth (**ma-ka-xa**) 167
muk tr. v. bury (**mu-ka**) 173
mukaj pass. v. buried (was) (**mu-ka-ja**) 173

N

-naj verbal ending (?); part of the PSS dedication phrase (**na-ja**) 179
najiy tr. incom. v. fills up (**na-ja-yi**) 180
nak tr. v. conquer (**na-ku**) 180
nak intr. v. ascend, rise, elevate (**na-ku**) 180
nawaj pass. v. adorned (was) (**na-wa-ja**) 182

O

och intr. v. enter (**OCH, OCH-chi**)..191, 192, 193
och b'i tr. v. phr. entered the road; "death" (**OCH B'I**) 192
och b'i-aj pass. v. phr. entered the road (was); "death" (**OCH B'I-ja**) 192
och b'ij-jiy tr. v. phr. road-entered; "death" (**OCH B'I-ji-ji-ya**) 193
och ja' tr. v. phr. entered the water, water-entered; "death" (**OCH JA'**) 194
och ja'-aj pass. v. phr. entered the water (was); "death" (**OCH JA'-ja**) 194
och k'ak' tr. v. phr. entered the fire, fire-entered; "dedication"
    (**OCH-chi K'AK', OCH K'AK'**)...193, 194
och ta chaan/ok ta kaan tr. v. phr. entered into the sky, became the sky,
    sky-entered (**OCH TA CHAAN-na/OK TA KAAN-na**) 195
och te'/ok te' tr. v. phr. entered the tree (**OCH TE'/OK TE'**) 195
ototaj pass. v. housed (was) (**OTOT-ja**)...197
ox ajal v. phr. thrice said (**OX aj-ja-li**)..198
ox ajal v. phr. thrice manifested (**OX aj-ja-li**)..198

P

paj tr. v. choose (**pa/PAJ**)...199
paklaj pos. v. faced down (was) (**pa-ka-la-ja**) 200
paklaj pos. v. doubled over (was) (**pa-ka-la-ja**) 200
pakax v. phr. reference to "coming back" (**pa-ka-ax**) 201
pak' tr. v. mold (**pa-k'a**)...201
pak' tr. v. form in clay (**pa-k'a**)...201
pak' tr. v. plant (**pa-k'a**)...201
pak' tr. v. hoist (**pa-k'a**)...201
pak'ajiy intr. com. v. molded (**pa-k'a-ji-ya**) 201
pak'ajiy intr. com. v. phr. formed in clay (**pa-k'a-ji-ya**) 201
pak'ajiy intr. com. v. planted (**pa-k'a-ji-ya**) 201
pak'ajiy intr. com. v. hoisted (**pa-k'a-ji-ya**)..201
pas/pasaj tr. v. open (**PAS/PASAJ, pa-sa**) 202
pat tr. v. form; "dedication" (**PAT, pa-ti, PAT-ta**) 202, 203, 204
pat tr. v. make; "dedication" (**PAT, pa-ti, PAT-ta**) 202, 203, 204
pat b'uj tr. com. v. made, formed; "dedication" (**PAT-ta-b'u-ji**) 205

pat b'uy tr. com. v. formed, made; "dedication" (**PAT-b'u-ya**) 204
patlaj pos. com. v. formed, made; "dedication" (**PAT-[la]-ja**) 204
patwan com. v. made, formed; "dedication" (**PAT-ta-wa-ni, PAT-wa-ni**)....................205
pet intr. v. turn, rotate (**PET**) 206
petjiy intr. com. v. turned, rotated (**PET-ji-ya**) 206
pitzal intr. v. play ball (**pi-tzi-la**) 209
pitzalaj pos. com. v. played ball (**pi-tzi-la-ja**)...209
pixom tr. v. wrap (**pi-xo-ma**) 209
puliy intr. com. v. burned (**pu-lu-yi, PUL-[yi]**) 210
puliy intr. com. v. sprinkled (**pu-lu-yi, PUL-[yi]**) 210

S

sat tr. v. destroy (**sa-ta**) 216
sat tr. v. lose (**sa-ta**) 216
satay intr. com. v. destroyed (**sa-ta-yi**) 216
satay intr. com. v. lost (**sa-ta-yi**) 216
si intr. v. be born (**SI**) 217
sij-ya intr. com. v. born (**SI-ji-ya**) 217
siyaj pass. v. born (was) (**SI-ya-ja**) 218
susaj pass. v. cut up (was) (**su-sa-ja**) 219
susaj pass. v. rasped (was) (**su-sa-ja**) 219

T

tab' tr. v. ascend, rise up, go up; dedication (**TAB'**)...223
tab' tr. v. present; dedication (**TAB'**)...223
tab'iy intr. com. v. ascended, rose up, went up; dedication (**TAB'-[yi]**) 223, 224
tab'iy intr. com. v. presented; dedication (**TAB'-[yi]**) 223, 224
takaj pass. v. come (was), come (have) (**ta-ki-ja**) 225
tal intr. v. come, arrive (**TAL, ta-li**) 226
tan lamaj pass. v. half diminished (was); "half period" (**[TAN] LAM-ja**) 227
tek' tr. v. phr. step on (**te'-k'a**) 230
tek'aj pass. v. phr. stepped on (was) (**te'-k'a-ja**) 230
tupaj pass. v. ear-flared (was), adorned (was) (**tu-pa-ja**) 239

TZ

tzak tr. v. grasp, grab (**tza-[ka]**) 241, 242
tzak tr. v. conjure (**tza-[ka]**) 241, 242
tzak intr. v. appear (**tza-[ka]**) 241, 242
tzakaw tr. v. grasp, grab (**tza-[ka]-wa**) 242
tzakaw tr. v. conjure (**tza-[ka]-wa**) 242
tzakaw tr. v. make appear (**tza-[ka]-wa**) 242
tzakaw ch'ul/tzakaw k'ul tr. v. phr. conjure/manifest/make appear
    god/divinity/holiness (**tza-[ka]-wa CH'UL/tza-[ka]-wa K'UL**) 242
tzik ja'ab'?/tzik ab'? intr. v. phr. the count of years (?); Initial Series
    Introductory Glyph (**tzi-ka JA'AB' (?)/tzi-ka AB'**) 243
tzutz tr. v. end, terminate, expire (**TZUTZ**) 244, 245
tzutz tr. v. join (**TZUTZ**) 244, 245
tzutzaj pass. v. ended (was), terminated (was), expired (was)
    (**TZUTZ-ja, tzu-tzu-ja**) 245
tzutziy intr. com. v. ended, terminated, expired (**TZUTZ-yi**) 246

TZ'

tz'a tr. v. give (**tz'a/TZ'A**) 247
tz'ak tr. v. put in order (**TZ'AK**) 247

tz'ak tr. v. count, increase (**TZ'AK**) 247
tz'akaj pass. v. put in order (was) (**TZ'AK-aj**) 247
tz'akaj pass. v. counted (was), increased (was) (**TZ'AK-aj**) 247
tz'ak b'ul tr. v. put in order (**TZ'AK b'u-li**) 248
tz'ak b'ul tr. v. count, increase (**TZ'AK b'u-li**) 248
tz'ap pos. v. plant upright (**tz'a-[pa]**) 248
tz'ap pos. v. hoist (**tz'a-[pa]**)...248
tz'ap tr. v. stack, pile up (**tz'a-[pa]**) 248
tz'apaj pass. v. planted upright (was) (**tz'a-pa-ja, tz'a-[pa]-ja**) 248, 249
tz'apaj pass. v. hoisted (was) (**tz'a-pa-ja, tz'a-[pa]-ja**) 248, 249
tz'apaj pass. v. stacked (was), piled up (was) (**tz'a-pa-ja, tz'a-[pa]-ja**) 248, 249
tz'apajiy intr. com. v. planted upright (**tz'a-pa-ji-ya**)............................249
tz'apajiy intr. com. v. hoisted (**tz'a-pa-ji-ya**) 249
tz'apajiy intr. com. v. stacked, piled up (**tz'a-pa-ji-ya**) 249
tz'apwa pos. v. plant upright (**tz'a-[pa]-wa**) 249
tz'apwa pos. v. hoist (**tz'a-[pa]-wa**)..249
tz'apwa pos. v. stack, pile up (**tz'a-[pa]-wa**) 249

U

uch' intr. v. drink (**UCH'**) 256
ut intr. v. happen, occur, come to pass (**u-ti**) 257
utiy intr. com. v. since it happened, since it occurred, since it came to pass;
    Anterior Date Indicator (ADI) (**u-ti-ya**) 257, 258
utjiy intr. com. v. since it happened, since it occurred, since it came to pass;
    Anterior Date Indicator (ADI) (**u-ti-ji-ya**) 257
utom intr. incom. v. it will happen, it will occur, it will come to pass;
    Future Date Indicator (FDI) (**u-to-ma**) 258, 259
u . . . wa tr. com. verbal affix pattern (**U . . . wa**) 259
u we'y tr. incom. v. phr. his/her/its eating of (**U we'-ya**) 259
u . . . wi tr. com. verbal affix pattern (**U . . . wi**)...................................259
uxul intr. v. carve, sculpt (**u-xu-[lu]**) 260

W

wa pos. suf. -*w* (**wa/WA**) 261, 262
wa pos. v. erect (**wa/WA**)..261, 262
wa prog. aspect marker on transitive verbs (?) (**wa/WA**) 261, 262
way intr. v. sleep (**WAY, WAY-ya**) 266, 267
wa yak'aw tr. v. give (**wa-ya-k'a-wa**) 266
wa yalaw tr. v. say (**wa-ya-la-wa**) 266
. . . wiy verbal suffix pattern used to derive an intransitive out of a
    transitive root (**. . . wi-ya**) 271
wol tr. v. make round (**wo-la**) 273
wol tr. v. wrap up (**wo-la**) 273

X

xan intr. v. go (**XAN-na, xa-XAN-na**)..275, 276
xan intr. v. walk (**XAN-na, xa-XAN-na**) 275, 276
xan intr. v. travel (**XAN-na, xa-XAN-na**) 275, 276

Y

ya background marker indicating the completive aspect (**ya**) 279, 280
. . . yan pos. com. verbal affix pattern (**. . . ya-ni**) 285
yataj tr. v. bathe, water (**ya-ta-ji**) 285

yatij tr. v. bathe, water (**ya-ti-ji**) 286
yax ch'am K'awil v. phr. first receiving [of] K'awil (**YAX CH'AM K'AWIL**) 288
yax ch'am K'awil v. phr. first harvesting [of] K'awil (**YAX CH'AM K'AWIL**)...............288
yax k'al tun v. phr. closed the first *tun*, closed the first stone
    (**YAX K'AL TUN-ni**) 288
yilaj pass. v. phr. seen/witnessed by he/she/it (was) (**yi-IL-la-ja, yi-la-ji**) 296
yilajiy pron. + intr. com. v. saw/witnessed (he/she/it) (**yi-li-aj-ji-ya**) 297
yilij pron. + intr. com. v. saw/witnessed (he/she/it) (**yi-IL-ji**) 295, 296

PRONOUNS

a 2nd pers. pron. you, yours (**a/AJ**, T228 and T229) 25
aj masc. agentive pron. he (**a/AJ**) 25, 26
aj masc. agentive pron. he of (**a/AJ**) 25, 26
in 1st pers. pron. I (**IN**) 98
in 1st pers. poss. pron. my (**IN**) 98
u 3rd pers. pron. he, she, it (**u/U**) 253, 254, 255
u 3rd pers. poss. pron. his, hers, its (**u/U**) 253, 254, 255
ya 3rd pers. prev. pron. he, she, it (**ya**); used with words beginning in *a* 279, 280
ya 3rd pers. prev. poss. pron. his, her, its (**ya**); used with words
    beginning in *a* 279, 280
ye 3rd pers. prev. pron. he, she, it (**ye/YE**); used with words beginning in *e* 290, 291
ye 3rd pers. prev. poss. pron. his, her, its (**ye/YE**); used with words
    beginning in *e* 290, 291
yi 3rd pers. prev. pron. he, she, it (**yi**); used with words beginning in *i* 294
yi 3rd pers. prev. poss. pron. his, her, its (**yi**); used with words
    beginning in *i* 294
yo 3rd pers. prev. pron. he, she, it (**yo**); used with words beginning in *o* 298
yo 3rd pers. prev. poss. pron. his, her, its (**yo**); used with words
    beginning in *o* 298
yu 3rd pers. prev. pron. he, she, it (**yu**); used with words beginning in *u* 304
yu 3rd pers. prev. poss. pron. his, her, its (**yu**); used with words
    beginning in *u* 304

ADJECTIVES

beloved *jun tan,* adj. (**JUN TAN-na**) 127
big *lakam,* adj. (**LAKAM, la-ka-ma**) 159
black *ek',* adj. (**EK'**) 88, 89
blue *yax,* adj. (**YAX, ya-xa**) 286, 287
blue-green *yax,* adj. (**YAX, ya-xa**) 286, 287
cherished *jun tan,* adj. (**JUN TAN-na**) 127
divine *ch'ul/k'ul,* adj. (**CH'UL/K'UL, CH'UL-lu/K'UL-lu**) 80, 81, 82, 84
divine *k'u,* adj. (**k'u/K'U**) 154, 155
first *b'a,* adj. (**b'a/B'A**) 39
first *na,* adj.; ordinal number (**na/NA/NAJ**) 177, 178
first *yax,* adj. (**YAX, ya-xa**) 286, 287
fresh *tzi,* adj. (**tzi/TZI**)..243
fruited (his/her/its) *yutal,* poss. adj.; component of the PSS
    (**yu-ta-{l}, yu-ta-la**)...305, 306
great *chak,* adj. (**CHAK**) 52, 53

great *lakam,* adj. (**LAKAM, la-ka-ma**) 159
great *noj,* adj. (**NOJ**) 185, 186
great *nuk,* adj. (**nu-ku**) 188
green *yax,* adj. (**YAX, ya-xa**) 286, 287
heavenly *chaanal/kaanal,* adj. (**CHAAN-na-NAL/KAAN-na-NAL**) 51
holy *ch'ul/k'ul,* adj. (**CH'UL/K'UL, CH'UL-lu/K'UL-lu**) 80, 81, 82, 84
large *lakam,* adj. (**LAKAM, la-ka-ma**)..159
large *nuk,* adj. (**nu-ku**) 188
many *ox,* adj. (**OX**) 197, 198
many *b'olon,* adj. (**B'OLON**)...44, 45
new *tzi,* adj. (**tzi/TZI**) 243
precious *k'an,* adj. (**K'AN, K'AN-na**) 147
pure *sak,* adj. (**SAK**) 213
red *chak,* adj. (**CHAK**) 52, 53
resplendent *sak,* adj. (**SAK**) 213
revealed *yej,* adj. (**ye/YE**)..290, 291
sacred *ch'ul/k'ul,* adj. (**CH'UL/K'UL, CH'UL-lu/K'UL-lu**) 80, 81, 82, 84
sacred *k'u,* adj. (**k'u/K'U**) 154, 155
seasoned *tzi,* adj. (**tzi/TZI**) 243
strong *kelem,* adj. (**ke-KELEM, ke-le-ma**)..134
sun-eyed *k'ina/k'inich,* adj. (**K'INA/K'INICH, K'INICH, K'INICH-ni**) 152
sun-faced *k'ina/k'inich,* adj. (**K'INA/K'INICH, K'INICH, K'INICH-ni**) 152
tree-fresh *te'el,* adj. (**te'-TE'-le**)..231
unripe *ch'ok,* adj. (**ch'o-ko**) 79
white *sak,* adj. (**SAK**) 213
white flowery *sak nik,* adj. (**SAK NIK**)..215
wide *nuk,* adj. (**nu-ku**) 188
yellow *k'an,* adj. (**K'AN, K'AN-na**) 147
young *ch'ok,* adj. (**ch'o-ko, ch'o-[ko]**) 79
youthful *pitz,* adj. (**pi-tzi**) 208

T-NUMBERS

T1	u/U	253
T3	u/U	253
T4	na/NA/NAJ, NOJ	177, 185
T5	ICH'AK, MOL (?)	92, 171
T12	a/AJ	25
T13	u/U	253
T16	YAX	286
T17	yi	294
T18	yi	294
T19	mu	172
T21	b'u	45
T23	IK', na/NA/NAJ	94, 177
T24	-il, li	95, 161
T25	ka	129
T32	CH'UL/K'UL (CH'UJUL/K'UJUL)	80
T36	CH'UL/K'UL (CH'UJUL/K'UJUL)	80
T37	CH'UL/K'UL (CH'UJUL/K'UJUL)	81
T38	CH'UL/K'UL (CH'UJUL/K'UJUL)	81
T40	CH'UL/K'UL (CH'UJUL/K'UJUL)	82
T41	CH'UL/K'UL (CH'UJUL/K'UJUL)	82
T41	k'u/K'U	154
T44	to	233
T45	ju	120
T46	ju	120
T48	na/NA/NAJ, NOJ	178, 186
T51	ta/TA	221
T53	ta/TA	221
T57	si	217
T58	SAK	213
T59	ti/TI	231
T60	ji, JUN, NUUN, TAJ	112, 113, 125, 188, 224
T61	yu	304
T62	yu	304
T67	wo	272
T69	je	111
T74	ma/MA	165
T76	k'a/ch'a	141
T77	k'a/ch'a	141
T80	PAT	202, 203
T82	li	162
T83	li	162
T84	NAL	180
T86	NAL, wi/WI	180, 268
T86v	wi/WI	268
T87	te'/TE' (che'/CHE')	228
T87hv	te'/TE' (che'/CHE')	230
T88	ji	113
T89	EK', TU	88, 89, 236
T90	TU	236
T92	TU	236
T93	ch'a/CH'A	71
T99	o	189
T100v	ki	134
T100hv	ki	135

T102	ki	135
T103	ta/TA	221
T106	nu	186
T109	CHAK	52
T110	ko	136
T111	B'AK	41
T113	ta/TA	221
T114	xa/XA	275
T115	yo/YOP	298
T116	IN, ni	98, 183
T117	wi/WI	268, 269
T120	ne/NE	182
T122	K'AK'	143
T124	tzi, tzo	242, 243
T125	ya	279
T126	ya	279
T126hv	ya	280
T128	k'a/ch'a (K'A/CH'A?)	141
T130	wa/WA	261
T130hv	wa/WA	262
T134	o	189
T136	ji	113
T138	b'a	39
T140	ma	165
T142	ma	165
T145	che	59
T146	si	217
T148	che	59
T149	nu	186
T150	TZ'AM (?)	248
T151	nu	187
T152	ITZ'	99
T153	JAL	106
T155	o	190
T168	AJAW	27
T173	mi	169
T174	KUCH	138
T177	pi	206
T178	la	157
T179	SAK NIK	215
T181	ja	105
T183	LAK	159
T187	K'AB'A	142
T188	le	161
T190	ch'ak	74
T191	u/U	254
T203v	tz'u	252
T204	u/U	254
T206	CHAN/KAN	57
T207v	OCH	191
T212	KIX (?)	135, 136
T216	su	218
T218	JOM, TZUTZ	118, 244
T220	ke, k'o	134, 154
T220v	JUL	123
T227	EM	90
T228	a/AJ	25
T229	a/AJ	25

T231	u/U	254
T232	u/U	254
T237v	i	92
T238	a/AJ	25
T246	-ji-ya	115
T248	tz'i	249
T257	TOK'	234, 235
T264	nu	187
T278	sa/SA	211
T279	o	190
T281	K'AN	147
T282	nu	187
T287	ch'o	78, 79
T301	b'e/B'E	43
T329	JUN	125
T333	CH'AK-ka	74
T335	wa/WA	261
T350	te'/TE' (che'/CHE')	228
T360	li	162
T361	OCH	192
T364	AJAW	27
T366v	tz'a/TZ'A	247
T367	WAK	263
T501	b'a/B'A, IMIX	39, 97
T501v	JA', NAAB'	109, 110, 178
T502	ma/MA	166
T503	IK'	94
T504	ak'/AK', AK'AB'	34, 35
T506	K'AN, OL, wa/WA	147, 196, 261
T507b	tzi	243
T507hv	tzi	243
T508	CHIKCHAN	61
T510	EK', LAMAT	89, 161
T511v	PET	206
T512	ye/YE	290
T513	MULUK, te'/TE' (che'/CHE'), u/U	174, 229, 255
T514	je, te'/TE' (che'/CHE')	111, 229
T514v	te'/TE' (che'/CHE')	229
T515a	chu	64
T516b	ak'/AK'OT, k'a/ch'a	35, 141
T520	cha/ka, CHUWEN, se	47, 69, 216
T520v	cha/ka	48
T521	WINAL, WINIK	269
T524	IX	102
T525	KIB'	135
T526	KAB', KAB'AN	130
T527	ETZ'NAB'	90
T528	KAWAK, ku, TUN	133, 137, 237
T529	WITZ	270
T533	AJAW	27
T533v	NICH/NIK	183
T534	la	157
T535	NICH/NIK	183
T536	xo	277
T537	na/NA/NAJ	178
T539v	WAY	266
T542a	e	87
T544	K'IN	151

T544hv	K'IN	152
T548	AB', JA'AB', TUN	26, 110, 237
T549hv	PAX	206
T551	POP	210
T552	at	36
T559	tzu/TZU	244
T560v	tzu	244
T561c	CHAAN/KAAN	49
T563a	tz'i	250
T563b	tz'i	250
T565	ta/TA	222
T566	ma	166
T568	lu	163, 164
T569	MUTUL	174
T570	B'AK	41
T571	CH'EN	77
T573	TZ'AK	247
T574	je, K'IN (?)	112, 151
T575	yi	294
T579v	JUB'	121
T580	CHIT, lo	62, 163
T581	MOL	171
T582	mo	170
T584	B'EN	43
T585	b'i/B'I	43
T586	pa/PAJ	199
T589	jo	116
T590	cho	63
T590v	CHAK	52, 53
T592	nu	187
T598v	CH'EN	77
T601	chu	65
T602	pa/PAJ	199
T604	k'u	155
T606	TAN	226
T607	jo	116
T608	nu, tz'u	187, 252
T609	JUN	125
T618v	IL, IL-ja	96, 97
T624	[JANAAB'] PAKAL	107
T624v	JANAAB'	106
T630	sa	211
T632v	MUYAL	176
T644	CHUM	66
T644b	CHUM-[mu]	67
T645	ta/TA	222
T646	NIKTE'	184
T669a	k'a/ch'a	141
T669b	k'a/ch'a	142
T671	chi/CHI, K'AB', MANIK'	61, 142, 168
T672	JOM	118
T673	yo	298
T676	TAL	226
T678	KOJAW	136
T679	i/I	91
T683	ja	105
T683a	K'AL	144
T683v	JUL	123

T684a	JOY-ja	119
T687a	po	209
T694	o	191
T699v	[TAN] LAM	227
T699v	tza	241
T700	CHUM (?)	66
T702v	CHUM (?)	67
T710	ye/YE	290
T710v	ye/YE	291
T712	CH'AB'	72
T713a	K'AL	144
T714	tza-[ka]	241
T714v	tza	241
T736v	CHAM, xi	55, 276
T738	ka	129
T738v	u/U	255
T740	ju, SI	120
T741v	e	87
T743	a/AJ	26
T743v	mo/MO'	171
T744a	K'UK'	155
T746	CHAAN/KAAN	49
T747	ti/TI	231
T747a	AJAW	28
T751	B'ALAM	42
T752	TZ'I	250
T753	TZ'I	250
T753v	CHITAM	62
T756	SOTZ'	218
T756b	tz'i, xu	251, 277
T756c	xu-[lu]	278
T756d	xu-[ku]	277
T757	b'a/B'A	39
T758	ch'o, ch'o-[ko]	79
T758b	ji	114
T758c	KAB'	129
T758v	TIL, TUL, tz'o	232, 236, 252
T761b	AT	36
T764	CHAN/KAN, CHIKCHAN	57, 62
T765	OCH/OK	192
T765a	OK	195
T767	LAKAM	159
T769a	WAY	266
T774	OL	196
T778	MUTUL	175
T844	AYIN	37
T854	pu/PU/PUJ	210
T1000a	JUN, na/NA/NAJ	126, 178
T1000b	IX/IXIK	103
T1000d	AJAW	28
T1000v	tzi/TZI	243
T1004v	sa	212
T1006	WAXAK	265
T1008v	u/U	255
T1010	CHAN/KAN	57
T1011	CHAAK	48, 49
T1014v	MAM	168
T1016	k'u/K'U	155